"Nothing is more beautiful than the Nevsky
Prospekt, nothing, that is, in St Petersburg . . .
no element is lacking in the splendor of
this great thoroughfare, the jewel of
our capital . . ."
Nikolai Gogol

"The aspect of St Petersburg is more
conducive of astonishment than admiration ...
if it is not quite perfectly beautiful, it is none
the less completely strange.**"**

Olympe Audovard

"On the left was a little
black canal, which lay
against the colossus of the
Admiralty . . . gilded at
every edge, and adorned
by a glinting statue of
Fame, all in gold . . ."
Louis-Ferdinand Céline

EVERYMAN GUIDES
PUBLISHED BY DAVID CAMPBELL PUBLISHERS LTD, LONDON

TITLE: ISBN 1-85715-891-1

NUMEROUS SPECIALISTS AND ACADEMICS HAVE CONTRIBUTED TO THIS GUIDE:

AUTHORS AND EDITORS: Agnès Baubault, Sophie Benech, Ewa Bérard, Vera Biron, Natalia Brodskaia, Marie-Hélèlene Carpentier, Annie Civard, Igor Dimitriev, Philippe Dubois, Yann Le Duc, Emmanuel Ducamp, Carole Gaborit, Cécile Gall, Frédéric Jubien, Anne Klimoff, Tamara Kondratieva, Vladimir Léon, Annette Lefebvre, Vladimir Leftchenko, Jean-Louis Malroux, Sophie Mastelinck, Béatrice Méneux, Natalia Metelitsa, Brigitte de Montclos, Andreï Nakov, Alexei Nekrassov, Anne Nercessian, Antoine Nivière, Alandrre Noskov, Béatrice Picon-Vallin, Florence Piquot, Andrei Pounine, Alexandre Rivline, Prascovie de Saint-Hippolyte, Alexandra Schouwaloff, Odile Simon, Vitali Sychev, Riccardo Tremori Jean-Pierre Verdet.

ILLUSTRATORS AND ICONOGRAPHERS: Michel Aubois, Jean-François Binet, Catherine Boncenne, Frédéric Bony, Vincent Brunot, Jean-Philippe Chabot, Jean Chevallier, Paul Coulbois, François Desbordes, Claire Felloni, Henri Galeron, Xavier Garnerin, Éric Gillion, Jean-Marie Guillou, Jean-Michel Kacedan, Catherine Lachaux, Marc Lagarde, Dominique Mansion, Laure Massin, Patrick Merienne, Florence Piquot, Maurice Pommier, Pascale Robin, Sylvain Roueri, Amato Soro, Catherine Totems, John Wilkinson.

PHOTOGRAPHERS: V. Baranovsky, V. Buss, Roger Gain, Koncharov, V. Savik, V. Terebenin.

WE WOULD ALSO LIKE TO THANK:
Helena Asséeva, Vera Biron (Dostoevsky Museum, St Petersburg), Isabelle Haas, Cyril and Natialia Ilinsky, Martine Kahane (Opéra Garnier-Bastille), Anne Nercessian, Véronique Schiltz, Vladimir Terebebin, Galina Vassiliev (Historic Archives of St Petersburg), Georges Willembachov (Hermitage Museum)
and
Princess Katia Galitzine.

TRANSLATED BY ANTHONY ROBERTS.
PRACTICAL INFORMATION TRANSLATED BY YVONNE WORTH.
EDITED AND TYPESET BY BOOK CREATION SERVICES, LONDON.
PRINTED IN ITALY BY EDITORIALE LIBRARIA.

EVERYMAN GUIDES
79 Berwick Street
London W1V 3PF

St Petersburg

Everyman Guides

CONTENTS

▲ St Petersburg

Palace Square

The Arrow

The Fortress

Smolny

The Admiralty and St Isaac's Cathedral

HOW TO USE THIS GUIDE

(Sample page shown from the guide to Venice)

The symbols at the top of each page refer to the different parts of the guide.

■ NATURAL ENVIRONMENT

● KEYS TO UNDERSTANDING

▲ ITINERARIES

◆ PRACTICAL INFORMATION

The itinerary map shows the main points of interest along the way and is intended to help you find your bearings.

The mini-map locates the particu[lar] itinerary within the wider area covered by the guide.

CANNAREGIO

Santa Lucia Station.

136

★ The star symbol signifies that a particular site has been singled out by the publishers for its special beauty, atmosphere or cultural interest.

● ▲ ■ ◆
The symbols alongside a title or within the text itself provide cross-references to a theme or place dealt with elsewhere in the guide.

At the beginning of each itinerary, the suggested means of transport to be used and the time it will take to cover the area ar[e] indicated:

⛵ By boat
🚶 On foot
🚲 By bicycle
⊙ Duration

THE GATEWAY TO VENICE ★

PONTE DELLA LIBERTA. Built by the Austrians 50 years after the Treaty of Campo Formio in 1797 ● 34, to link Venice with Milan. The bridge ended the thousand-year separation from the mainland and shook the city's economy to its roots as Venice, already in the throes of the industrial revolution, saw

🚶 Half a day

BRIDGES TO VENICE

NATURE

The St Petersburg region extends 280 miles west to east and between 65 and 200 miles north to south. Its southeast extremity is washed by the waters of the Gulf of Finland; and to the north of it is Lake Ladoga. The region lies to the northwest of the Russian plateau, the substratum of which is crystalline rock. The various ice ages produced morainic elevations and lakes, which in general give the land its undulating aspect. The climate is one of strong contrasts, being conditioned on the one hand by the movement of air masses off the Atlantic and on the other by polar continental air, which is dry and very cold in winter. St Petersburg itself is situated more or less where the northern and temperate climatic regions meet.

0 3 miles	Isthmus of Carelia
Kotlin Island	
Bay of Neva	Neva

Sandy banks along the seaboard

Argillaceous plains, with forests and marshes in sandy soil areas

Plains and plateaux with glacial moraines (mixed and coniferous forests)

Marshes and peat-bogs

Arable land and conifer forests (foothills)

Calcareous plateau with deciduous or coniferous forests and grassland

Prone to flooding

Autumn weather is characterized by frequent depressions, with strong winds causing occasional floods.

In December Atlantic depressions bring rain and snow; in January and February the arrival of dry air from the Arctic makes for cloudless skies.

The black tern lives in noisy colonies among the marshes skirting the Bay of the Neva.

On the island of Kotlin the construction of a dyke was begun in the 1980's as a measure to protect the city from flooding. The dyke is still unfinished, because it has been shown to disturb the Neva estuary's ecosystem.

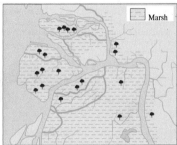

Marsh

The marshy, island-strewn delta in which Peter the Great chose to build his capital ● 78 benefits from Atlantic weather, without which the region would probably be icebound for much of the year.

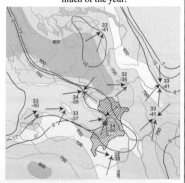

AVERAGE TEMPERATURES AT GROUND LEVEL (°C)

—16— July isotherm (61°F)

—-8— January isotherm (18°F)

33 Maximum temperatures (91°F)

-40 Minimum temperatures (-40°F)

AVERAGE PRECIPITATION (mm)

less 650 700 750 800 more

——— Isohyet

PREVAILING WINDS

⟶ July

⟶ January

In the spring the weather changes frequently on account of the continual confrontation of air masses.

In July the average temperature is 67° F. July is also a season of thunderstorms; cloudbursts can be very violent.

THE NEVA

SPARLING
Between March and May this deep-sea fish runs
up the Neva to Lake Ladoga, where it spawns.
At this time of year hundreds of fishermen
stand on the Neva bridges, waiting for the
sparling (*koriuchka*) to come up river.

The Neva flows out of Lake Ladoga, then crosses the isthmus of
Carelia to form a delta at its junction with the Gulf of Finland.
The river's entire length is less than 50 miles, but at its widest
point it is some 500 yards across, with a depth of not more than
80 feet. The Neva's vast volume of water makes it the sixth
largest river in Europe.

ROACH
The roach frequents the
lower stretches of the Neva,
as far as the mouth; here it
seeks the sandy substratum of
the river bed.

PERCH
The strong currents of the
Neva are a perfect habitat for
the perch, which lays its eggs
on aquatic plants.

BREAM
Well-adapted to the water
quality of the Neva, bream
tend to frequent areas where
the river bottom is muddy.

PIKE PERCH
The voracious fish, very common in Eastern
Europe, prefers still waters but may also be
found where the current flows strongly.

RUFFE
A bottom-dwelling fish confined
to lakes and big rivers, the ruff
habitually moves in shoals.

House martin

Swift

These birds nest on the great riverfront buildings of St Petersburg, notably the Hermitage ▲ *168*. They feed on insects, skimming close to the water's surface.

During the winter the Neva may be impassable for a period varying between two and five months. In the winter of 1941–2 ● *50* the Neva was covered by ice over 3 feet thick. The river's powerful current sometimes brings very high water.

The worst flooding on record took place in 1824 ● *35*. Dykes have been constructed in the bay of the Neva to protect the city.

Following the thaw the Neva may still remain impassable to ships for over a month, as great blocks of ice sweep downstream from Lake Ladoga to the open sea. The "walrus club" are a sturdy group of people who, in winter, cut a hole in the ice around Peter and Paul Fortress and dip themselves into the below freezing water. Apparently this makes you live longer.

BLACK-HEADED GULL
Present on the river all year round, this half-tame gull will often eat from the hand during the winter.

The Summer Garden ▲ *186* is a combination of rigorous landscaping and exuberant animal life.

The building of the city of St Petersburg led inevitably to a significant change in the vegetation of the surrounding region. The new artificial plantations brought with them a number of foreign exotic plant species to live alongside the indigenous varieties. Nowadays St Petersburg still remains a "green city", with historic spaces – such as the Summer Garden and the enormous parks of Krestovsky and Elagin islands – which serve as urban reminders of the great forests that lie further afield.

RED SQUIRREL
The shy, agile rodent is widespread throughout the parks and cemeteries of St Petersburg.

PINE MARTEN
A carnivorous member of the weasel family, which habitually feeds on birds as well as small mammals, beetles and carrion.

F. Desbordes

HOODED CROW
Omnipresent in the city, this crow is especially numerous in the smaller parks and around the Alexander Nevsky Monastery
▲ 253.

SISKIN
The siskin is common in the mountain and forest regions of Europe – and in the parks of St Petersburg.

Male

Female

SCARLET ROSEFINCH
The oriental species is currently expanding its range deep into Western Europe.

FIELDFARE
The fieldfare nests in noisy colonies, especially in the Summer Garden.

THRUSH NIGHTINGALE
A legendary songbird, the eastern European version of our common nightingale.

Men scything the grass by hand in Elagin Park ▲ 154, in the center of St Petersburg.

ALDER
The berries of this small tree, which favors cool, humid soils, attracts birds like the siskin during the winter months.

LIME TREE
The lime is very common in and around St Petersburg. In June and July the gardens are richly scented with its blooms.

HORNBEAM
Hornbeams, widely planted in Russia during the 19th century, supply generous shade and easily worked wood.

THE CARELIAN FOREST

WILLOW WARBLER
This long-distance migrant nests in large numbers in the woods around St Petersburg, where willows, rowans and birches predominate.

The forests of the St Petersburg region straddle a transitional zone between the northern taiga, where conifers proliferate, and the mixed woodlands of the temperate regions. The latter, a blend of deciduous trees and conifers, seem to have receded southward following a very cold, wet period over four thousand years ago. In the Carelian forest there are fewer deciduous trees, with rowans predominating. Numerous lakes, interspersed with marshes and heather-covered peat bogs, give this area a charm that is properly more Scandinavian than Russian, yet this is the quintessential "Russian forest" described by novelists.

CHAFFINCH
Large numbers of chaffinches populate the St Petersburg region in summer, migrating to southern Europe in the winter.

NORWAY PINE
Abundant on the sandy soils around the northern rim of the Gulf of the Neva.

BIRCH
One of the principal hardwood trees in the St Petersburg region; it often grows with conifers.

SPRUCE
Typical of the Carelian forest. Its fruits are a rich source of food for woodland birdlife.

BEARBERRY
The *tolmanka* is very similar to the bilberry and is widely used in pharmacology.

MILITARY ORCHID
The military orchid flowers in May and June on calcareous sunny banks and along the margins of woods.

SWAMP-BERRY
The deep blue fruit of the swamp-berry is a common sight in marshy areas during the autumn.

COTTON GRASS
In June, when the *puchitsa* is in flower, its fluffy seedballs cover the ground like new-fallen snow.

ELK (MOOSE)
In the 1970's elk were still present in large numbers up to the edge of the city. Stocks have declined steeply in recent years.

GRAY WOLF
A small wolf population survives around St Petersburg, but is now under severe pressure from hunters.

■ CEMETERIES

The cemeteries of St Petersburg come as a surprise to most visitors to the city. From the outside they appear impenetrable, but those who persevere will be rewarded with the sight of an unkempt riot of graves, bushes and sprawling wild plants. During the Soviet era the cemeteries were not maintained, with the result that the growth of lush vegetation remained unchecked; this in turn attracted abundant wild creatures which took advantage of the near-natural conditions that prevailed there.

The tangle of plants and ruined tombstones offers a quiet refuge from the din of the surrounding city.

RED FOX
The parks and cemeteries of St Petersburg have made it possible for the red fox to survive in the heart of the city. Foxes may often be glimpsed by daylight, hunting for mice, rats and voles.

PIED FLYCATCHER
Very numerous in temperate woodlands, this migrant nests in older trees.

ROBIN
Unlike robins in western Europe, those in Russia migrate southward in winter.

BLACKCAP
This warbler arrives in St Petersburg in May, migrating south in August.

TREE SPARROW
Very common in the open green spaces of St Petersburg, it is seldom seen in the built-up areas, unlike its cousin the house sparrow.

POPLAR
In the early summer the cotton-like seeds of the catkin carpet the surrounding vegetation in white.

RUSSIAN ELM
These elms are especially common in St Petersburg's cemeteries; they seem less vulnerable to disease than the western European variety.

IVY
Most of the older graves in the cemeteries are completely obscured by ivy.

RASPBERRIES
In the autumn wild raspberries are a delight to strollers and birds alike.

NORWAY MAPLE
St Petersburg lies roughly at the northernmost limit of the Norway maple.

■ LIGHT AT MIDNIGHT

*"Across the sky, gilded
By the sun's perpetual rays
Dawn hurries to relieve
The unconsummated dusk
And night endures for barely an hour."*
Pushkin, *The Bronze Horseman*

As St Petersburg is not within the Arctic
Circle, there is no midnight sun, but its
latitude is sufficiently high (almost 60°N)
to bring some light throughout the night.
The sun only just dips below the horizon
and the earth's atmosphere continues to
diffuse its beams. Most plants are in full
bloom at this time of year.

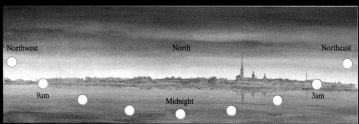

Northwest   North   Northeast

9am   Midnight   3am

Toward the earth's poles, the sun rises less directly over
the horizon, and the more the days vary in length over
the year.

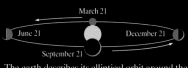

March 21

June 21   December 21

September 21

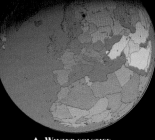

The earth describes its elliptical orbit around the
sun in 365 days and 6 hours. During this
revolution the inclination of the earth varies in
relation to the sun, determining the lengths of the
days and seasons.

▼ **SUMMER SOLSTICE**
On June 21 the night, or rather twilight, lasts
only five hours at St Petersburg. At midnight
the sun lies only 6° beneath the horizon. In
London at the same time of year the night
lasts for seven hours and the sun drops 23°
below the horizon. In New York the night
lasts for nine hours and twenty minutes and
the sun drops 25° below
the horizon.

▲ **WINTER SOLSTICE**
On December 21 at noon the sun stands at
slightly over 6° above St Petersburg. In
London it is at 26° and in New York at 27°.
From mid-afternoon onward the Gulf of
Finland is under cover of night.

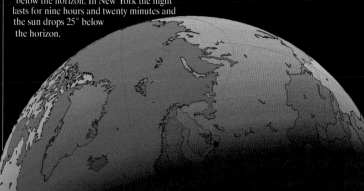

HISTORY AND LANGUAGE

1700

1750

1682–1725
Reign of Peter the Great, who
proclaimed himself Emperor

1700–21
Northern War: the Russians annex
Estonia, Latvia and Carelia

1703–25 "A WINDOW ON EUROPE"

A NEW ETERNAL CITY

On May 16, 1703 a village by the Neva, recently abandoned by its Finnish inhabitants, began to resound to the din of saws and axes. On June 29, the Feast of Saint Peter and Saint Paul, the foundations of a church were laid within the precinct of the future fortress of the same name: Sankt-Piter-Bourkh (pronounced in the Dutch manner) identified the Czar with the names of the two saints. In doing so, Peter the Great sought to endow Russia with an imperial, messianic destiny, of which Rome was the paramount model.

The arms of the city of St Petersburg borrow from the emblems of Rome and the Vatican: thus the crossed anchors refer both to the papal keys, which symbolize faith, and to the fleet created by Peter the Great, which could also "open the gates of Paradise". From the first years of its construction, the city of St Petersburg was known to Russians as "paradise".

THE CONQUEST OF NATURE FOR REASONS OF STATE

Peter's city gradually grew out of the marshes. In September 1703 the wooden fortress was completed, along with the Czar's house. But soon stone was brought in as the principal construction material. The richest families were obliged by law to build their mansions of stone, and were heavily fined if they failed to do so. According to an *ukaze* (edict) of 1714, which remained in force for sixty-five years, every boat, vessel or waggon entering the city had to bring with it a certain amount of cut stone. On the building sites labored vast numbers of convicts and serfs (40,000 on average between 1709 and 1716), adventurers, soldiers, Russian craftsmen and foreign specialists. The foreigners came in the hope of gain and were sometimes detained by force. Hunger and cold killed nearly 100,000 people during the first years of building, sacrificed to the will and ambition of the Czar. Strategic and commercial considerations justified the choice of his apparently unpromising site. By May 1703 Peter was promising substantial grants to the first three merchant vessels to drop anchor in the new port.

| 1795 | 1812 | June 18, 1815 | 1853–6: |
| Third partition of Poland between Austria, Prussia and Russia | Napoleon in Moscow | Battle of Waterloo | Crimean War |

1800

| 1809 | September 26, 1815 |
| Annexation of Finland | Foundation of the Holy Alliance |

1725–1856: ORIGINALITY AND IMITATION

THE "PALMYRA OF THE NORTH"

In a letter dated September 28, 1704, Czar Peter referred to the city under construction as his "new capital". The inauguration took place in 1712, at which time the Russian court, the Senate and the foreign embassies all moved to St Petersburg from Moscow; Peter was subsequently married there, to a Lithuanian peasant girl. The first museums, a library, a theater, an observatory and the Academy of Sciences were quickly opened. In the vicinity of St Petersburg were built the palaces of Oranienbaum and Peterhof, while a road was built to Tsarskoe Selo, the future summer residence of the Czars.

of both Russian and foreign-born artists, St Petersburg "... became distinct from the other cities of Europe, precisely because it so nearly resembled each one of them". Travelers called it the "London", "Venice", "Rome", "Berlin" or "Paris" of Russia, as it struck them. But the city's new attractions obliged its inhabitants to adapt: some social groups to luxury and extravagance, the rest to the behavior of their superiors in the hierarchy. Poets and writers, meanwhile, became intrigued by the mystery of this seductive but far from traditional city.

THE DISAPPEARING CITY

After the death of Peter the Great half the Russian court and at least half of the population of St Petersburg fled the city. The *ukaze* of 1729, which threatened fugitives with exile and the confiscation of their property, had little effect. New, harsher measures sparked a revolt, and in 1737 the city was burned down. Nevertheless the Empress Elizabeth I (right), Peter the Great's daughter, pressed on with the construction of the Winter and Anichkov palaces and the Gostiny Dvor, realizing her father's dream. Catherine II ● *40* lifted the restrictions, enticed the population back with perquisites, and initiated major construction projects such as the Tauride Palace and Marble Palace, the Hermitage, the Peter and Paul Fortress, the bridges and the granite river embankment. Toward the mid-19th century, thanks to the talents

31

| February 19, 1861 | December 1865 | | 1889–92 |
| Abolition of serfdom in Russia | Abolition of slavery in the USA | | Counter-reforms |

1861 **1880**

| **1863–5** | **1864–76** | **March 1, 1881** | **1883** |
| Liberal reforms of Alexander II | Marx and Engels: the First International | Assassination of Czar Alexander | Marxist propaganda appears in Russia |

1856–1914 St Petersburg in the Forefront of Modernism

The industrial center of the Empire

The first steamships and the Moscow–St Petersburg railway line (1851) opened a new era in the city's history. By 1868 the Putilov factory was already a major producer of rails, locomotives and carriages. In 1900, 13,000 workers were employed there, with about a hundred more metallurgical factories developing in related sectors. Other factories, using modern British and German equipment (Nobel, Nevsky, Lessner) built ships and typographical machines and (in competition with Obukhov) supplied the needs of the Army. There was also a number of textile mills in and around St Petersburg. A new port, constructed in 1885, was added to that of Kronstadt, expanding the city's potential for international trade: corn and wood were exported in vast quantities, balancing imports of steel and machine tools. Banks, many of whose shareholders were foreigners, proliferated during the boom of the 1890's.

The St Petersburg civil servant

According to the poet Grigoriev, Russian civil servants – whose uniforms varied from one ministry to the next – were the "alpha and omega" of St Petersburg. Schoolboys, university students, soldiers, sailors, policemen and ecclesiastics completed the picture. Right from the time of its foundation, St Petersburg was a heavily regulated city: the aspect of the roofs and chimneys, the construction materials, the color and height of all buildings (which might on no account be taller than the Winter Palace), the width of the streets, the hours by which the gates had to be closed, and the arrangements for street cleaning were all carefully ordained by bureaucratic rules.

A center for free thought

Paradoxically, it was in this tightly controlled environment that free thought blossomed – thanks to the culture of an intellectual elite, naturally, but also thanks to the special receptiveness of St Petersburgers. Seventy percent of the workers in the capital knew how to read and write, as opposed to an average of 21 percent in the rest of the Russian Empire. St Petersburgers spread the word on avant-garde art, along with technical innovation (airplanes) and new diversions (cinema, football).

1904–5	1912–13	June 28, 1914	1924
Russo-Japanese War	Balkan Wars	Assassination of Franz-Ferdinand of Austria at Sarajevo	England, France, Sweden and other European nations recognize the USSR

1900   1920

12 March 1918	1918–20	March 2–6, 1919	December 30, 1922
Moscow replaces St Petersburg as capital	Civil War and foreign intervention	First Congress of the Third International (Komintern) in Moscow	The USSR is officially inaugurated

1914–24: PETROGRAD: WAR AND REVOLUTION

THE COMING OF THE REVOLUTION

On July 20, 1914, from a balcony of the Winter Palace, Nicholas II read the declaration which brought Russia into the Great War. On August 18 the German name of the capital was changed to the more Russian-sounding Petrograd – much closer to "Pieter", as ordinary people had always called it. For the writer Solzhenitsyn, who described the war years practically from day to day (*The Red Wheel*, 4,000 pages), the declaration of war was the beginning of the greatest drama of the century, whilst for Lenin it represented a great gift offered by the Czar to the nascent Revolution.

According to Lenin, in an underdeveloped nation revolution could come about only as a consequence of war: while Karl Marx thought revolution improbable anywhere but within the most advanced capitalist systems. History began to prove Lenin right in February 1917.

On the night of October 24–5, 1917 insurgents attacked the Winter Palace, seat of the provisional government. With a roar that drowned the stutter of machine-gun fire, a wave of humanity swirled around the great building. The October Revolution was under way.

THE DESTRUCTION OF ST PETERSBURG

The October Revolution – so glorified for seventy-six years thereafter – led to many irreparable losses for St Petersburgers. The city was transformed in two ways. On the edge of the central area quantities of dilapidated buildings in which tens of thousands of workers lived were emptied and destroyed. Meantime the historic capital began to fall apart from the very first months of Soviet supremacy. Spacious apartments were divided up among working families, and the original décor, of two-headed eagles, crowns and statues, removed; a decree abolishing private ownership deprived houses and shops, fountains and gardens of ordinary maintenance; and railings, stained glass, stair carpets, bas-reliefs and weathercocks simply vanished. The campaigns against religion brought about the destruction or conversion into offices of a large number of churches. Much-needed capital was raised by the sale of works of art abroad. At the same time the names of streets and squares were altered, short-circuiting the collective memory: about 500 names were changed, including that of the Nevsky Prospekt, which became Avenue 25 October. About 400 names vanished altogether, along with the things they referred to. Finally, on Lenin's death in January 1924, the Soviet Congress, "at the request of the workers", abolished the name of the capital altogether.

33

1938	1939	1940	1941
Munich Agreements (September)	The Russo-German Pact (August). Partition of Poland (September)	Pact with Finland (March) Annexation of the Baltic States and Bessarabia (June)	The Germans invade Russia (June). They are halted outside Moscow (December)

| 1924 | | 1940 | |

1929	1936	April 8–11, 1940	1949
First attempts at collectivization	The Anti-Komintern Pact (Germany and Russia)	Massacre of 1,400 Polish prisoners at Katyn by Russian security services	Creation of NATO (April)

1924–91: LENINGRAD, GLORY AND CALAMITY

A NEW IMAGE OF THE CITY

The houses of one and a half million emigrants and victims of war and revolution were occupied by workers and peasants fleeing collectivization (1928–33). These people became city workers and were distinct from the native St Petersburgers in their language and way of life. The atmosphere of the city, in which before the revolution the cream of the aristocracy and the intelligentsia had flourished, became envenomed as Leningrad found itself increasingly sidelined and provincialized. Nevertheless, the Soviet government in Moscow continued to regard Leningrad as a free-thinking potential rival. The Party's purges and wholesale arrests uprooted many recently arrived families, adding to the prevailing loss of identity in the city.

A new image was to emerge later, in consequence of the heroic resistance during the siege of Leningrad (1941–4), although the city's troubles did not come to an end until the 1960's and 1970's, with the stabilization of the population and an improvement in living conditions.

THE OPENING OF LENINGRAD TO TOURISM

The work of restoration which had continued ever since the end of the siege had taken on a different character by the end of the 1970's, the purpose of which was to recreate the city's former charm. After the opening of an initial underground railway in 1955, new lines were built on a regular basis; the length of the Neva embankment was tripled (nearly 100 miles of it were reinforced with granite); park space in the city was increased to 22,500 acres, and the number of bridges was increased to 310 by 1989. Meantime cheap high-rise housing began to make its mark on the various islands (42 new projects were completed in 1970). Soviet tourists arrived to visit the "glorious city", and with the new policy of detente toward the West even foreign visitors began to appear.

March 5, 1953	August 1, 1975	April 25, 1986	June 12, 1991
Death of Stalin	Helsinki conference. Signature of the final act on Human Rights	Nuclear disaster at Chernobyl	First election by universal suffrage in Russia: Yeltsin elected President

1960   1980   1990

February 1956	March 11, 1985	November 1989	December 25, 1991
Krushchev denounces Stalin's personality cult	Gorbachev is elected First Secretary of the Soviet Communist Party	Fall of the Berlin Wall	The USSR becomes the Commonwealth of Independent States

THE PALACES AROUND LENINGRAD

The environs of Leningrad suffered terribly from the German occupation, and after the Allied victory in World War Two the towns in the region were so badly damaged that they had to be reconstructed rather than restored. With their 18th-century palaces and parks, these museum-towns are very much a part of Leningrad and are well worth visiting. They are also highly functional: Petrodvorets, with its university campus, is populated by students; Tsarskoe Selo trains farmers from all over the country at its Agricultural Institute; Gatchina is a scientific research center with a number of different institutes. Pavlosk, Oranienbaum and the isthmus of Carelia now serve as popular summer resorts.

ST PETERSBURG SINCE 1991

REBIRTH OF THE CITY

On June 12, 1991, 54 percent of the city's inhabitants voted to restore its historic name. "St Petersburg" has come back, but with more difficulty than the Kirov Ballet experienced in readopting the name of Mariinsky, or the University in jettisoning the name of Zhdanov. Russian and foreign sponsors, notably the organizers of the "Goodwill Games" (July–August 1994), support the ongoing embellishment projects for the city: the houses along the Nevsky Prospekt have been repainted, the streets remetalled, and foreign cafés are opening apace. But the real sign of a renaissance, foreshadowing St Petersburg's tricentenary, has been the resumption of literary work on and about it: the appearance of a first major collection entitled *The Petersburg Metaphysic* has confirmed this trend.

A SOLUTION TO THE PROBLEM OF FLOODING

On several buildings in the city are plaques indicating the levels of the worst floods among the 253 which have afflicted St Petersburg since 1703. One of these recalls the bitter catastrophe of November 7, 1824, when the water rose 12 feet. Today, the reformist administrators of St Petersburg and their Finnish neighbors are committed to renewing the city's flood protection facilities, while respecting the ecology of the region.

> GEDENKE
> DES HOHEN WASSERS
> AM 7 NOVEMBER
> 1824

THE ROMANOV DYNASTY

Czar Alexander I presents his army to Napoleon.

 MIKHAIL FYODOROVICH (1613–45)*. The first of the Romanov Czars, son of Fyodor Nikitich, better known as Filaret, patriarch of Tuchino and descendant of the Riurik family (founder of the Kiev state, the first state of Russia).

 ALEXEI I (1645–76)*. The son of Mikhail Fyodorovich. In the early years of his reign, the state was run by his tutor, the boyar B. Morozov. This reign was marked by a major social crisis and ecclesiastical reforms initiated by the Patriarch of Moscow, Nikon.

 SOPHIA (1682–9)*. In 1689 Sophia Alexeyevna was assigned to the monastery of Novodyvichy (Moscow) and the regency passed to Natasha Naryshkin (second wife of Alexei I and mother of Peter I).

 FYODOR III (1676–82)*. The son of Alexei I and Maria Ilinychna, Fyodor was bored by affairs of state and allowed his advisors to run the country. He died at 21.

CATHERINE (1691–1733)

 ANNA IVANOVNA (1730–40). Niece of Peter I, Anna was chosen by the supreme council (over her daughters Anna and Elizabeth) to succeed Peter II. Hers was an arbitrary regime.

ALEXEI (1690–1718). After joining the conspiracy against his father, Alexei was condemned by the Czar, imprisoned and tortured.

 PETER II (1727–30). Grandson of Peter I. Peter's brief reign was marked by the return of the court to Moscow and the eviction of Prince Menshikov.

IVAN VI (1740–1)*
Regency of Anna.

 ALEXANDER I (1801–25)* (left). The adored grandson of Catherine II. Russia in his reign joined the coalition against Napoleon; later, Alexander instigated major reforms and founded many new institutions.

 ALEXANDER III (1881–94)*. Son of Alexander II. The assassination of his father led him to bring a halt to the reform movement and re-establish a conservative regime.

NICHOLAS II ● 44 (1894–1917). Son of Alexander III. The dynasty's last emperor. His reign ended in the upheaval of the Revolution in 1917, which cost Nicholas and his family their lives (July 17, 1918).

IVAN V (1682–96)*
Brother of Fyodor III. Co-Czar with his half-brother Peter (the future Peter the Great), during the regency of Sophia Alexeyevna.

PETER I (1682–1725)*. ● *38*. On the death of his mother, Peter the Great seized the reins of power. His second wife, Catherine I (1725–7) was a Lithuanian peasant girl. On his death, she became the first Empress of Russia.

ANNA (1708–28)

ELIZABETH PETROVNA ● *31 (1741–61)***
Daughter of Peter the Great, she organized a coup d'etat in 1741, deposing Ivan IV, great-nephew of Anna Ivanovna.

PETER III (1761–2). Son of the Duke of Holstein-Gottorp. In 1745 he married Sophia of Anhalt-Zerbst (the future Catherine II).

CATHERINE II ● *40 (1762–96)*
Ordered the assassination of her husband by Alexei Orloff, and took power in a 1762 coup d'etat.

PAUL I (1796–1801)*. Son of Peter III and Catherine II, whom he loathed. Assassinated in the Engineer's Castle.

NICHOLAS I (1825–55). Brother of Alexander I. His reign was marked by the Decembrist uprising and the Crimean War.

ALEXANDER II (1855–81)*
Son of Nicholas I. From the end of the Crimean War, he undertook a reform program (abolition of serfdom in 1861) but was assassinated by terrorists.

* Dates of reign.

RASPUTIN ▲ *202 (1872–1916)*
Born a peasant (his real name was Grigor Novykh), Rasputin was introduced into the court of Nicholas II on account of his healing powers. Very quickly he gained huge influence over the Czar's political decisions. On December 16, 1916 he was assassinated by Prince Yusupov.

● PETER THE GREAT

By inviting Western technicians and military officers to Russia, Peter the Great was able to form a regular Army and Navy capable of defending his country's interests. As Czar, his principal objective was to make Russia a great military power, not to transplant into it European civilization. But a century after his death the Russian intelligentsia was divided between the Slavophiles, who wished to eradicate Peter from Russian history, and the Occidentalists, who recognized his openness to progress while acknowledging that civilization was beaten into Russia "by blows of the knout".

> "He sought first to make Germans and Englishmen, when he should have been making Russians."
> J.-J. Rousseau

SAILOR, SOLDIER AND CRAFTSMAN . . .
At the age of ten, and on his own initiative, Peter formed an army. This "child's game" led to the founding of the three elite regiments which later spearheaded Russia's victory over Napoleon. The Czar, who grew up far from the sea, was forever dreaming of it. An abandoned English ship in one of his grandfather's dry-docks sparked his longing for a great Russian fleet. In 1697, at Saardam, he learned for himself about naval construction: the first frigate of Russia's fleet was partly built by his hands.

A "NOBLE SAVAGE"
In the European vogue, Peter had an African prince called Ibrahim brought to his court – the man who organized the kidnapping was an ancestor of Tolstoy's. Ibrahim became a general (Hannibal) in the Russian Army, and was the great-grandfather of the poet Pushkin ● 114.

ECCENTRIC VALUES
Culturally, Peter was an innovator; but many of his changes were frankly viewed as sacrilege. Beards had to be shaved in homage to the true faith; clothes were "teutonized" in styles which had formerly been thought of in Russia as carnival disguises. The Czar also instituted a Council of Drunkenness as a parody of the Ecclesiastical Council, and arranged elaborate marriages and funerals for dwarves, whom he pilloried to amuse his court. Russian culture somehow remained in place, but with its values knocked topsy-turvy.

THE DESPOT
Peter, as Czar, pitied no man and respected nothing. During his reign the nobles were forced to educate themselves; if they did not, they were forbidden to marry. They also had to "divert themselves": in other words, frequent cafés and drink vodka, and serve vodka on all occasions, on pain of forfeiting all their possessions. The Czar's son Alexei ▲ *147* was accused of plotting against him, arrested, condemned to death – and tortured by Peter's own hand.

BRONZE GROTESQUE ▲ *148*
In 1991 Chemiakin, a Russian-French-American sculptor, offered to the city of St Petersburg a symbol of the fallen empire, in the form of a statue of Peter fixed in his chair. The head, sculpted after a mask done by Rastrelli in 1719, is completely disproportionate to the body.

On her arrival in Russia Sophia of Anhalt-Zerbst, Princess of Pomerania and fiancée of Peter III, noted in her journal: "I will reign alone over Russia." Shortly after, while Russophobia and disdain for the orthodoxy of her husband were causing outrage in St Petersburg, she converted to the Orthodox religion. In 1762 she acceded to the throne as Catherine II, supported by the officers who had assassinated her husband.

A CIVILIZING INFLUENCE
When Catherine acceded, the state of academic faculties in the city was such that there might be only one student per class; police had to recruit pupils on the day schools opened.

A PHILOSOPHER ON THE THRONE
Catherine wished her reforms to answer the desires and interests of her subjects. Quoting Montesquieu, Quesnay and Beccaria, she put forward her ideas in a treatise, the *Nakaz*, whose triumph is depicted in the allegory at right. In 1767 Catherine formed a legislative committee, but came up against deputies who were ignorant of both government and the mechanics of the modern state, and unanimously defended the right to possess serfs.

At the close of the 18th century Russia had nearly 300 schools, promoting the rise among ordinary Russians of an intelligentsia. The nobility was educated at home, but 200 of its daughters were taught at the Smolny Institute, which opened in 1764 ▲ *250*.

MILITARY GLORY
The victories of Marshal Alexander Suvarov over the Turks in 1790 and then over the French Army in the Alps in 1799 not only earned him the title of Prince of Italy but also gave Russia a decisive role on the European scene.

PUGACHOV'S REVOLT
In 1774, Pugachov, an illiterate cossack calling himself Peter III, threatened the throne of Catherine II.

People from the Volga regions, peasants working in the factories of the Urals and serfs flocked to Pugachov's banner.

"A WORSE REBEL THAN PUGACHOV"
This was Catherine's note on Radishchev's book *A Voyage from St Petersburg to Moscow* (1790). Its author, a Russian noble who had studied at the University of Leipzig, was influenced by "half-baked scholars like Rousseau and Raynal". Observing the wretched state of the serfs in the two capitals, Radishchev condemned the regime of the "enthroned philosopher", who according to him was "... a deformed monster, impudent, obese, with a hundred yapping heads".

THE NOTES OF CATHERINE II
Kurakin, the Czar's best friend, secretly collected the only copy of the notes of Catherine II, sealed by Paul I. These notes did not appear until 1858, when they were published in French, in London, on the initiative of the revolutionary Herzen – who also published Radishchev.

MÉMOIRES

DE

L'IMPÉRATRICE CATHERINE II

ÉCRITS PAR ELLE-MÊME,

ET PRÉCÉDÉS D'UNE PRÉFACE

PAR

A. HERZEN.

(ÉDITION DE N. TRÜBNER & CIE.)

LONDRES,
TRÜBNER & CIE, 60, PATERNOSTER ROW
1859.

During the military campaigns against Napoleon (1813–14) aristocratic Russian officers, educated from an early age by foreign tutors and (later) professors, saw at first hand constitutional regimes which had rid themselves of serfdom, and whose masses were moved by revolutionary ideals. On their return to Russia they formed secret societies with the aim of transforming their own country along the same lines. From 1822 onward these societies had polarized into two opposing groups, the Northern and the Southern.

CONSTITUTIONAL MONARCHY OR REPUBLIC?
Lively debates pitted Pestel, republican leader of the Southern Society, against Nikita Muraviev, the Northern leader, who proposed a constitutional monarchy. Some of the conspirators saw Pestel as a new Robespierre.

THE SENATE SQUARE
The conspirators decided to act on December 14, 1825, when the regiments of St Petersburg were scheduled to swear their oath of loyalty to Nicholas I. While some caused a diversion among the soldiers drawn up on the Senate Square ▲ *194*, others (including Prince Trubetskoy, the instigator of the coup) hesitated so long that the Czar's troops were able to foil the revolt, killing 1,271 people.

HANGED REBELS
The five leaders of the Decembrist insurrection were led to the gallows on July 14, 1826, with signs reading "Assassins of the Czar" hung around their necks. Three of the ropes broke, and the hangings had to be carried out again.

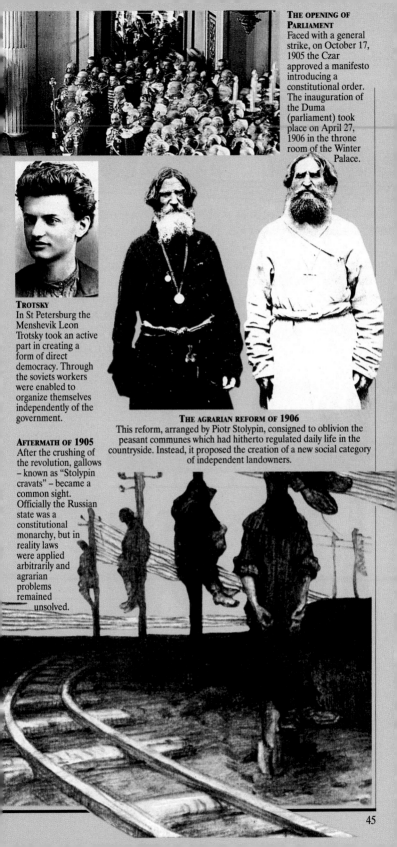

Faced with a general strike, on October 17, 1905 the Czar approved a manifesto introducing a constitutional order. The inauguration of the Duma (parliament) took place on April 27, 1906 in the throne room of the Winter Palace.

TROTSKY

In St Petersburg the Menshevik Leon Trotsky took an active part in creating a form of direct democracy. Through the soviets workers were enabled to organize themselves independently of the government.

AFTERMATH OF 1905

After the crushing of the revolution, gallows – known as "Stolypin cravats" – became a common sight. Officially the Russian state was a constitutional monarchy, but in reality laws were applied arbitrarily and agrarian problems remained unsolved.

THE AGRARIAN REFORM OF 1906

This reform, arranged by Piotr Stolypin, consigned to oblivion the peasant communes which had hitherto regulated daily life in the countryside. Instead, it proposed the creation of a new social category of independent landowners.

45

THE 1917 REVOLUTION

Nicholas II and his family, prisoners at Tsarskoe Selo.

Russia's problems were compounded by World War One. The economy was unable to accelerate its rate of production to meet the new needs. Prices rose and inflation attained alarming proportions. Nicholas II was no longer a credible monarch, being perceived as the protector of Rasputin, a debauched charlatan who had cured his son Alexei; and as he was commander-in-chief of the Army a series of military defeats were sufficient to destroy the Czar altogether. The 4th Duma, which had remained loyal to him until 1915, finally stiffened in its opposition and resolved to depose him.

THE FALL OF THE CZARIST SYSTEM

The Czarist regime collapsed in five days, between February 23 and 27. Two plots, one in the Czar's immediate entourage, the other fomented by deputies in the Duma, projected the Czar's replacement by his brother. But the conspirators were forestalled by a spontaneous uprising by workers and soldiers in Petrograd, who seized the Arsenal and proclaimed a republic.

TWO POWERS

A power struggle ensued between the members of the provisional government, led by Prince Lvov, who wished to install a parliamentary regime and thereafter maintain the status quo, and the Petrograd Soviet, which advocated radical change.

FRATERNITY

While the streets of Petrograd resounded to the strains of the "Varsovienne" in honor of the martyrs of international revolution, the April Crisis suddenly struck. The Soviet offered the allies a "peace without annexations or reparations", which the provisional government affected to ignore.

SOCIALIST POWER
The socialist Kerensky, who became Prime Minister in July, was unable to control the radicalization of the masses.

"ALL POWER TO THE SOVIETS"
From April onward this was the rallying cry of the Bolsheviks. Their role in crushing a *putsch* led by General Kornilov, a monarchist rival of Kerensky, enabled them to attract both revolutionary socialists and Mensheviks to their cause during August. The bolshevization of the soviets was then quickly accomplished.

THE BOLSHEVIK TRIUMPH
This poster, which has since become an icon, was at first little understood. The failure of the Kornilov *putsch* drew Western attention away from Russia. In France and England the fall of Kerensky and the October Revolution ▲ *248* were passed over almost without comment, even in well-informed socialist circles. The bolshevization of the soviets likewise went unnoticed.

The Terror, or Purge, is often explained in terms of the personal motivations of Stalin himself, who was bent on revenge against the older Bolsheviks and on gaining absolute power. In fact, Stalin's ambitions were quickly outstripped by the sheer enormity of the phenomenon he had instigated. After the assassination of Kirov the Purge reached a paroxysm, with over two million political prisoners between 1934 and 1938. The State-Party system never succeeded in overcoming the socio-economic difficulties stemming from violent collectivization and accelerated industrialization. Confronted with social tensions, officials at every level of Soviet society promoted the fear of Stalin, along with his virtual deification.

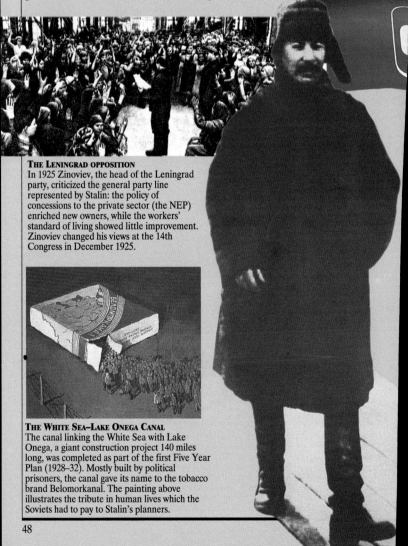

THE LENINGRAD OPPOSITION
In 1925 Zinoviev, the head of the Leningrad party, criticized the general party line represented by Stalin: the policy of concessions to the private sector (the NEP) enriched new owners, while the workers' standard of living showed little improvement. Zinoviev changed his views at the 14th Congress in December 1925.

THE WHITE SEA–LAKE ONEGA CANAL
The canal linking the White Sea with Lake Onega, a giant construction project 140 miles long, was completed as part of the first Five Year Plan (1928–32). Mostly built by political prisoners, the canal gave its name to the tobacco brand Belomorkanal. The painting above illustrates the tribute in human lives which the Soviets had to pay to Stalin's planners.

THE ASSASSINATION OF KIROV

Kirov (below), the party chief, was very popular in Leningrad on account of his attempts to raise the workers' standard of living. On December 1, 1934 Kirov's assassination allowed those responsible for Russia's economic chaos to direct the popular fury against "spies", "saboteurs" and other "turncoats".

ИСКОРЕНИМ
ШПИОНОВ и ДИВЕРСАНТОВ!

"NIGHT TERROR"

The great show trials held in Moscow unleashed a widespread sense of insecurity, the "night terror". Arrests were invariably carried out at dawn.

THE PURGE OF COSMOPOLITANS

Leningrad artists and intellectuals were the first victims of a campaign led by Zhdanov, the ideological head of the Central Committee, who demanded "proletarian science and art".

1948: THE LENINGRAD AFFAIR

Popov, the party chief (below), was shot along with a number of other officials on a charge of seeking to turn Leningrad into the capital of a federal Russia.

THE SIEGE OF LENINGRAD

CONDEMNED TO DEATH
The three million inhabitants under siege by the
Wehrmacht had fuel and provisions for only two
months: their water and electricity supplies were
cut by the bombardments. Only a quarter of the
sixty-eight armaments factories supplying the
defenders of Leningrad were operational.

Soviet agents and diplomats rapidly
informed Stalin of alarming German
troop movements along the frontier.
Having underestimated the threat,
Stalin found himself obliged to
intervene personally when Nazi troops
flooded into the USSR. The ensuing
battle, as sudden as it was
catastrophic, took a huge toll in
Russian lives. The siege of Leningrad,
which was to last nine hundred days,
was one of the most tragic
consequences of Stalin's giant error.
On September 8, 1941 the front had
come within 4 miles of the city's
southwestern edge, and Leningrad was
linked to the rest of the country only
by air and by way of the frozen waters
of Lake Ladoga.

FAMINE IN LENINGRAD
Famine took hold from the autumn of 1941 onward, and
was sharpened by the loss by fire of most of the
warehouses containing the city's meager reserves of
food. By December over 53,000 people had died, and
the daily bread ration was down to 9 oz for workers and
4½ oz for the unemployed and for children. During the
siege over 800,000 people died of hunger, 17,000 were
killed, and 35,000 were wounded in the fighting.

THE LIFELINE
One of the few ways out of besieged Leningrad lay
across the frozen waters of Lake Ladoga. From
November 1942 a track was made across the ice which
allowed the city to be supplied with bread. In the
summer a network of pipes and cables running across
the bed of the lake carried electricity and gasoline to the
beleaguered citizens.

> "WE HAVE NO FEAR OF BULLETS
> NOR DO WE GRIEVE FOR OUR HOUSES,
> BUT WE ARE RESOLVED TO PRESERVE OUR MOTHER TONGUE
> IN ALL ITS TRUTH AND FORCE."
>
> ANNA AKHMATOVA, FEB. 23, 1942

HOPE RETURNS

By the end of 1942 Leningrad was gradually coming back to life: factories reopened and the nightmare of famine faded. In January 1943 the Red Army succeeded in breaking the German blockade along the lake shore: a railway was constructed via Schlisselburg, known as the "Victory Line".

A SYMBOL OF LIFE

The composer Dmitry Shostakovich, who volunteered for military service, was assigned for his own safety to sentry duty on the roof of the Conservatoire and ordered to compose a special work for the People's Theater. Evacuated from Moscow at the age of 35, he completed his work in the Urals: the *7th ("Leningrad") Symphony* ▲ *228* was performed at Kubichev and Leningrad in 1942.

IMPERISHABLE GLORY

The celebratory fireworks of January 27, 1944 clothed the city in a lasting aura of heroism. After the war a million citizens were decorated for their part in the siege. At the coming of *perestroika*, the Museum of the Defense of Leningrad (instituted 1946–9), reopened its doors; an association of survivors was founded, and September 8 was declared a day of national mourning.

Russian belongs to the Eastern Slavic group of languages, along with Ukrainian and Byelorussian. These three languages, with Serbian, Macedonian and Bulgarian, are all (with very slight variations) written with the cyrillic alphabet.
(Below left, a table of cyrillic characters given with their Roman equivalents.)

IMPRI-MERIE	ÉCRITURE	APPEL-ATION	IMPRI-MERIE	ÉCRITURE	APPEL-ATION
А а	*A a*	a	Р р	*P p*	erre
Б б	*Б б*	bé	С с	*C c*	esse
В в	*B в*	vé	Т т	*T т*	té
Г г	*Г г*	ghé	У у	*У у*	ou
Д д	*Д д*	dé	Ф ф	*Ф ф*	effe
Е е	*Е е*	yé	Х х	*Х х*	kha
Ж ж	*Ж ж*	jé	Ц ц	*Ц ц*	tsé
З з	*З з*	zé	Ч ч	*Ч ч*	tché
И и	*И и*	i	Ш ш	*Ш ш*	cha
й	*й*	i krat koé (i bref)	Щ щ	*Щ щ*	chtcha
I i	*У i*	i	Ъ ъ	*ъ*	tvoerdy znak (signe dur)
К к	*К к*	ka	Ы ы	*ры*	i dur miagky znak (signe mou)
Л л	*Л л*	elle	Ь ь	*ь*	
М м	*М м*	emme	Э э	*Э э*	è
Н н	*Н К*	enne	Ю ю	*Ю ю*	iou
О о	*О о*	o	Я я	*Я я*	ia
П п	*П п*	pé			

THE CYRILLIC ALPHABET

In 863 the monk Cyril and his brother Methodus perfected the glagolitic alphabet, although this was soon supplanted by a simplified equivalent, the cyrillic. This alphabet includes several characters taken from both the Greek and Roman alphabets. In 1710 Peter the Great, with his *grajdnka* (civil alphabet), suppressed the graphic survivals of nasal vowels, and simplified the forms of certain letters. The orthographic reform of 1917 replaced the Ѣ by e, and almost did away with the use of the hard sign Ъ. The cyrillic alphabet in its present form contains thirty-two letters.

THE SLAVIC LANGUAGE

Common Slavic was the only language spoken in the plains of Northern Europe toward the middle of the first millennium AD. Old Slav as spoken in the 9th century (at the beginning of the differentiation between the Slavic languages and peoples) is still understood by most Slavs. From it came Slavonic, a literary and religious language still used in the liturgy of Orthodox Slavs.

FOREIGN CONTRIBUTIONS

For centuries thereafter the Psalter was to be the principal reading matter of Russians. Their many contacts with Byzantium, both peaceful and belligerent, eventually led to the conversion of the Kiev prince Vladimir in 988, followed by that of his people; this event marked the entry of the pagan Slavs into Christendom. Later Western influences contributed to the development of oral and folk art, in

Cyril and Methodus were sent to Moravia by the Byzantine Emperor Michael III to evangelize the Slavs. Their new alphabet allowed them to translate the New Testament into the old Slav language.

addition to an original and precocious body of literature, notably *The Sayings of Prince Igor*. After the 11th century old Russian texts, such as the Ostromir New Testament, were written in a mixture of authentic Russian and Slavonic, the proportions of which varied from period to period and genre to genre. The interaction of these two languages eventually determined the form of what we know as literary Russian.

LOMONOSOV

In his *Russian Grammar* (1755) Lomonosov, a brilliant self-taught scholar, historian and philologist, purged the written language of obsolete Slavonic expressions, then reordered the lexicon into three categories: Slavonic, mixed and Russian terms. Three styles emerged from the combination of these elements: low, medium and high. This rigid classification had the merit of giving spoken Russian the place it deserved in literature (including song, epigram, private correspondence, comedy), the Slavonic terms being relegated to a more abstract, elevated linguistic register.

THE AWAKENING NATION

The Mongol invasion (13th century) and the domination of the "Golden Horde" (Tartar state) condemned the Russian language to centuries of isolation, which was eventually shaken off by a new religious and national awareness. This turning inward, at first forced but later deliberate, was generally damaging, but after a period of difficulty, in 1613 the Romanovs took over: intellectual inquiry again appeared along with literature. The Slavonic, Greek and Latin Academy, founded in Moscow in 1682, used a ponderous, artificial, heavily russified Slavonic language which stifled poetic creativity; yet it laid the groundwork for the blossoming of Russian literature in

the century that followed, by bringing *belles-lettres* to the forefront of Russian life.

LITERATURE AND THE RUSSIAN LANGUAGE

THE LANGUAGE OF POETS

Even more than grammarians, writers like Sumarokov, Derzhavin and Karamzin (left) were the architects of the modern Russian language. At the turn of the 18th into the 19th century they prepared the ground for the great works of Pushkin. Under Catherine the Great intellectual and artistic life intensified in richness and was marked by a desire to imitate French classicism as well as scrupulously to respect the hierarchy of genres and styles established by Lomonosov. Karamzin rejected all distinctions between the spoken language and the written one: his ambition was to elevate spoken Russian to the status of a literary language.

MODERN RUSSIAN

Thus modern literary Russian emerged by stages, enriched by the language spoken by ordinary people. Russian songs and *bylines* (song epics) passed into print and, thanks to the discovery of *The Sayings of Prince Igor*, the master story-writer Ivan Krylov was able to contribute to a synthesis between popular and academic Russian. Nevertheless, it was Alexander Pushkin who perfected literary expression in the Russian language, with his motto: "When things are simple, say them simply."

THE SPREAD OF THE RUSSIAN LANGUAGE

With the creation of the Soviet Union and its fifteen republics, twelve of which were non-Slav, Russian became the official language of the Federation.

Learning the language was made compulsory, not only for Soviet youth but also for the youth of the other Eastern countries. Many Africans, Asians and Latin Americans went to study in the Soviet Union and learned to speak fluent Russian.

spread. Under the cultural influence of the West the language has borrowed heavily (and sometimes inelegantly) from foreign tongues, absorbing words which have often supplanted Russian ones. Yet Russian is also acquiring new home-grown terms to describe the political, economic, social and moral upheavals of the era.

Today Russian is one of the five official languages of the United Nations, even though the difficulties of Russia at the close of the 20th century have begun to impede its

УЧИСЬ СЫНОК

ARTS AND TRADITIONS

Today, as in the past, foreign visitors to Russia are amazed by the magnificence of the Orthodox liturgy, the gold of its icons and its polyphonic choral music. The Russians themselves cherish the beauty and symbolism of their Byzantine rite; a beauty which, according to the old chronicles, originally motivated their conversion to Christianity. Beyond their esthetic value these rites embody theological and spiritual teachings which remain unaltered since the 17th-century schism of the traditionalist "Old Believers". The Orthodox liturgy was the sole vehicle of faith permitted by the Soviet regime.

THE LITURGY
The length and the sheer splendor of Orthodox services tend to reinforce the idea of eternity and holiness, while its informality seems to welcome all comers.

The Orthodox year, with its round of feasts and fasts, is extremely rich and varied. The Russian Church still observes the Julian Calendar, which is thirteen days out of step with the Gregorian Calendar. The linchpin of church life is the Sunday Eucharist, during which clergy and congregation, including young children, take Communion.

RUSSIAN CLERGY
Parish priests (often married men) form the "white" clergy, while the "black" clergy are monks who have taken vows. Formerly the color of their vestments showed the difference between them. The bishops are appointed from among the monks and celibate or widowed priests; the principal of these bishops, the Patriarch of Moscow, is the titular head of the Russian Orthodox Church.

THE ICONOSTASIS
Covered with five rows of icons ● 58 and topped by a cross, the iconostasis is a central element in every Russian Orthodox church. It depicts the prophets, the feasts of the liturgical year and the dëesis (prayer) of the saints in company with Christ. The larger lower row is made up of the icons of Christ, the Virgin and the various saints. It has three doors, used by the clergy: the central one (the "royal door"), reserved for the most solemn rites of the Orthodox Church, symbolizes the entrance to the kingdom of God.

ORTHODOX CHURCHES
As the meeting point of God and mankind, the church signifies heaven on earth. Orthodox churches can be square or cruciform, and have a central dome; important churches have five domes, symbolizing Christ and the four Evangelists.

THE SEVEN SACRAMENTS
The Orthodox rite of baptism is followed by Chrismation (or Confirmation). The other sacraments are the Eucharist, marriage, ordination of the clergy, penitence, and the anointing of the sick.

ORTHODOX EASTER
Called the "feast of feasts", Easter is the climax of the Orthodox year. After the forty-day Lenten fast and the ceremonies of Holy Week, the celebration rite begins with a candlelit procession, followed by the announcement of Christ's Resurrection. At Matins the victory of life over death is exalted; later, friends and relatives gather round the Easter table, with its Easter eggs and cakes blessed at church.

The Orthodox Church, which rejected the charge of idolatry made during the iconoclastic controversy in Byzantium (8th century), defines the icon as bearing witness to divine revelation, and thus justifiable in terms of the dogma of incarnation (God may not be represented in a picture but Christ, who was made man, can be). The icon is neither a work of art nor a pious image: it has a clear liturgical function, as well as a teaching role.

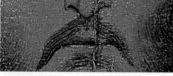

THE ORIGINS
Icons, which came to Russia with Christianity from Byzantium, reached a degree of perfection following the iconoclastic crisis. The Greek mosaic artists who decorated the churches of Kiev in the 11th century trained the first Russian iconographers. In the *Head of Christ* below the influence of mosaic is clearly discernible, notably in the golden lines traced through the hair.

A PAINTED SCRIPT
The technique of icon-making has not changed for centuries. It employs only natural materials. The wooden panel is first covered with a fine layer of plaster, and the image is painted on the wet surface; the powdered mineral colors are blended with an egg-based emulsion. The painting is then embellished with gold leaf and varnished, and the title is inscribed in vermilion lettering. In the Slavonic language a single word is used for the functions of writing and painting; therefore the artist does not merely paint his icon but he "writes" it too. Above: *Life of Saint Serge of Radonega* (16th century).

A WINDOW ON ETERNITY
This *Christ in Majesty* (16th century) shows all the symbolism and sanctity of the icon, through the use of concentric circles and inverted perspective to express a relationship between time and space which is very different to that of the world in which we live. In this way the icon becomes a kind of window on eternity. Such rules were codified in manuals, which also laid out guidelines for icon composition, the ordering of themes and use of color.

ANONYMOUS WORKS
Novgorod, Pskov, Suzdal and later Moscow succeeded one another as schools of iconography, each with its own tradition. The icon was never signed by an individual, but the fine rendering of the *Presentation of Christ* (right) is probably the work of Andrei Rublev, the great Muscovite icon-painter of the 15th century.

DECADENCE
From the 17th century onward the art of the icon was affected by excessive symbolism and borrowings from the West. The detailed and naturalistic *Trinity* (1671) by Simeon Uchakov, the official Kremlin painter, differs greatly from the icon by Rublev which inspired it.

REDISCOVERY OF THE ICON
In the 16th century a tradition arose of covering almost the entire work with precious metals. In the *Virgin of Kazan* (above, late 19th century) only the faces are visible. In the early 20th century the icon regained its original esthetic and theological aspects.

GOLD AND SILVER WORK

In the 18th century gold and silver work made in St Petersburg differed little from that of the rest of northern Europe, because the craft was essentially the preserve of foreigners who had moved to Russia's new capital. Even so, while the second half of that century was strongly marked by the influence of France, St Petersburg gained a high reputation for the sheer quantity and refinement of the objects produced by its jewelers. Although luxury items they were often in everyday use at court and in the houses of the rich. As a result this specifically Russian taste for enamel and precious stones had a strong influence on local production.

Part of a harness (1730).

STEEL WORK

The Tula works, founded in 1712, produced a wide variety of objects. Although its specialty was weapons it was also famous for its domestic products; later it turned to the manufacture of furniture, the finest examples of which may be seen at Pavlovsk. The technique used was that of "blueing" the steel, and subsequently decorating it with gold, silver or copper. The cutting of the steel to resemble facetted pearls, as well as its polish, produced an effect which is still highly valued by collectors.

JEWELRY AND GEMSTONES

Jérémie Pauzié, who made the gemstone flowers above, was born in Switzerland in 1716. At the age of thirteen he was apprenticed to a St Petersburg jeweler and, although he belonged to no special guild, was made court jeweler in 1740. This bouquet, mounted in a vase in the 19th century, was originally made to be worn at the shoulder or on a belt. It is typical of the court's pronounced taste in gems, which Pauzié used in profusion.

MASTERWORKS

This gilded silver platter, decorated by the *repoussé* technique, resembles the work being done at the same period in Germany. There is no hallmark on the piece but the dedication to Peter the Great dates it to between 1721 and 1725.

Chessmen, Tula, late 18th century.

TOBACCO BOX

Tobacco boxes of this type were very much the fashion at the Russian court; they were frequently presented by monarchs as diplomatic gifts, and were also given as lovers' pledges. Pauzié made scores of them for the Empress Elizabeth I.

● FABERGÉ

Cigarette box, gold and enamel (1908).

"If you compare my creations to those of Tiffany, Boucheron and Cartier you will conclude that they are of lesser value . . . but what, in fact, are these companies? They are sellers of jewelry, they are not artists. Hugely valuable objects interest me little, if their value resides in nothing more than an infinity of diamonds and pearls." This remark by Fabergé neatly expresses the spirit of his world-famous firm.

CARL FABERGÉ
Born in St Petersburg in 1846, the son of a modest jeweler of Huguenot stock, Peter Carl Fabergé took over the family business in 1870 and began by producing jewelry to conform with the prevailing taste for all things French. The arrival of his brother Agathon, an imaginative artist, contributed to the blossoming of the business after 1882.

THE FLOWERS
Fabergé's naturalist compositions are executed with astonishing skill: oatgrass and cornflowers on golden stalks rise from a translucent vase of rock crystal.

THE EGGS
Fabergé's eggs are marvels of inventiveness and delicacy. They are still copied today.

ENAMELS
Worked in *champlevé* or applied in successive layers on a checkered background, enamelwork was produced in over a hundred different hues.

PRECIOUS METALS
Fabergé's metals were also very finely worked: up to four shades of gold might be blended to produce the desired effect. Silver was deliberately left in its original state.

IMPERIAL COMMISSIONS
Under the aegis of the master Mikhail Perkhin, in the 1890's Fabergé's workshops produced large quantities of objects and gems, many of them commissioned by the Czar's family. Fabergé Easter eggs were given by Nicholas II to his mother and his wife.

SEMI-PRECIOUS STONES
Pink and black rhodonite, mouse-gray Kalkan jasper and pale green nephrite (mined in the Urals) gave Fabergé's designers all the imaginative scope they needed to create their confectionery dishes, figurines and quaint animal sculptures.

● PORCELAIN

1749

Peter the Great had tried to reproduce Delft and Meissen "porcelain" (in fact it was faience) in Russia, without success. It was not until the appearance of Dmitry Vinogradov (1720–58), a friend of the famous savant Lomonosov, that the technique was achieved with any degree of success. Later, in the reign of Elizabeth I, the process of manufacture was perfected, a fact mentioned in a contemporary publication. The first imperial porcelain works on the banks of the Neva produced buttons, cane tops and knife handles (1745–50). Then, as technical skills improved, complete table services were manufactured for the court, along with statuettes whose imperfections were often masked by lavish gilding.

MADE-TO-ORDER TABLE SERVICES
Private factories soon made their appearance, competing directly with the imperial works; they created made-to-order table services, some commissioned by Catherine II. These services, which might include up to a thousand pieces, reflect the growing luxury of the imperial table, particularly in the 19th century.

FIGURINES
The production of figurines, typically Russian, has never ceased in St Petersburg. The only changes brought to it by the Revolution were in the types of figures portrayed.

GUREEV TABLE SERVICE (1807)

This service bears the name of the head of Alexander I's Imperial Cabinet. The various pieces are remarkably diverse, with beautifully defined figures.

FROM REVIVED STYLES TO ART NOUVEAU

Following its approximation to the Sèvres style in the late 18th century, Russian porcelain went through a historicist period in the first quarter of the 19th century. Later it regressed into a multicolored, richly gilded Rococo style. At the close of the 19th century the imperial porcelain works came under the influence of Copenhagen, adopting modern simplified forms and new colors and designs in the Art Nouveau style.

CONSTRUCTIVIST PORCELAIN

Porcelain manufacture was a domain in which the modernization of designs and ideas could immediately be applied. This meant that propaganda themes coexisted with Constructivist work, often produced by such renowned artists as Malevich and Kandinsky, who in no way disdained this unusual medium. Above, a tea-service in porcelain designed by Malevich; the link with his paintings

● *109, 110* is evident.

As a rule the palaces of St Petersburg were decorated with furniture designed on French, English and German models, when these pieces were not directly imported from Western Europe. Furniture made in Russia remained simple and massive until the reign of Peter I, but its quality developed rapidly throughout the second half of the 18th century. The extensive building projects of Catherine II and her court stimulated a marked increase in demand, which eventually could be satisfied only by locally made products.

In the time of Peter the Great, the furniture trade specialized in marquetry as well as carved, painted and gilded pieces.

FREEDOM OF MOVEMENT
In the 18th century the work of cabinet-making in Russia was shared between the master-craftsmen of St Petersburg and trained serfs on aristocratic estates. Their virtuosity proved the innate skills of Russian woodworkers: the materials they used were many and varied, and they did not hesitate to blend indigenous wood species, which had an undeserved reputation for poor quality, with more exotic ones.

CARELIAN BIRCHWOOD In the early 19th century new types of furniture – tiered consoles, serpent-shaped elbow rests and claw-foot armchairs – were introduced. Between 1820 and 1840 the use of natural woods became generalized, emphasizing the ornate aspect of Carelian birchwood.

NEW MATERIALS
An instinct for variety in materials is characteristic of this aspect of Russian decorative art. Already in the reigns of Elizabeth I and Catherine II steel-based furniture manufactured at the Tula works had made its appearance ● *60* near Moscow.

SCHOOL OF TALACHKINO
At the close of the 19th century the predominant furniture style still had its roots in Russian culture. Furniture of the Talachkino School reflected the carved geometrical shapes of the empire's Byzantine origins.

"RUSSIAN JACOB"
Another exclusive style of the late 18th century was "Russian Jacob" (strips of brass inlaid in mahogany, in geometrical patterns).

GILT AND SEMI-PRECIOUS STONES
In the 19th century Russia produced remarkable pieces of furniture (such as tables and monumental candelabra) incorporating colored crystal and stones mined in the Urals, which added to the exoticism of the new Italianate palaces then being built.

In their own way the theaters of St Petersburg bear witness to Russian political history, since their names invariably changed to reflect the party in power. As the custodians of Russia's great dramatic, lyrical and choreographical works the imperial Mariinsky and Alexandrinsky theaters mounted the masquerades of the early 20th century, which are evoked in Anna Akhmatova's *Poem without a Hero*. These illustrated the dreams of a society in crisis; they included Lermontov's legendary *Masked Ball*, with lavish décor by Alexander Golovine. With *perestroika*, new theaters emerged; and recent productions directed by Lev Dodin have demonstrated the enduring vitality of the Russian theater.

ALEXANDRINSKY THEATER ▲ *230*. As the Academy of Drama in 1920, renamed the Pushkin Theater in 1937, the Alexandrinsky was, along with the Maly Theater in Moscow, one of the two great centers of 19th-century Russian culture. Between 1908 and 1918 it was profoundly influenced by the work of the great reformer Vsevolod Meyerhold.

MARIINSKY THEATER ▲ *202*
This great institution was inaugurated in 1860, with the purpose of presenting the classical repertoire. Renamed the Kirov Theater in 1935, it later became the mecca of the Russian Ballet ▲ *200*. It reverted to its original name in 1993.

LITTLE THEATER OF OPERA AND BALLET
▲ *225*
Also known as the Maly or Mussorgsky Theater, at one time this was named the Mikhailovsky Theater. As the third of the former imperial playhouses it was the home of a French company from 1879 to 1917. Renamed the Little (Maly) Theater, it was one of the few experimental institutions for opera and ballet in Russia during the 1930's.

BDT (TOVSTONOGOV THEATER)
"Theater of tragedy, romantic drama and high comedy" – or so its original purpose was described.

The theater was known as the Gorky Theater between 1932 and 1993. For thirty years it mounted the classic plays of G.A. Tovstonogov, after whom it was renamed in 1993.

THEATER OF MUSICAL COMEDY (1929)
The director and satirical artist Nicholas Akimov (left) worked here from 1930 to 1950. This theater is known for its original repertoire.

LITTLE (MALY) DRAMATIC THEATER ▲ *238*
This repertory theater, founded in 1944, acquired a wider reputation in the 1980's under its director Lev Dodin. The Maly Theater Company gained worldwide fame with new plays like *Brothers and Sisters* (1985, from a novel by F. Abramov) and *Gaudeamus* (1990, by Sergei Kaledin). The Maly's style is notable for its realism and its often acrobatic stagecraft.

St Petersburg, where the first school of Russian dance opened in 1738, well in advance of Moscow, is the cradle of ballet. The entire history of classical dance is marked by Russian emotion and poetry, which enriched a technique originally imported from Europe. This enabled Russian dancers, while mastering both Italian virtuosity and French academic rigor, to apply themselves to the expression of the inner life of their roles. From the *divertissements* and interludes devised by 18th-century ballet masters such as Landé and Fossano to the worldwide phenomenon of the Diaghilev ballets, Russia has raised this particular art to the highest level of her cultural heritage.

BALLETS RUSSES (1908–29)
The success of the Ballets Russes gave a new stimulus to European ballet, as dance in Russia became the focus of a wide variety of artistic movements and interests. The research of the choreographer Fokine and the painters Bakst and Benois resurrected images of antiquity, the Orient, Old Russia and traditional festivals.

LEON BAKST (1866–1924)
As a scene-painter and decorator working for Serge Diaghilev, Leon Bakst moved to Paris in 1909. Above, a costume design for *Narcisse*, Saisons Russes, Paris 1911. Baskt's sketches are on show at the Theater Museum, Ostrovsky Square ▲ *231*.

SERGE DIAGHILEV (1872–1929)
As the founder of the World of Art association Diaghilev masterminded the successful Saisons Russes tours abroad. He brought together the most brilliant and innovative artistic talents of his time: Bakst and Picasso, Fokine and Nijinsky, Karsavina and Pavlova, Rimsky-Korsakov, Stravinsky, Prokofiev and many more.

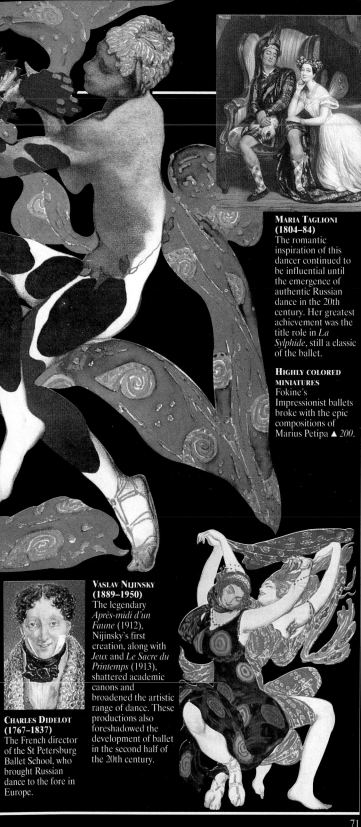

MARIA TAGLIONI (1804–84)
The romantic inspiration of this dancer continued to be influential until the emergence of authentic Russian dance in the 20th century. Her greatest achievement was the title role in *La Sylphide*, still a classic of the ballet.

HIGHLY COLORED MINIATURES
Fokine's Impressionist ballets broke with the epic compositions of Marius Petipa ▲ *200*.

VASLAV NIJINSKY (1889–1950)
The legendary *Après-midi d'un Faune* (1912), Nijinsky's first creation, along with *Jeux* and *Le Sacre du Printemps* (1913), shattered academic canons and broadened the artistic range of dance. These productions also foreshadowed the development of ballet in the second half of the 20th century.

CHARLES DIDELOT (1767–1837)
The French director of the St Petersburg Ballet School, who brought Russian dance to the fore in Europe.

71

● MUSIC

The Capella, the Conservatoire and the Philharmonia, as the centers of St Petersburg's musical establishment, made it their business to encourage artistic creativity and the expression of musical talent. In the 20th century the musical traditions of the St Petersburg School are associated with the esthetic of the Group of Five, which included the composers Balakirev, Borodin, Cui, Mussorgsky and Rimsky-Korsakov. While the historic past and folktales of Russia were the main sources of inspiration, the music itself remained thoroughly European.

THE CAPELLA

Founded in 1479 in the reign of Ivan III, the original purpose of the Capella was to train church choirs. In the 18th century, at St Petersburg, it became an imperial chapel, with the most talented musicians serving as its directors. Later it offered a wide variety of musical training, from directing of choirs (1846) to folk music (1918). In 1920 the Capella introduced women's voices into Russian choirs for the first time.

THE CONSERVATOIRE

The fame of the Conservatoire, founded in 1862, rests on the extraordinary creative activity which at one time was centered upon it. The musicologist and art historian Stasov was the catalyst for the Group of Five composers, who were inspired by folktales and historical legends such as Boris Godunov; these were very different from the Moscow School, represented by Tchaikovsky and Rachmaninov, whose musical inspiration was more European in style.

THE PHILHARMONIA

This institution, founded in 1921, was named after Shostakovich in 1974. Dmitry Shostakovich (1906–75), although a quasi-official Soviet composer, fell out of favor with the authorities in 1947. Encouraged by Zhdanov, he belonged to the tradition of Bach and Mussorgsky. His work includes fifteen symphonies, among them the famous *7th* ("*Leningrad*") *Symphony* ● *51.*

SERGEI PROKOFIEV (1891–1953)

Trained as a pianist and composer at the St Petersburg Conservatoire, Prokofiev began his career as a concert artist. Between 1918 and 1932 he lived outside Russia; on his return to the Soviet Union he suffered political persecution. His work sums up the finest achievements of Russian music, from Glinka through to Rachmaninov (*Romeo and Juliet*, 1938).

IGOR STRAVINSKY (1882–1971)

A pupil of Rimsky-Korsakov, Stravinsky lived in Russia until 1914. Later he was a permanent member of the Saisons Russes in Paris, where his ballets *The Firebird* (1910), *Petrushka* (1911) and *The Rite of Spring* (1913) were performed. The themes of these ballets were inspired by Russian folklore.

● RECIPE: "BLINIS"

Blinis, made from one of the oldest of flour-based recipes, were originally eaten "in communion" with the souls of deceased loved ones in Russia: at Christmas with *koutia* (broth made with cracked wheat), at funerals and during Carnival. Following the 1917 Revolution *blinis* became everyday fare in Russia, unconnected with the Orthodox calendar.

PREPARING THE MIXTURE

Ingredients
(for six people):
2lb 3 oz/10 cups flour
1½ oz yeast
½ tsp salt
1 tsp caster sugar
10 fl. oz lukewarm water
1 pint lukewarm milk
3 tbsp oil
3 eggs

1. Prepare in advance: in a warm bowl dissolve the yeast, salt and sugar in the lukewarm water. Pour the mixture into a mixing bowl.

2. Mixing well with a whisk, add the flour, milk and egg yolks, working till smooth.

3. Allow the mixture to rise in a warm place for 40 minutes. Cover the bowl. Then whip the egg whites until stiff.

ПОЖАЛУЙ ПОДИ ПРОЧЬ ОТЪМЕНА МНЕ ДЕЛА НЕТ ДАТЕБА
ПРИШЕЛЪ ЗАЖЕПУ ХВАТАЕШЬ БЛИНОВЪ ПЕЧЬ МЕШАЕШЬ
ЗАЖЕПУ ХВАТАТЬ НЕВЕЛАТЪ ДЛАТОГО ЧТО БЛИНЫ
ПОДГОРАТЪ АТОТЪ ЧАСЪ РЕСОНЪ СЫШУ СКОВОРОДНЕМЪ ХВ
АЧЮ МНЕ ХОТА ІСТЫДНО ДТЕ БУДЕТЪ УЖЕ ОБИДНО А ВИТЬ

4. Gently fold the egg whites into the mixture with a spatula.

6. Pour a little of the mixture into the heated frying pan, turning the pan to make the mixture spread as thinly as possible.

5. Lightly grease a 5-inch frying pan with a half-potato dipped in melted butter.

7. Cook at medium heat, as with pancakes (the first is often a disaster).

8. The *blinis* are then covered with melted butter and thick cream (*smetana*), and eaten with *zakouskis* (hors d'oeuvres): smoked salmon, tarama, herring, salmon eggs, or similar tasty accompaniments. Traditionally, Russians serve *blinis* with an assortment of chilled red and black caviar and ice-cold vodka.

CAVIAR

● RUSSIAN
SPECIALTIES

SHAWLS
Light and warm, Russian shawls come in many colors, usually with bright flower patterns. They are available in most department stores in St Petersburg.

ZEFIRS
Sweets resembling meringues coated in chocolate.

RUSSIAN VODKA
As the Russian national drink, vodka is sold everywhere; but beware of imitations.

MATRYOSHKAS
These little dolls, usually made by Muscovite craftsmen, are very popular with tourists. The quality of the painted design may vary considerably.

CRAFTS
Lacquered Palekh boxes (right) echo the art of this former school of iconography. Look, too, for objects made of amber or semi-precious stones, such as this green malachite box (right).

ARCHITECTURE

THE TOWN PLAN: THE FOUNDING OF ST PETERSBURG

PETER I'S SKETCH FOR PETERHOF (1712)

This "Trident" design, copied from Versailles, was used on the left bank of the Neva, the Admiralty supplying the point of convergence of the three avenues.

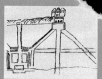

In May 1703 Peter I, then at war with the Swedes, captured a stronghold at the mouth of the Neva river. To consolidate his victory he began building a new fortress 4 miles downstream dedicated to saints Peter and Paul, later adding the Admiralty and shipyards on the left bank. The site was unhealthy and ill-protected; nevertheless, by 1712 the Czar was determined to build his new capital there. St Petersburg, ". . . the window through which Russia looked out on Europe", evolved into a huge experiment, whereby patterns borrowed from Western cities were assimilated into Russian tradition.

ПЛАНЪ
МѢСТНОСТИ
САНКТПЕТЕРБУРГА.
въ 1700 году.

HISTORY AND LEGEND

The legend of this city, which was born of the will of a single man, has left an indelible mark on history. Built "on the corpses of thousands of men", popular tradition has it that St Petersburg will one day return to the waves from which it rose.

THE MOUTH OF THE NEVA IN 1698

Apart from one or two settlements of Carelians, the flat, sea-level islands of St Petersburg were uninhabited and clothed with forest. They were subject to floods made even more fearsome by the current flowing out of Lake Ladoga where it meets the powerful waves of the Gulf of Finland.

THE PETER AND PAUL FORTRESS (1703)

A symbol of autocratic military power, the Peter and Paul Fortress stands directly across the Neva from the Imperial Palace. The gilded spires of the Peter and Paul Cathedral, the Admiralty and Mikhail Palace add bright verticals to the flat, gray urban landscape.

THE DEVELOPMENT OF THE CITY

The plans drawn up by Jean-Baptiste Leblond, the chief architect for St Petersburg, were remarkable for a system of Dutch-style canals, supposed to absorb the flood waters and facilitate communications. Other features were an arrangement of the various districts to suit different sections of the population, and an attempt (eventually abandoned) to surround the city with ramparts.

● St Petersburg in 1725

Although in 1725 St Petersburg was far from completed, the planning options governing its later construction were already fixed. There were two fortresses to guard the mouth of the Neva (Peter and Paul on the right bank and the Admiralty on the left); the Menshikov Palace and the Kunstkammer endowed Vasilyevsky Island with its first architectural features; the Summer Palace and the gardens bounded the city to eastward; the river's tributaries had been channeled; and the Nevsky Prospekt had been laid out.

WAREHOUSES
The first constructions in the city were of wood, always abundant in Russia.

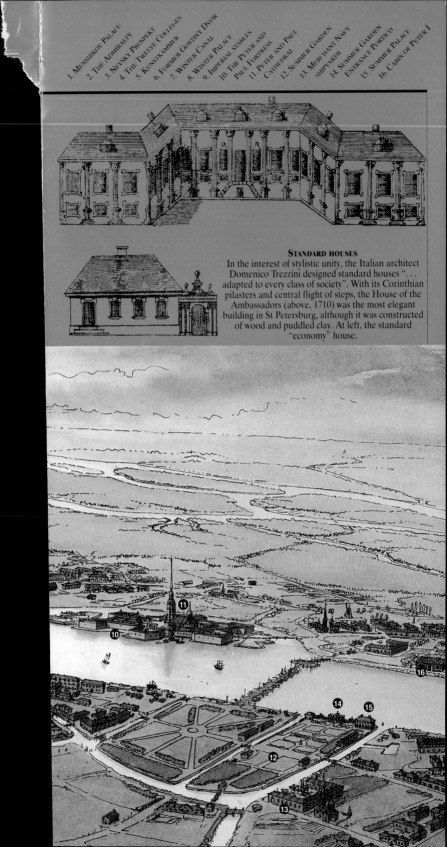

STANDARD HOUSES

In the interest of stylistic unity, the Italian architect Domenico Trezzini designed standard houses ". . . adapted to every class of society". With its Corinthian pilasters and central flight of steps, the House of the Ambassadors (above, 1710) was the most elegant building in St Petersburg, although it was constructed of wood and puddled clay. At left, the standard "economy" house.

In his haste to jettison Muscovite traditions Peter the Great engaged foreigners to build his modern city, naval installations and cultural center. Dutch engineers and Italian and German architects succeeded one another, until the arrival in 1716 of the French master builder Leblond. Leblond and his team were commissioned both to build, and to train the Russians in contemporary Western architectural concepts. "Naryshkin Baroque", characteristic of late 17th-century Moscow, gave way to Dutch pediments cheek by jowl with Italianate superimposed orders, German staircases and French curb-roofing.

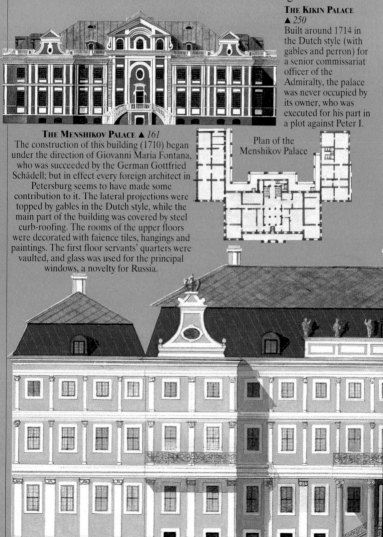

THE KIKIN PALACE
▲ 250
Built around 1714 in the Dutch style (with gables and perron) for a senior commissariat officer of the Admiralty, the palace was never occupied by its owner, who was executed for his part in a plot against Peter I.

THE MENSHIKOV PALACE ▲ 161
The construction of this building (1710) began under the direction of Giovanni Maria Fontana, who was succeeded by the German Gottfried Schädell; but in effect every foreign architect in Petersburg seems to have made some contribution to it. The lateral projections were topped by gables in the Dutch style, while the main part of the building was covered by steel curb-roofing. The rooms of the upper floors were decorated with faience tiles, hangings and paintings. The first floor servants' quarters were vaulted, and glass was used for the principal windows, a novelty for Russia.

Plan of the Menshikov Palace

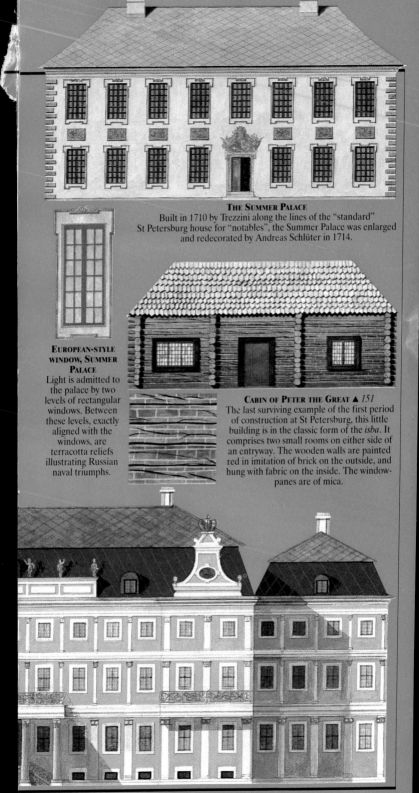

THE SUMMER PALACE
Built in 1710 by Trezzini along the lines of the "standard"
St Petersburg house for "notables", the Summer Palace was enlarged
and redecorated by Andreas Schlüter in 1714.

**EUROPEAN-STYLE
WINDOW, SUMMER
PALACE**
Light is admitted to
the palace by two
levels of rectangular
windows. Between
these levels, exactly
aligned with the
windows, are
terracotta reliefs
illustrating Russian
naval triumphs.

CABIN OF PETER THE GREAT ▲ 151
The last surviving example of the first period
of construction at St Petersburg, this little
building is in the classic form of the *isba*. It
comprises two small rooms on either side of
an entryway. The wooden walls are painted
red in imitation of brick on the outside, and
hung with fabric on the inside. The window-
panes are of mica.

Born in Paris in 1700, Bartolomeo Rastrelli arrived in St Petersburg in 1716 with his father, a sculptor. During the thirty years spanning the reigns of Anna Ivanovna and Elizabeth I he set a strong imprint on the city's architecture. As the designer of the imperial palaces, from 1734 onward he introduced Rococo into the Summer Palace, becoming Empress Elizabeth's court architect. The blossoming of Baroque art was also favored by Peter the Great, who paid for Russian students to be trained in Western Europe: in this sense, the assimilation of Western models led to an authentically creative result.

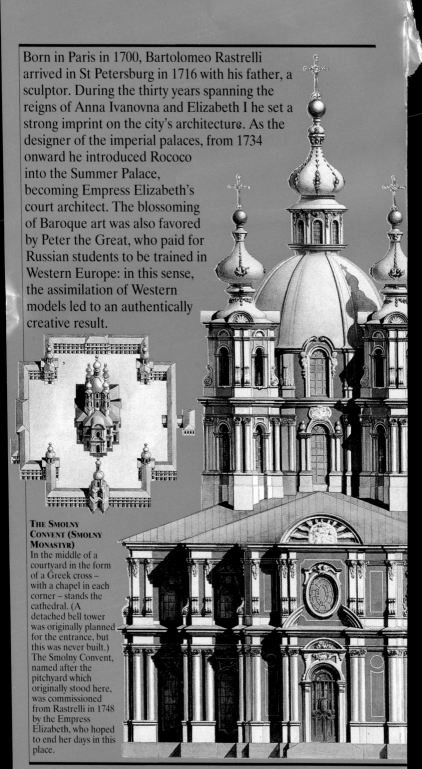

THE SMOLNY CONVENT (SMOLNY MONASTYR)
In the middle of a courtyard in the form of a Greek cross – with a chapel in each corner – stands the cathedral. (A detached bell tower was originally planned for the entrance, but this was never built.) The Smolny Convent, named after the pitchyard which originally stood here, was commissioned from Rastrelli in 1748 by the Empress Elizabeth, who hoped to end her days in this place.

**ST NICHOLAS'
CATHEDRAL ▲** *204*
Isolated, Russian
style, from the main
church, Savva
Chevakinsky's
campanile (1756–8)
is a model of elegant
mid-18th-century
Baroque. The
concave façades of
the lower floor
contrast with
the circular
designs of the
two upper ones,
with their small
dome and drum.

ATLAS FIGURES
The Atlas figures at Tsarskoe Selo
▲ *264* were covered with tin sulphate
in the form of leaves of crystal, in
color resembling gold.

DECORATIVE STUCCOS
The stucco décor was
made up of powdered
marble, slaked lime
and plaster,
heightened with paint
or gilt.

SMOLNY CATHEDRAL
▲ *247*
The cathedral has five
cupolas, in accordance
with Russian tradition.
The central one,
supported by a
windowed drum, is
flanked by four smaller
domes on towers. The
rhythm of the
projections, columns
and pilasters framing
pedimented bay
windows lends the two
lower levels originality
and liveliness. This
impression is
strengthened by the
blue color, of which
Elizabeth was
especially fond.

BAROQUE FAÇADES
Above the basement level the Winter Palace
(above left) comprises a single Ionic order,
followed by a double one, along with a
balustrade. At Tsarskoe Selo (above right)
the level of the galleries connecting the
projections on the front of the building is
handled like a stylobate, with Atlas figures
supporting the two upper floors.

85

● CLASSICISM AND THE EMPIRE STYLE

The New Holland Arch

On the accession of Catherine II, Bartolomeo Rastrelli was no longer in favor. The Czarina, who preferred sober lines, imposed a return to the canons of antiquity and the 17th century, surrounding herself with European architects such as Vallin de la Mothe, Antonio Rinaldi, the Scottish court architect Charles Cameron, Yuri Felten and Giacomo Quarenghi. Later, Alexander I brought the Empire style to St Petersburg (known in Russia, as the "classic" style), as a statement of imperial power. After the accession of Nicholas I in 1825 the major town planning review of the capital was entrusted to the Italian Carlo Rossi. It was Rossi who conceived the great colonnaded squares, so strong   a feature of the city today.

THE TAURIDE PALACE ▲ *251*
Built between 1783 and 1789 by Ivan Starov for Prince Potemkin, the Tauride Palace is austere to a fault, with smooth walls, rectangular unadorned bays, an upper level topped by a frieze of alternating triglyphs and bare metopes, and a Doric portico.

PLAN OF THE TAURIDE PALACE
The central axis leading to the main gallery is flanked by pavilions linked to the main body of the building by wings; one of these contains the theater, the other the private apartments.

A DECORATIVE PROJECT
Devised for the state bedroom of the Grand Duchess Maria Fyodorovna, the wife of the future Paul I, in the Catherine Palace of Tsarskoe Selo ▲ *264*. The designer was Charles Cameron.

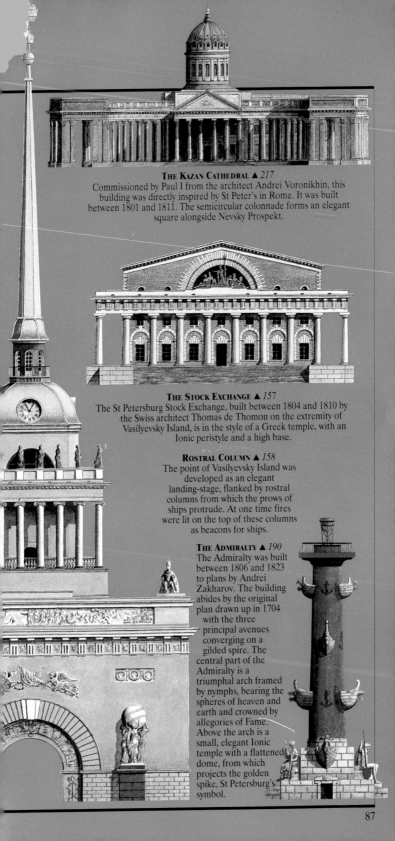

THE KAZAN CATHEDRAL ▲ 217
Commissioned by Paul I from the architect Andrei Voronikhin, this
building was directly inspired by St Peter's in Rome. It was built
between 1801 and 1811. The semicircular colonnade forms an elegant
square alongside Nevsky Prospekt.

THE STOCK EXCHANGE ▲ 157
The St Petersburg Stock Exchange, built between 1804 and 1810 by
the Swiss architect Thomas de Thomon on the extremity of
Vasilyevsky Island, is in the style of a Greek temple, with an
Ionic peristyle and a high base.

ROSTRAL COLUMN ▲ 158
The point of Vasilyevsky Island was
developed as an elegant
landing-stage, flanked by rostral
columns from which the prows of
ships protrude. At one time fires
were lit on the top of these columns
as beacons for ships.

THE ADMIRALTY ▲ 190
The Admiralty was built
between 1806 and 1823
to plans by Andrei
Zakharov. The building
abides by the original
plan drawn up in 1704
with the three
principal avenues
converging on a
gilded spire. The
central part of the
Admiralty is a
triumphal arch framed
by nymphs, bearing the
spheres of heaven and
earth and crowned by
allegories of Fame.
Above the arch is a
small, elegant Ionic
temple with a flattened
dome, from which
projects the golden
spike, St Petersburg's
symbol.

Western Europe's fascination with the past was reflected in St Petersburg, where neo-Baroque, neoclassicism, neo-Gothic and neo-Renaissance vied for precedence. The architecture of St Isaac's Cathedral is reminiscent of St Paul's in London, while the lavish décor of its interior borrows from every conceivable style. The Church of the Resurrection (also known as the Church of the Redeemer, or the Church of the Spilt Blood) is an example of a specifically Russian form of historicism, which had its origin in Moscow. It was built on the spot where Alexander II was assassinated, and has magnificent mosaics.

ATLAS AT THE BELOSELSKY-BELOZERSKY PALACE
This was the first palace in St Petersburg built in specific reference to the Russian Baroque style created by Rastrelli a century earlier.

THE CHESME CHURCH
Built between 1777 and 1780 by Yuri Felten, in honor of Orlov's 1770 naval victory against the Turks, this church and the palace in front of it are the earliest examples of neo-Gothic in Russia.

ECLECTIC DÉCOR
Behind the classical exterior of St Isaac's is a lavish interior: here painted frescos have been supplanted by mosaics (right) and marble wall-surfaces. The columns of the iconostasis are covered with lapis lazuli and malachite.

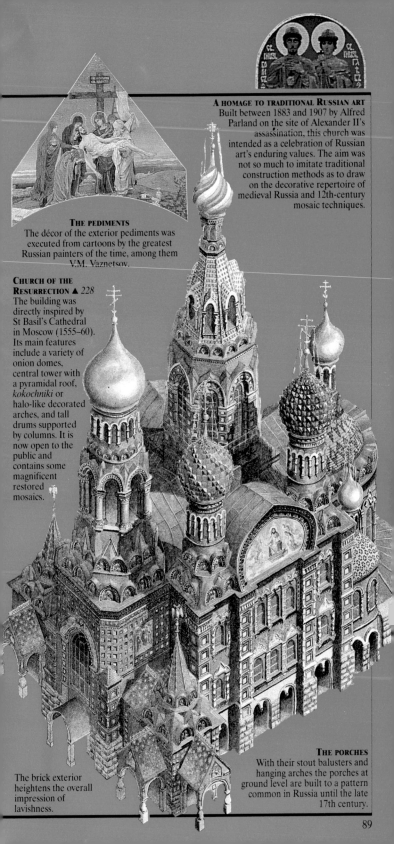

A HOMAGE TO TRADITIONAL RUSSIAN ART
Built between 1883 and 1907 by Alfred
Parland on the site of Alexander II's
assassination, this church was
intended as a celebration of Russian
art's enduring values. The aim was
not so much to imitate traditional
construction methods as to draw
on the decorative repertoire of
medieval Russia and 12th-century
mosaic techniques.

THE PEDIMENTS
The décor of the exterior pediments was
executed from cartoons by the greatest
Russian painters of the time, among them
V.M. Vaznetsov.

**CHURCH OF THE
RESURRECTION ▲ 228**
The building was
directly inspired by
St Basil's Cathedral
in Moscow (1555–60).
Its main features
include a variety of
onion domes,
central tower with
a pyramidal roof,
kokochniki or
halo-like decorated
arches, and tall
drums supported
by columns. It is
now open to the
public and
contains some
magnificent
restored
mosaics.

THE PORCHES
With their stout balusters and
hanging arches the porches at
ground level are built to a pattern
common in Russia until the late
17th century.

The brick exterior
heightens the overall
impression of
lavishness.

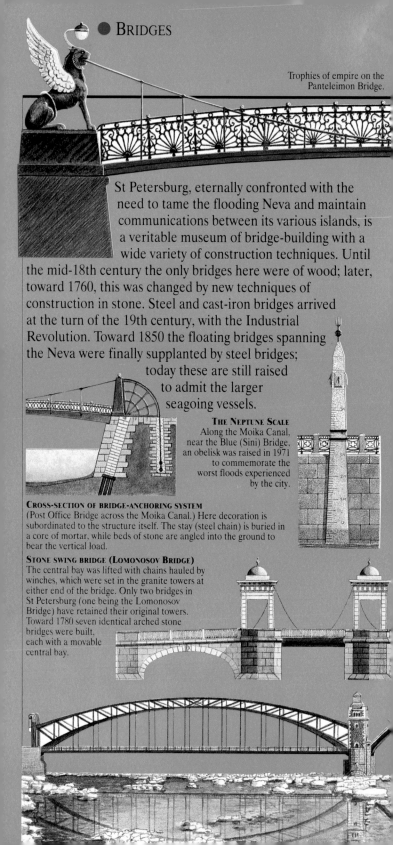

BRIDGES

Trophies of empire on the
Panteleimon Bridge.

St Petersburg, eternally confronted with the
need to tame the flooding Neva and maintain
communications between its various islands, is
a veritable museum of bridge-building with a
wide variety of construction techniques. Until
the mid-18th century the only bridges here were of wood; later,
toward 1760, this was changed by new techniques of
construction in stone. Steel and cast-iron bridges arrived
at the turn of the 19th century, with the Industrial
Revolution. Toward 1850 the floating bridges spanning
the Neva were finally supplanted by steel bridges;
today these are still raised
to admit the larger
seagoing vessels.

THE NEPTUNE SCALE
Along the Moika Canal,
near the Blue (Sini) Bridge,
an obelisk was raised in 1971
to commemorate the
worst floods experienced
by the city.

CROSS-SECTION OF BRIDGE-ANCHORING SYSTEM
(Post Office Bridge across the Moika Canal.) Here decoration is
subordinated to the structure itself. The stay (steel chain) is buried in
a core of mortar, while beds of stone are angled into the ground to
bear the vertical load.

STONE SWING BRIDGE (LOMONOSOV BRIDGE)
The central bay was lifted with chains hauled by
winches, which were set in the granite towers at
either end of the bridge. Only two bridges in
St Petersburg (one being the Lomonosov
Bridge) have retained their original towers.
Toward 1780 seven identical arched stone
bridges were built,
each with a movable
central bay.

SUSPENSION BRIDGE

The Bank Bridge (Bankovsky Most) was built by
Georg Tretter in 1825–6, across the Griboedov Canal.
The anchoring of the stays holding up the plank roadway
is hidden inside the bronze griffons, sculpted by Pavel
Sokolov. Of six similar bridges constructed between 1823
and 1826 only three have survived.

WOODEN PONTOON

The first bridges, built in about 1720, were of wood. The largest consisted of a succession of
connected barges. For the small canals Dutch-style drawbridges were used.

STRUCTURE

The cross-section above shows the
abutment pier of the steel arch and the
way its thrust is absorbed by the masonry.
The entire abutment pier rests on a
substructure of wooden pilings.

THE PANTELEIMON BRIDGE

Built in 1907–8 by the engineer Andrei
Pchenitsky, this bridge spans the Fontanka near
the Summer Garden. For its decoration (parapets
and lampposts) the architect Lev Ilin used
Empire motifs.

METAL SWING BRIDGE

The Peter the Great bridge (Bolshoy Okhtinsky), built
between 1908 and 1911 to a prize-winning design by
V. Apychov, answered the need for a structure which would
allow ships to pass freely along the waterway. The lateral bays,
each about 400 feet in length, are the longest in St Petersburg.

● ART NOUVEAU

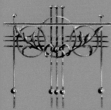

Wrought-iron "entrelac" design.

In the early 20th century St Petersburg, like other European capitals, was affected by modernist trends. The Art Nouveau style, popular almost everywhere, seems to have acquired certain typically regional characteristics when it reached the banks of the Neva. The majestic architecture of the classical age, the exuberance of Baroque and the innovations of Art Nouveau in Europe and Scandinavia were metamorphosed in a highly original manner in St Petersburg.

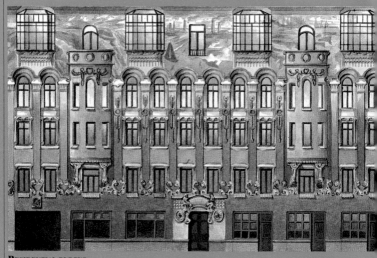

RESIDENTIAL BLOCKS

In the Petrograd district a number of Art Nouveau buildings were constructed, notably that of no. 28 Bolshaya Zelenina (19th century), which included both artists' studios and ordinary apartments. The façade is varied by two oriels, and crowned by an extensive mosaic.

THE PRIVATE TOWNHOUSE

The townhouse of the ballerina Mathilda Kseshinskaya, on Kronversky Avenue, is a typical example of a picturesque yet elegant Art Nouveau structure in the European mode. It was built (1904–6) by the architect A.I. Hogen.

THE COMMERCIAL BUILDING

The Azovsko-Donskoy bank was built (1908–9) by the architect F.I. Lidval and the sculptor V.V. Kuznetsov. Designed in every way to reflect the grand scale of the capital, this building was inspired by the classicism of Catherine II's reign.

BAS-RELIEFS

Neoclassical Art Nouveau also had its place, in the bas-reliefs, decorative friezes and medallions of the bank's façade.

MATERIALS OF ART NOUVEAU

The door of the Zimmerman Building, built in 1906 on Avenue Kamennoostrovsky, shows the diversity of the materials and construction techniques used in Art Nouveau. Rough-hewn projecting stones, bricks and mortar surfaces combine for a colorful yet formal effect.

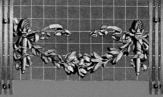

BLUE CERAMIC AND WROUGHT IRON

These supply the decorative motif for the cornice, which is handled in the classical manner. Note the foliated ribbon pattern on the flambeaux, with their pine-cone tops.

PROFILING

The profusion of glass, wrought iron, natural stone and vegetable ornamentation in the details of the surrounding balustrade and the projecting window show that the architect has fully mastered the new style without succumbing to eclecticism.

● CONSTRUCTIVISM

The Revolution of October 1917 marked a turning point in the development of Russian architecture. Thereafter the vogue was for the "Soviet style", or Constructivism, which could suitably represent the new ideology and exonerate architects from the charge of Formalism. Soon enough, Russian architects accomplished a stylistic transition, assimilating their classical heritage into a relatively human brand of Constructivism. This style, which developed in the 1940's and 1950's, was later baptized "Stalinist Empire".

RATIONALISM AND FUNCTIONALISM
This 1929 project, with its extensive glass and its concrete-covered walls, is typical of Constructivism.

ABSENCE OF DECORATION
Constructivism sought to respond to the needs of society, and condemned all embellishments as "bourgeois" and superfluous. Nevertheless, the residential building above (Karpovka Embankment, 1931) displays an example of Constructivist sculpture.

THE REVIVAL OF DECORATION
Later attitudes changed and decoration became "useful" again. The frieze on the façade of the Moscow cinema (top) assimilated – and interpreted – the Russian classical heritage.

THE CLASSICAL MANNER
This building on Kamennoostrovsky Avenue was designed by the architect N. Lanser in 1936. The central part is flanked by slightly projecting wings, and the profiling is carefully worked, with faceted stonework, pilasters, arabesques and medallions.

MONUMENTALISM (THE KIROV SOVIET)
This effect is achieved by emphasizing the horizontal lines in contrast to the vertical tower.

ART IN THE SERVICE OF THE STATE (KIROVSKY ZAVO METRO STATION)
The building of the metro system, of the highest quality and very costly indeed, was meant to serve the Soviet ideal.

A MOVE TOWARD THE OUTSIDE WORLD
The Finland Station (Finlyandsky Voksal), built in 1957, represented a timid gesture toward international modernism.

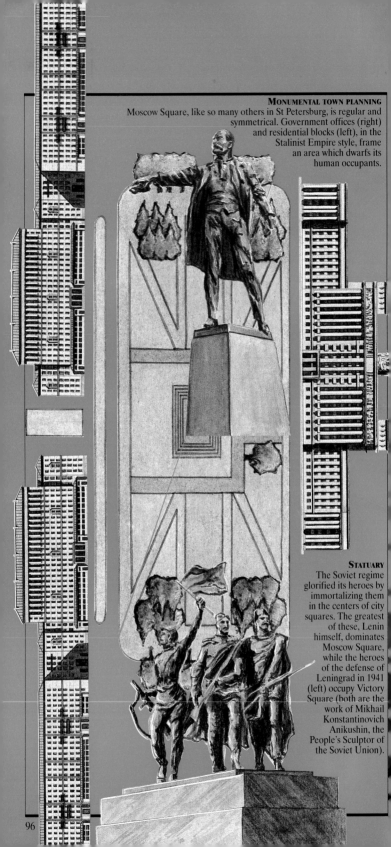

MONUMENTAL TOWN PLANNING
Moscow Square, like so many others in St Petersburg, is regular and symmetrical. Government offices (right) and residential blocks (left), in the Stalinist Empire style, frame an area which dwarfs its human occupants.

STATUARY
The Soviet regime glorified its heroes by immortalizing them in the centers of city squares. The greatest of these, Lenin himself, dominates Moscow Square, while the heroes of the defense of Leningrad in 1941 (left) occupy Victory Square (both are the work of Mikhail Konstantinovich Anikushin, the People's Sculptor of the Soviet Union).

St Petersburg
AS SEEN BY PAINTERS

L ike many of his Swedish compatriots Benjamin Patterssen (1750–1815) came to seek his fortune in St Petersburg. His arrival coincided with an important moment in the history of the city. The avenues were under construction and the people were impatient to see how their town would look once they were completed; above all, they had become acutely planning-conscious and were fascinated by major architectural ensembles. Profiting from this vogue, Patterssen began painting detailed views of St Petersburg in 1793; these were very popular on account of their refined technique and architectural exactitude. Patterssen also excelled as an engraver and draftsman; but his paintings of the city's monuments belong in the realm of poetry. His *View of the Kutuzov and Palace Embankment* (opposite) is remarkable for its rendering of the atmosphere and luminosity of springtime.

Fyodor Alexeyev (1753–1824) was launched by the Fine Arts Academy as a painter of theater décors and a master of perspective. The result was that he was unable to give free rein to his own brand of classicism until 1790, at which time his views of St Petersburg had become so successful that Czar Paul I commissioned Alexeyev to paint several other cities in the empire, most notably Moscow.

Below, his *View of the Palace Embankment from the Peter and Paul Fortress*.

99

St Petersburg as seen by painters
Chernetsov

Grigory Chernetsov (1801–65) shifted the artistic focus from topography to portraiture. As a former pupil at the Fine Arts Academy, he followed his master Maxim Vorobiov (1787–1855) on the path of Romanticism. His *Neva Embankment in Front* of the Fine Arts Academy: Night (2) (about 1830) is a subject also treated by Vorobiov. This picture is not so much a representation of the city but more a picture of the river itself, and of the dreamlike atmosphere investing it during the hours of darkness, while *Parade on the* Marsovo Pole (Field of Mars) (1831–7) (3), commissioned by Czar Nicholas I is a veritable portrait of St Petersburg society. The main interest of this huge painting lies in the figures that people it, which include, most notably, literary lions such as Krylov, Pushkin, Griboedov and Zhukovsky (1).

At the St Petersburg Fine Arts Academy the art of interior painting reached its apogee in the mid-19th century. The teaching of perspective was revived by the efforts of Maxim Vorobiov (1787–1855). One of his pupils, Constantin Ukhtomsky (1818–81), along with two St Petersburg-based foreign painters (Edward Hau, 1807–87, and Luigi Premazzi, 1814–91), were chosen to paint the Winter Palace and the rooms of the New Hermitage (Novy Ermitazh) designed for the imperial collections. The three artists faced an identical challenge: to paint as much space as possible with the maximum number of details, juggling angles of view from perspectives that were impossible in real life. The commission was brilliantly carried out, as attested by Ukhtomsky's *Cimmerian Bosphorus Antiquities Room* (**2**), Hau's *Italian School Gallery* (**3**) and *History of Painting Gallery* (**4**), and Premazzi's *Artist's Apartment, Winter Palace* (**1**). The three artists' talents as watercolorists and their mastery of trompe l'oeil were also much admired by contemporaries, who followed the Czar's example in having the interiors of their palaces and houses similarly recorded.

1	
2	4
3	

St Petersburg as seen by painters
Benois

From the time of their arrival in Russia in the late 18th century until the October Revolution of 1917 the Benois family remained implacably French. Nevertheless the painter Alexander Benois (1870–1960) was able to make the connection between the culture of his origins and that of St Petersburg, which he always considered his home. An avid historian, he maintained that his feelings about the past were "... more tender and affectionate" than his feelings about the present. As leader of the World of Art movement Benois created a completely new genre, the historical landscape, which allowed him to bring the 18th century back to life. His city of St Petersburg, whose image he held so clearly in his mind that he tirelessly painted it from memory, is peopled by courtesans and more or less enlightened monarchs. In much of his work St Petersburg is the background for ballet and theater décors. Real landscapes, personal memories and Benois' own deep knowledge allowed him to fill these décors with childlike innocence and freshness, as in *Holy Week Fair on Admiralty Square, about 1830* (right).

Anna Ostrumova-Lebedeva (1871–1955) illustrated another aspect of the historical landscape, with St Petersburg as the central theme. For her the only significant epoch was that of classicism, whose architecture and ambiance she painted in preference to people, as seen in *Columns of Our Lady of Kazan* (1903) (**2**). Until her death, she continued to perfect her art, using watercolors and xylographs to depict the four elements and above all the waters of the Neva, which she viewed as the fountainhead of the city's poetry. *The Fontanka and the Summer Garden* (1922) (**1**).

THE RUSSIAN
AVANT-GARDE

In the early 20th century the intellectual and artistic catalyst of St Petersburg (renamed Petrograd in 1914 and Leningrad in 1924) produced several avant-garde movements, led by creative talents of the first rank. Russian artists felt themselves on a par with their European counterparts, notably the French Cubists and Italian Futurists. They also expressed themselves within the context of various trends dominated by the new painting.

The Young Movement 1910–14), which generated most of the avant-garde's initiatives, attracted artists as different as Matiushin, Rozanova, Malevich, Tatlin and Filonov. Their links with Parisian Cubists and the Expressionists of Munich Kandinsky) eventually produced a conceptual structure Rozanova, 1913) which led to the blossoming of Cubo-Futurism and the abstract art associated with Malevich. The movement which was to reverberate through the rest of the 20th century came to the forefront in December 915 with the "Last Futurist Exhibition: 0, 0", at which Tatlin's counter-reliefs" firmly established the trend toward Constructivism. Thus the dialectic of the decades that followed was inaugurated in St Petersburg. The 1917 Revolution led many of the most prominent artists to migrate to Moscow, but after 921 the focus of modern art, now subordinated to Productivism, again shifted to Petrograd. Artists met at the Institute of Artistic Culture (GINHUK), by whose agency their works were assembled in the Russian

Museum ▲ 226 and the Zubov Art History Institute. The latter, which was opened in 1912, was intended to give St Petersburg's art an international dimension. Formalist (or Abstract) art, as championed by the Institute, fell into disfavor in the later 1920's, and eventually disappeared altogether.

MIKHAIL LARIONOV
Autumn (1912), a Primitivist work

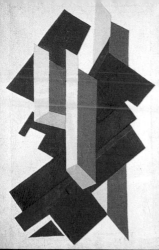

OLGA ROZANOVA, *Suprematist Composition* (1916–17)

KASIMIR MALEVICH
Portrait of Ivan Klium (1913)

Goncharova (1881–1962) and Larionov (1881–1964), the leaders of Futurism in Moscow, featured strongly in the exhibitions of 1910–14.

NATALIA GONCHAROVA
Peasants Carrying Fruit (1911–12)

The brilliant Cubo-Futurist theories of Matvejs (1877–1914) were championed by Olga Rozanova (1886–1918). This artist, whose notions of color emerged in the form of Futurist-Expressionist paintings between 1911 and 1913, went on to produce striking "trans-rational" compositions (1915) in which the figurative element was used as a metaphor rather than an object. The Cubist work of Pavel Filonov (1883–1941) was inspired by Russian folklore and mystical aspirations, while the Suprematism of Malevich (1879–1935) took its cue from European culture. With its intuitive, abstract construction, Malevich's work moved away from material reality to celebrate "pure sensibility" (Suprematism, or "pure non-objectivity" as he himself defined it). Malevich's approach, inspired by Cubism but refined by him, demonstrates a basic unity; and it was this above all which characterized his first Suprematist constructions.

PAVEL FILONOV
Orient and Occident (1912–13)

MIKHAIL MATIUSHIN
Movement in Space (1919–22)

OLGA ROZANOVA
Office (1915)

This passage to the "third dimension" led to a theorization of his thought and an individual approach to spatial reality, to which the artist applied himself in the 1920's. Mikhail Matiushin (1861–1934), a friend of Malevich, was one of the most original artists in the Futurist group. A musician, painter, sculptor and theorist of the plastic arts, he developed an original view of the multi-dimensional space revealed by supra-sensorial experience. According to his theory of "enlarged vision" our perception of the world can go beyond the real to a different level of subjective and intuitive experience. His work as a teacher and publisher established the literary and theoretical validity of the Russian Avant-Garde.

The most famous work of Vladimir Tatlin (1885–1953), the model for his monument to the Third International, was created in Petrograd in 1919–20. This emblematic Constructivist piece, inspired by the Eiffel Tower, was supposed to ally the "logic of materials" which had fascinated Tatlin since 1914 with the Functionalist demands of the dawning technical age. The fame of the monument eclipsed the purely pictorial decline of this artist, who embraced the ideology of "renunciation of painting" in 1920–21. After the brief Formalist (Abstract) period epitomized by the work of Altman and Lebedev (which is now in the Russian Museum), the Avant-Garde period was supplanted by Socialist Realism, which faithfully reflected the new "restrictive" ideology.

VLADIMIR TATLIN
Project for the Monument to the Third International (1920)

Relief (1914)

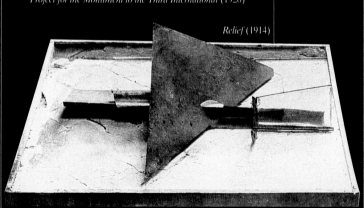

● ALEXANDER PUSHKIN

"An extraordinary phemonemon and a unique expression of the Russian spirit," said Nikolai Gogol ● *122* of Alexander Sergeivich Pushkin (1799–1837). One of Russia's greatest poets, he was born into ancient Russian gentry on his father's side and, on his mother's, was descended from the Ethiopian Ibrahim Hannibal. After a rebellious childhood and the restrictive life of a courtier in St Petersburg, he lived through censorship, exile, close surveillance . . . and complete isolation. Revered as a national genius and a liberator of the Russian language, he is still considered to be a major figure in world literature. At his funeral a distraught elderly man, asked if he was close to the poet, replied "No, but I am a Russian."

A CLASSICAL EDUCATION
At an early age Pushkin discovered the major classical writers in the extensive family library. His taste for French writers (Voltaire especially) earned him the nickname of "Frenchman" at the Tsarskoe Selo Lyceum ▲ *267* (1811) where he was a pupil. It was here, at this famous school for the sons of nobility, that Pushkin first began writing poetry at the age of fifteen.

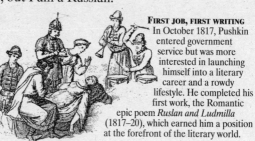

FIRST JOB, FIRST WRITING
In October 1817, Pushkin entered government service but was more interested in launching himself into a literary career and a rowdy lifestyle. He completed his first work, the Romantic epic poem *Ruslan and Ludmilla* (1817–20), which earned him a position at the forefront of the literary world.

"DEAR FRIEND HAVE FAITH . . . RUSSIA SHALL FROM HER AGE-OLD SLEEP ARISE"
In 1819, Pushkin belonged to a circle known as "The Green Lamp"; the Tsar's discovery of his revolutionary writings led to his exile (1820–4) in the south, followed by a period under close surveillance in Mikhailovskoe. The Decembrists' rising ● *42* changed his life. In a letter to the Tsar, he swore he had had nothing to do with this plot and requested permission to leave Mikhailovskoe. In exchange, Nicolas I offered his protection . . . and his own personal censorship.

"BORIS GODUNOV"

Following publication of the historical drama *Boris Godunov*, Nicolas I decided to make Pushkin a court poet insisting he must write a novel in the style of Walter Scott."

AN UNHAPPY BUT CREATIVE EXILE

During his exile in the south of Russia, Pushkin was given subaltern duties under the governor of Bessarabia. He was allowed, however, to visit the Caucasus and the Crimea, where he was introduced to Eastern and Greek culture. Pushkin's *Southern Poems:* "The Prisoner of the Caucasus", "The Fountain of Bakhchisarai" (1823) and "The Gypsies" (1824) bear witness to these new and exotic influences and also demonstrate his admiration for the poetry of his contemporary, Lord Byron.

"EUGENE ONEGIN"

A mirror of 19th-century Russian society, *Eugene Onegin* (1823–30) is considered by some to be the first Russian novel worthy of that title. Its eponymous hero is a frivolous dandy based in St Petersburg, leading a life of excess. He eventually wearies of the tedious merry-go-round and retreats to the provinces, a reflection of Pushkin's own fate.

Les Grands-Croix, Commandeurs et Chevaliers du Sérénissime Ordre des Cocus réunis en grand Chapitre sous la présidence du vénérable grand-Maître de l'Ordre, S. E. O. L. Narychkine, ont nommé à l'unanimité Mr Alexandre Pouchkine coadjuteur du grand Maître de l'Ordre des Cocus et historiographe de l'Ordre.

Le sécrétaire perpétuel: Cte J. Bor...

"THE BRONZE HORSEMAN" AND "THE QUEEN OF SPADES"

"I earn money from my work and my work demands solitude ..." Despite feeling oppressed by a difficult and turbulent life during his enforced stay at the family home of Boldino in 1833, Pushkin wrote two of his most celebrated works: "The Bronze Horseman" ● 118 and *The Queen of Spades*. The latter is the story of an obsession which turns into a nightmare: it tells of the secret of three cards the last of which, the Queen of Spades, brings about the downfall of the protagonist.

A LIBELOUS LETTER
On November 4, 1836, Pushkin received an unsigned letter dishonoring him and his wife. The writer was Baron Haeckeren, the adopted father of George Dantes, a French emigrant who was devoted to Pushkin's wife. The last thing that Pushkin wrote was a letter of reply to Baron Haeckeren.

СРЕДА. **ТОМ. I. № 8.** ФЕВРАЛЯ 5

ЛИТЕРАТУРНАЯ ГАЗЕТА.

1830 ГОДЪ.

LITERARY CRITICISM

Pushkin was one of the first Russian writers to make a living almost entirely from writing. Following his return from exile, he became involved with his friend Delvig's *Literary Gazette*. In 1836, he obtained permission to start his own literary review, *Contemporary Life*, a collection of articles and critical studies on contemporary Russian and foreign literature. Only four editions were published during Pushkin's lifetime.

СОВРЕМЕННИКЪ,

ЛИТТЕРАТУРНЫЙ ЖУРНАЛЪ,

издаваемый

АЛЕКСАНДРОМЪ ПУШКИНЫМЪ.

THE DUEL

On January 26, 1837, George Dantes challenged the poet to a duel. On January 27, on the banks of the Moika Canal, Pushkin was mortally wounded and carried back to his home at 12, Moika Quay ● *82.* He died on January 29. Several days later the young Lermontov hurled these vengeful lines: "All of your vile blood can never wash away/The fair blood of the poet!"

"VENUS AND THE VULCAN"

On February 18, 1831, Pushkin and Natalia Goncharova were married in Moscow. The poet was then caught up in a whirl of celebrations (and growing debts). In 1831 at Tsarkoe Selo, Natalia was officially presented to the Empress . . . and was soon after courted by the Emperor.

MAJESTY

PETER'S CREATION

"The Bronze Horseman" (1833) is an epic poem in which Etienne-Maurice Falconet's statue of Peter the Great, erected by Catherine the Great, comes to life and chases a clerk through the city during the 1824 flood. In this poem Alexander Pushkin (1799–1837) ● 114 uses the contrast between the menacing equestrian statue and the hero Eugene to symbolize the destructive effect of Peter the Great's imperialist Russia upon the ordinary man.

❝I love you, Peter's creation, I love your stern
Harmonious look, the Neva's majestic flow,
Her granite banks, the iron tracery
Of your railings, the transparent twilight and
The moonless glitter of your pensive nights,
When in my room I write or read without
A lamp, and slumbering masses of deserted
Streets shine clearly, and the Admiralty spire
Is luminous, and, without letting in
The dark of night to golden skies, one dawn
Hastens to relieve another, granting
a mere half-hour to night. I love
The motionless air and frost of your harsh winter,
The sledges coursing along the solid Neva,
Girls' faces brighter than roses, and the sparkle
And noise and sound of voices at the balls,
And, at the hour of the bachelor's feast, the hiss
Of foaming goblets and the pale-blue flame
Of punch. I love the warlike energy
Of Mars' Field, the uniform beauty of the troops
Of infantry and of the horses, tattered
Remnants of those victorious banners in array
Harmoniously swaying, the gleam of those
Bronze helmets, shot through in battle. O martial
Capital, I love the smoke and thunder
Of your fortress, when the empress of the north
Presents a son to the royal house, or when
Russia celebrates another victory
Over the foe, or when the Neva, breaking
Her blue ice, bears it to the seas, exulting,
Scenting spring days.❞

"THE BRONZE HORSEMAN",
SELECTED POEMS OF ALEXANDER PUSHKIN,
TRANS. D.M. THOMAS, PUB. SECKER & WARBURG, LONDON 1982

ST PETERSBURG MORNING

Vladimir Nabokov (1899–1977) and his family left Russia for Germany in 1919, and he lived thereafter in Berlin, Paris, the US and finally Switzerland. He wrote mainly in Russian until he moved to the US in 1940.

❝How utterly foreign to the troubles of the night were those exciting St. Petersburg mornings when the fierce and tender, damp and dazzling arctic spring bundled away broken ice down the sea-bright Neva! It made the roofs shine. It painted the slush in the streets a rich purplish-blue shade which I have never seen anywhere since. On those glorious days *on aller se*

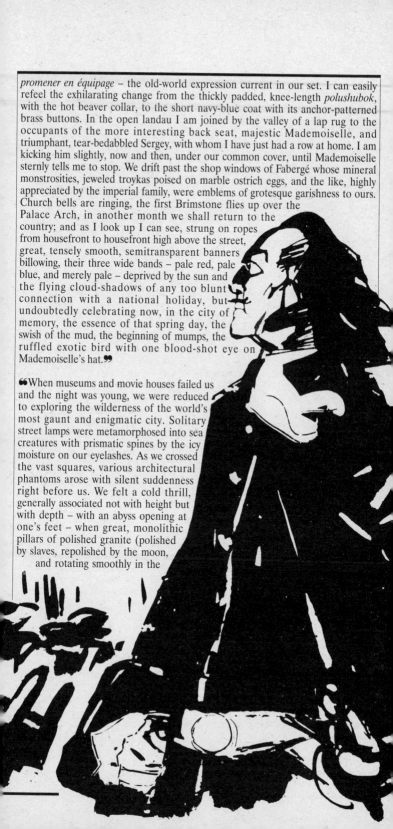

promener en équipage – the old-world expression current in our set. I can easily refeel the exhilarating change from the thickly padded, knee-length *polushubok*, with the hot beaver collar, to the short navy-blue coat with its anchor-patterned brass buttons. In the open landau I am joined by the valley of a lap rug to the occupants of the more interesting back seat, majestic Mademoiselle, and triumphant, tear-bedabbled Sergey, with whom I have just had a row at home. I am kicking him slightly, now and then, under our common cover, until Mademoiselle sternly tells me to stop. We drift past the shop windows of Fabergé whose mineral monstrosities, jeweled troykas poised on marble ostrich eggs, and the like, highly appreciated by the imperial family, were emblems of grotesque garishness to ours. Church bells are ringing, the first Brimstone flies up over the Palace Arch, in another month we shall return to the country; and as I look up I can see, strung on ropes from housefront to housefront high above the street, great, tensely smooth, semitransparent banners billowing, their three wide bands – pale red, pale blue, and merely pale – deprived by the sun and the flying cloud-shadows of any too blunt connection with a national holiday, but undoubtedly celebrating now, in the city of memory, the essence of that spring day, the swish of the mud, the beginning of mumps, the ruffled exotic bird with one blood-shot eye on Mademoiselle's hat.❞

❝When museums and movie houses failed us and the night was young, we were reduced to exploring the wilderness of the world's most gaunt and enigmatic city. Solitary street lamps were metamorphosed into sea creatures with prismatic spines by the icy moisture on our eyelashes. As we crossed the vast squares, various architectural phantoms arose with silent suddenness right before us. We felt a cold thrill, generally associated not with height but with depth – with an abyss opening at one's feet – when great, monolithic pillars of polished granite (polished by slaves, repolished by the moon, and rotating smoothly in the

polished vacuum of the night) zoomed above us to support the mysterious rotundities of St. Isaac's cathedral. We stopped on the brink, as it were, of these perilous motifs of stone and metal, and with linked hands, in Lilliputian awe, craned our heads to watch new colossal visions rise in our way – the ten glossy-gray atlantes of a palace portico, or a giant vase of porphyry near the iron gate of a garden, or that enormous column with a black angel on its summit that obsessed, rather than adorned, the moon-flooded Palace Square, and went up and up, trying in vain to reach the subbase of Pushkin's '*Exegi monumentum*'. 99

VLADIMIR NABOKOV, *SPEAK, MEMORY:*
AN AUTOBIOGRAPHY REVISITED,
WEIDENFELD AND NICOLSON, LONDON 1960

AMONG FRIENDS?
In which Dostoyevsky makes arrangements. . . .

66At the end of the Nevsky Prospekt is Alexander Nevsky Square . . . with the great convent and the church . . . and two ancient cemeteries, in one of which, Tikhvin, rests Dostoyevski, who had begged his wife not to bury him in the Volkovskoye cemetery among the literati. ('I do not want to lie in the middle of my enemies.') Around Dostoyevski are Glinka, Mussorgsky, Rimsky-Korsakov, Borodin, Tchaikovsky. Dostoyevski had never shown a particular inclination toward music; he appreciated Beethoven, Mendelssohn, and Rossini and could not bear Wagner. Destiny wished him to have as neighbors in death, besides his friend Nekrasov, the greatest musicians of Russia. After our companions in school, in military service, in hospital or prison, these are our final companions.99

ALDO BURGYS, "CHEKHOV IN SONDRIO",
TRANS. ANN GOLDSTEIN, PUB. *NEW YORKER*,
SEPT. 14, 1992

THE WINTER PALACE
After the great fire of 1837, the Winter Palace was rebuilt in a year.

66Under the Empress Elizabeth the palace had taken eight years to build; Kleinmichael completed it in one. True it is that almost the whole of the masonry resisted the fire, but the whole of the interior had to be reconstructed, and what a task that was! The work went on literally day and night; there was no pause for meals; the gangs of workmen relieved each other. Festivals were unheeded; the seasons themselves were overcome. To accelerate the work, the building was kept, the winter through, artificially heated to the excessive temperature of twenty-four to twenty-six degrees Réaumur. Many workmen sank under the heat, and were carried out dead or dying; a painter, who was decorating a ceiling, fell from his ladder struck with apoplexy. Neither money, health, nor life, was spared. The Emperor, who, at the time of the conflagration, had risked his own life by penetrating into the innermost apartments to save the lives of others, knew nothing of the means employed to carry out his will. In the December of the following year, and in proud consciousness of his power, he entered the resuscitated palace and rejoiced over his work. The whole was constructed on the previous plan, but with some improvements and many embellishments. With the Empress on his arm, and followed by his whole family, he traversed the apartments of this immense building, completed, in one year's time, by the labour of thousands of men. He reached the saloon of St. George, the largest and most beautiful of all, and the royal family remained there longer than anywhere else, examining the costly gold mouldings of the ceiling, the five colossal bronze chandeliers, and the beautiful relievo over the

throne, which represents St. George slaying the dragon. The Empress was tired, and would have sat down; – the patron spirit of Russia prevented her: as yet there was no furniture in the hall so she leaned on the Emperor's arm and walked into the next room, followed by the entire retinue. The last of these had scarcely passed through the door when a thundering crash resounded through the palace, which trembled to its very foundations, and the air was darkened by clouds of dust. The timbers of the ceiling of the saloon of St. George had yielded to the weight of the chandeliers; and the whole had fallen in, crushing everything beneath its enormous mass. The saloon, a moment before so brilliant, was a heap of ruins. The splendid palace was again partly destroyed, but the genius of Russia had watched over her destiny – the imperial family were saved. **99**

EDWARD JERRMANN, *PICTURES OF ST PETERSBURG*,
TRANS. BY FREDERICK HARDMANN, LONDON 1852

COLORS
The poet and novelist Andrey Biely (1880–1935) describes a walk along the Moika Canal.

66Below, to one side of them, the Moika Canal appeared blue; on the other side stood the familiar three-story colonnaded building with the same familiar series of modeled ornaments: ring after ring, and inside each ring a coat of arms – a Roman helmet between two crossed swords.

Before them, where the canal took a turn to the left of a stone projection, loomed the dazzling dome of St. Isaac's Cathedral against a background of exquisite turquoise.

They had reached the Embankment: the deep waters of the Neva looked green-blue. Far, far away, appearing ever so remote, the islands looked incredibly flat and low; and their buildings seemed so flat too that the deep green-blue waters threatened suddenly to wash over and submerge them. A pitiless sunset hovered above this green blue surface, scattering its gleams here and there: the Troitsky Bridge and the Winter Palace glowed purple.

Suddenly, a clearly defined silhouette appeared above these green-blue waters and against the background of the red sky; the flaps of a coat cape beat in the breeze like a pair of wings; carelessly, a waxen face with protruding lips came into view; the eyes seemed to search for something in the blue expanse of the Neva and, unable to find what they sought, took refuge under the visor of a modest cap; the eyes saw neither Sofya Petrovna nor Varvara Evgrafovna: they saw only the green-blue depths; they rose and fell – beyond the Neva, where the buildings glowed purple on the sunken banks of the island. A bulldog, carrying in his mouth a whip

with a silver handle, ran snorting ahead of the silhouette.
As he passed them, the young man barely blinked his eyes,
touched the band of his cap with his fingers, and walked
on without a word. The buildings glowed purple.**"**

ANDREY BIELY, *ST PETERSBURG*, TRANS. BY JOHN COURNOS,
PUB. GROVE PRESS INC., NEW YORK, 1959

PETERSBURG SOCIETY

WORKING PEOPLE

*Dramatist and prose writer Nikolai Gogol (1809–52) was
born in the Ukraine but moved to St Petersburg in 1828. He
wrote a series of short stories set in the city in the mid 1830's,
which are satirical and exaggerated in tone yet brilliantly
descriptive.*

"Let us begin with earliest morning when all Petersburg
smells of hot, freshly-baked bread and is filled with old
women in ragged gowns and pelisses who are making their
raids on the churches and on compassionate passers-by.
Then the Nevsky Prospect is empty: the stout shopkeepers
and their assistants are still asleep in their linen shirts or
washing their genteel cheeks and drinking their coffee;
beggars gather near the doors of the confectioners' shops
where the drowsy Ganymede who the day before flew round
like a fly with chocolate, crawls out with no cravat on, broom in
hand, and thrusts stale pies and scraps upon them. Working people
move to and fro about the streets: sometimes peasants cross it,
hurrying to their work, in high boots caked with mortar which even
the Ekaterinsky canal, famous for its cleanness, could not wash off.
At this hour it is not proper for ladies to walk out, because Russian
people like to explain their meaning in rude expressions such as they
would not hear even in a theatre. Sometimes a drowsy government clerk
trudges along with a portfolio under his arm, if the way to his department lies
through the Nevsky Prospect. It may be confidently stated that at this period,
that is, up to twelve o'clock, the Nevsky Prospect is for no man the goal, but
simply the means of reaching it: it is filled with people who have their occupations,
their anxieties, and their annoyances, and are thinking nothing about it. Peasants
talk about ten kopecks or seven coppers, old men and women wave their hands or
talk to themselves, sometimes with very striking gesticulations, but no one listens to
them or laughs at them with the exception perhaps of street boys in homespun
smocks, darting like lightning along the Nevsky Prospect with empty bottles or
pairs of boots from the cobblers in their arms. At that hour you may put on what
you like, and even if you wear a cap instead of a hat, or the ends of your collar stick
out too far from your cravat, no one notices it.**"**

NIKOLAI GOGOL, "THE NEVSKY PROSPECT",
FROM *THE OVERCOAT & OTHER STORIES*,
TRANS. BY CONSTANCE GARNETT,
PUB. CHATTO & WINDUS, LONDON, 1923

EXODUS

*Born in Moscow, Fyodor Dostoevsky (1821–81) first moved to St Petersburg in 1838 to
study at the St Petersburg Engineering Academy. During the 20th century, Dostoevsky
has become the most widely read and influential of Russian writers in Britain and the
US. He was a powerful thinker, influenced by Socialism and liberal ideas in the first
half of his life, and then by the Russian Orthodox Church. In this extract from his short
story "White Nights", written in 1848, is Dostoevsky's description of what he considered
to be an alarming trend in St Petersburg society.*

"It was only this morning that at last I discovered the real cause of my unhappiness. Oh, so they are all running away from me to the country, are they? I'm afraid I must apologise for the use of this rather homely word, but I'm not in the mood now for the more exquisite refinements of style, for everybody in Petersburg has either left or is about to leave for the country; for every worthy gentleman of a solidly-prosperous and dignified position who hails a cab in the street is at once transformed in my mind into a worthy parent of a family who, after his usual office duties, immediately leaves town and, unencumbered by luggage, hastens to the bosom of his family – to the country; for every passer-by now wears quite a different look, a look which almost seems to say to every person he meets, 'As a matter of fact, sir, I'm here by sheer chance, just passing through, you understand, and in a few hours I shall be on the way to the country.' If a window is thrown open and a most ravishing young girl, who a moment ago had been drumming on it with her lovely white fingers, pokes out her pretty head and calls to the man selling pots of plants in the street, I immediately jump to the conclusion that the flowers are bought not for the purpose of enjoying the spring and the flowers in a stuffy old flat in town, for very soon everybody will anyway be leaving for the country and will take even the flowers with them. Why, I've got so far in my new discovery (quite a unique discovery, you must admit) that I can tell at once, just by looking at a man, in what sort of a cottage he lives in the country. The residents of the Stone and Apothecary Islands can be recognised by their studied exquisiteness of manners, their smart summer clothes, and their wonderful carriages in which they come to town. The inhabitants of Pargolov and places beyond 'inspire' your confidence at the first glance by their solidly prosperous position and their general air of sobriety and common sense; while the householder of Krestovsky Island is distinguished by his imperturbably cheerful look. Whether I happen to come across a long procession of carters, each walking leisurely, reins in hand, beside his cart, laden with whole mountains of furniture of every description – tables, chairs, Turkish and non-Turkish divans, and other household chattels – and, moreover, often presided over by a frail-looking cook who, perched on the

very top of the cart, guards the property of her master as though it were the apple of her eye; or whether I look at the barges, heavily laden with all sorts of domestic junk, sailing on the Neva or the Fontanka, as far as the Black River or the Islands – both carts and barges multiply tenfold, nay, a hundredfold in my eyes. It really seems as though everything had arisen and set off on a journey, as though everything were moving off in caravan after caravan into the country; it seems as though the whole of Petersburg were about to turn into a desert, and it is hardly surprising that in the end I am overwhelmed with shame, humiliation, and sadness.**"**

DOSTOEVSKY, "WHITE NIGHTS",
FROM *THE BEST SHORT STORIES OF DOSTOEVSKY*,
TRANS. BY DAVID MAGARSHACK,
PUB. THE MODERN LIBRARY, NEW YORK, 1955

ENTRANCE TO A BALL

It took Count Lev Nikolaevich Tolstoy (1828–1910) almost seven years to write "War and Peace", an epic novel following the fortunes of three aristocratic families through the Napoleonic invasion.

❝Natasha had not had a moment free since early morning and had not once had time to think of what lay before her.

In the damp chill air and crowded closeness of the swaying carriage, she for the first time vividly imagined what was in store for her there at the ball, in those brightly lighted rooms – with music, flowers, dances, the Emperor, and all the brilliant young people of Petersburg. The prospect was so splendid that she hardly believed it would come true, so out of keeping was it with the chill darkness and closeness of the carriage. She understood all that awaited her only when, after stepping over the red baize at the entrance, she entered the hall, took off her fur cloak and, beside Sonya and in front of her mother, mounted the brightly illuminated stairs between the flowers. Only then did she remember how she must behave at a ball, and tried to assume the majestic air she considered indispensable for a girl on such an occasion. But, fortunately for her, she felt her eyes growing misty, she saw nothing clearly, her pulse beat a hundred to the minute and the blood throbbed at her heart. She could not assume that pose, which would have made her ridiculous, and she moved on almost fainting from excitement and trying with all her might to conceal it. And this was the very attitude that became her best. Before and behind them other visitors were entering, also talking in low tones and wearing ball-dresses. The mirrors on the landing reflected ladies in white, pale-blue, and pink dresses, with diamonds and pearls on their bare necks and arms.

Natasha looked in the mirrors and could not distinguish her reflection from the others. All was blent into one brilliant procession. On entering the ball-room the regular hum of voices, footsteps, and greetings deafened Natasha, and the light and glitter dazzled her still more. The host and hostess, who had already been standing at the door for half an hour repeating the same words to the various arrivals, '*Charmé de vous voir,*' greeted the Rostovs and Peronskaya in the same manner.

The two girls in their white dresses, each with a rose in her black hair, both curtsied in the same way, but the hostess's eye involuntarily rested longer on the slim Natasha. She looked at her and gave her alone a special smile, in addition to her usual smile as hostess. Looking at her she may have recalled the golden, irrevocable days of her own girlhood and her own first ball. The host also followed Natasha with his eyes and asked the count which was his daughter.

'Charming!' said he, kissing the tips of his fingers.

In the ball-room guests stood crowding at the entrance doors awaiting the Emperor. The countess took up a position in one of the front rows of that crowd. Natasha heard and felt that several people were asking about her and looking at her. She realized that those noticing her liked her, and this observation helped to calm her.

'There are some like ourselves and some worse,' she thought.❞

LEO TOLSTOY, *WAR AND PEACE*,
TRANS. BY LOUISE AND AYLMER MAUDE,
PUB. EVERYMAN'S LIBRARY, LONDON,
AND ALFRED A. KNOPF, NEW YORK, 1992

BACKSTABBING

Anton Chekhov (1860–1904) deplored theatrical society in St Petersburg. The premiere of "The Sea Gull" at the State Theatre in 1896 was disastrous yet it was later a great success when staged at the Moscow Arts Theatre, and he took all his subsequent plays to the latter.

❝I am tired out, like a ballerina after five acts and eight tableaux. Banquets, letters which one is too lazy to answer, conversations and all sorts of bosh. Right now I've got to take a cab to Vasilievsky Island, to dine there, yet I am bored and I have to work. I will stay here for three days more and see: if this ballet continues I'll either go home or to Ivan in Sudoroga.

I am enveloped by a dense atmosphere of ill will, extremely vague, and to me inexplicable. They are tendering me dinners and chanting banal dithyrambs to me and at the same time are all set to devour me. Why? The devil knows. If I had shot myself I would have afforded great pleasure to nine-tenths of my friends and admirers. And in what petty ways people express their pettiness! Burenin berates me in a *feuilleton*, even though it is not customary for newpapers to berate their own contributors; Maslov (Bezhetsky) no longer goes to dine with the Suvorins; Shcheglov tells all the gossip current about me, and so on. All this is dreadfully foolish and boring. They're not people, but some sort of mold.**99**

> LETTER TO M.P. CHEKHOVA, ST PETERSBURG, JANUARY 14, 1891,
> IN *LETTERS OF ANTON CHEKHOV*, TRANS. BERNARD GUILBERT GUERNEY,
> PUB. VIKING PRESS, NEW YORK, 1968

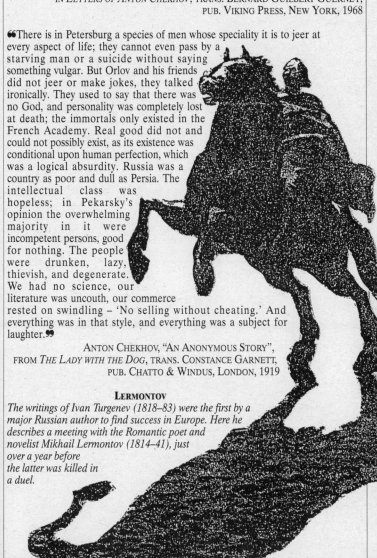

66There is in Petersburg a species of men whose speciality it is to jeer at every aspect of life; they cannot even pass by a starving man or a suicide without saying something vulgar. But Orlov and his friends did not jeer or make jokes, they talked ironically. They used to say that there was no God, and personality was completely lost at death; the immortals only existed in the French Academy. Real good did not and could not possibly exist, as its existence was conditional upon human perfection, which was a logical absurdity. Russia was a country as poor and dull as Persia. The intellectual class was hopeless; in Pekarsky's opinion the overwhelming majority in it were incompetent persons, good for nothing. The people were drunken, lazy, thievish, and degenerate. We had no science, our literature was uncouth, our commerce rested on swindling – 'No selling without cheating.' And everything was in that style, and everything was a subject for laughter.**99**

> ANTON CHEKHOV, "AN ANONYMOUS STORY",
> FROM *THE LADY WITH THE DOG*, TRANS. CONSTANCE GARNETT,
> PUB. CHATTO & WINDUS, LONDON, 1919

LERMONTOV

The writings of Ivan Turgenev (1818–83) were the first by a major Russian author to find success in Europe. Here he describes a meeting with the Romantic poet and novelist Mikhail Lermontov (1814–41), just over a year before the latter was killed in a duel.

66Lermontov, too, I saw only twice: at the house of Princess Sh[akhovskoy], a Petersburg high society woman, and a few days later at a New Year's fancy dress ball at the Noblemen's Club on the eve of 1840. At Princess Sh[akhovskoy]'s I, a very rare and unaccustomed visitor at high society parties, saw him only from a distance, observing the poet, who had become famous in so short a time, from a corner where I had secreted myself. Lermontov sat down on a low stool in front of a sofa on which, wearing a black gown, was sitting one of the society beauties of those days, the fair-haired Countess [Emilia] Mussin-Pushkin, who died young and who really was a strikingly beautiful girl. Lermontov wore the uniform of the Life Guards Hussar Regiment. He had removed neither his sword nor his gloves and, frowning and hunching his shoulders, gazed sullenly at the Countess. She only exchanged a few words with him, talking mostly to Count Sh[akhovskoy], also a Hussar officer, who was sitting beside him. There was something ominous and tragic in Lermontov's appearance: his swarthy face and large, motionless dark eyes exuded a sort of sombre and evil strength, a sort of pensive scornfulness and passion. His hard gaze was strangely out of keeping with the expression of his almost childishly tender, protruding lips. His whole figure, thick-set, bow-legged, with a large head on broad, stooping shoulders, aroused an unpleasant feeling; but everyone had at once to acknowledge its immense inherent strength. It is, of course, a well-known fact that he had to some extent portrayed himself in Pechorin. The words: 'His eyes did not laugh when he laughed,' from *A Hero of Our Time*, etc., could really have been applied to himself. I remember that Count Sh[akhovskoy] and the young Countess suddenly burst out laughing at something and went on laughing for some time; Lermontov, too, laughed, but at the same time he kept looking at them with a sort of offensive astonishment. For all that I could not help feeling that he was fond of Count Sh[akhovskoy] as a fellow-officer and that he was also well-disposed towards the Countess. There could be no doubt that, following the fashion of those days, he was trying to assume a Byronic air together with a number of other even worse eccentricities and whimsicalities. And he paid dearly for them! At heart Lermontov was probably terribly bored; he felt stifled in the airless atmosphere where fate had forced him to live.99

<small>I<small>VAN</small> T<small>URGENEV</small>, L<small>ITERARY</small> R<small>EMINISCENCES AND</small> A<small>UTOBIOGRAPHICAL</small> F<small>RAGMENTS</small>,
TRANS. BY D<small>AVID</small> M<small>AGARSHACK</small>, PUB. F<small>ABER</small> & F<small>ABER</small>, L<small>ONDON</small>, 1959</small>

F<small>ASHION</small>
Russian revolutionary Alexander Herzen (1812–70) combined his personal life and his opinions with political views in his autobiography published in 1885.

66The Petersburghers laugh at the costumes seen in Moscow; they are outraged by the caps and Hungarian jackets, the long hair and civilian moustaches. Moscow certainly is a non-military city, rather careless and unaccustomed to discipline, but whether that is a good quality or a defect is a matter of opinion. The harmony of uniformity, the absence of variety, of what is personal and whimsical, a traditional obligatory dress and external discipline are all found on the largest scale in the most inhuman condition in which men live – in barracks. The uniform and a complete absence of variety are passionately loved by despotism. Nowhere are fashions followed so respectfully as in Petersburg, and that shows the immaturity of our culture; our clothes are alien. In Europe people dress, but we dress up, and so are terrified if a sleeve is too full, or a collar too narrow. In Paris all that people are afraid of is being dressed without taste; in London all that they are afraid of is catching cold; in Italy every one dresses as he likes best. If one were to show an Englishman the battalions of fops on the Nevsky Prospect, all wearing exactly similar, tightly buttoned coats, he would take them for a squad of 'policemen'.99

<small>A<small>LEXANDER</small> H<small>ERZEN</small>, M<small>Y</small> P<small>AST AND</small> T<small>HOUGHTS</small>,
TRANS. BY C<small>ONSTANCE</small> G<small>ARNETT</small>,
PUB. C<small>HATTO</small> & W<small>INDUS</small>, L<small>ONDON</small>, 1924</small>

FESTIVITIES

English tutor William Coxe (1747–1828) witnessed an enormous and ultimately rather dangerous party in St Petersburg.

❝On the 6th of December we were witness to a very singular entertainment given to the public by a Russian, who had acquired a large fortune by farming, during four years only, the right of vending spirituous liquors. On surrendering his contract, he gave, as proof of his gratitude to the lower class of people, by whom he had enriched himself, a feast near the garden of the summer-palace . . . announced by hand-bills distributed throughout the city . . . which commenced at two o'clock in the afternoon. A large semicircular table was covered with all kinds of provision, piled in different shapes, and in the greatest profusion. Large slices of bread and caviare, dried sturgeon, carp, and other fish, were ranged to a great height, in the form of pent-houses and pyramids, and garnished with craw-fish, onions, and pickles. In different parts of the grounds were rows of casks full of spirituous liquors, and still larger vessels of wine, beer, and quass. Among the decorations, I observed the representation of an immense whale in pasteboard, covered with cloth and gold or silver brocade, and filled in the inside with bread, dried fish, and other provisions.

All sorts of games and diversions were exhibited for the amusement of the populace. At the extremity of the grounds was a large square of ice well swept for the scaters; near which were two machines like the swinging vehicles at Bartholomew Fair. One of these machines consisted of two cross-beams fixed horizontally to a pole in the center by means of a pivot; from the ends of the beams hung four sledges, in which people seated themselves, and were turned round with great velocity; the other had four wooden horses suspended from the beams, and the riders were whirled round in like manner. . . . Beyond these were two ice-hills. . . . Two poles, above twenty feet in height, were also erected, with colours flying; and at the top of each was placed a piece of money, as a prize for those who could swarm up and seize it. The poles, being rubbed with oil, soon froze in this severe climate; many and tedious were the attempts of the various competitors in this slippery ascent to fame. The scene was lively and gay; for about 40,000 persons of both sexes were assembled on the occasion. . . .

It was preconcerted, that, on firing a rocket, the people were to drink a glass of spirituous liquor, and, on the discharge of a second, to begin the repast. But the impatience of the populace anticipated the necessity of a second signal; and the whole multitude was soon and at once in motion. The whale was the chief object of contention; within the space of a few minutes he was entirely divested of his gaudy trappings, which became the spoils of his successful invaders. . . . They rend him into a thousand pieces, to seize the provision with which his inside was stored. The remaining people . . . were employed in uncovering the pent-houses, and pulling down the pyramids. . . . Others crowded around the casks and hogsheads; and with great wooden ladles lapped incessantly wine, beer, and spirits. The confusion and riot, which soon succeeded, is better conceived than described; and we thought it expedient to retire. . . .

But the consequences of this feast were indeed dreadful. The cold had suddenly increased with such violence, that Fahrenheit's thermometer, which at mid-day

stood only at 4, sunk towards the close of the evening to 15 below freezing point. Many intoxicated persons were frozen to death; not a few fell a sacrifice to drunken quarrels; and others were robbed and murdered in the more retired parts of the city, as they were returning late to their homes. From a comparison of various reports, we had reason to conclude, that at least 400 persons lost their lives upon this melancholy occasion. (The following day I counted myself no less than forty bodies, collected in two sheds near the place of entertainment.)"

WILLIAM COXE, "TRAVELS IN RUSSIA",
SEVEN BRITONS IN IMPERIAL RUSSIA 1698–1812,
ED. PETER PUTNAM,
PUB. PRINCETON UNIVERSITY PRESS, 1952

CATHERINE THE GREAT

The first of the two following extracts tells of the beginnings of the Hermitage picture collection; the second, a love letter, tells of Catherine's difficulties in communicating with Prince Grigory Potemkin in the Winter Palace.

"[Catherine] entered into negotiations with the dealer Gotskowski. This gentleman also regularly supplied pictures to Frederick II of Prussia, who had done so much to further Catherine's marriage (which, incidentally, in no way inhibited her from calling him her mortal enemy once she was on the throne, nor yet from subsequently signing a Treaty of Alliance with him: she had, in fact, lost no time in mastering the rules of politics). Gotskowski was in debt and Catherine was delighted to strike a bargain with him and thus secure for herself in Berlin itself 225 pictures which should normally have gone to Sans Souci to delight the eyes of Frederick. Spite may, indeed, have been the mainspring of Catherine's love of art collecting."

PIERRE DESCARGUES,
THE HERMITAGE, TRANS.
K. DELAVENAY, LONDON, 1961

"My little darling, good morning! As so often happens, I could not enter your apartments as the Palace is full of human cattle, wandering about in the passages. I greet you from afar and pray for your good health."

*LETTRES D'AMOUR DE CATHERINE II
À POTEMKIN*,
ED. G OUDARD,
PARIS 1934, TRANS. FROM THE FRENCH BY
MARIE NOËLE KELLY

A COMIC WEDDING

In 1740 Empress Anne, displaying an extraordinary sense of humour, organized Prince Galitzine's bizarre wedding to Avdotaya Ivanovna.

❝The winter of 1739–40 was unusually cold, and the scientists of the Academy embarked on a programme of experiments to test the properties of ice that was available in such abundance. Knowing this, a court Chamberlain called Alexander Tatishchev thought of combining it with a new entertainment for the court – building a palace of ice on which artists and artisans as well as scientists could exercise their skills. In the end it turned out to be a setting for another of the Empress's macabre jokes for which poor Golitsyn was again the butt. . . . One morning a huge and astonishing procession formed up in the streets. Goats, pigs, cows, camels, dogs and reindeer were seen harnessed to various vehicles each of which contained a representative pair from each of the 'Barbarous Races' in the Empire. There were Lapps and Kirghiz, Tunguses and Tatars, Bashkirs and Finns – each couple in 'national dress'. But the centrepiece was an elephant with an iron cage on its back. The cage contained Golitsyn and his unlovely bride. To the accompaniment of cymbals, bells and the occasional roaring of an angry beast, the procession passed the Palace and eventually arrived at Ernest Biron's covered riding school, where a banquet had been prepared for the captive bridal pair and their guests. By the Empress's express command each couple was served with its own traditional dishes – including such culinary delights as reindeer meat, horse-flesh and fermented mare's milk. There was entertainment too. A poet named

Tredyakovski declaimed an ode composed specially for the occasion entitled: 'Greetings to the Bridal Pair of Fools', and each pair of guests was made to dance its own 'national dance' for the amusement of onlookers. Then the procession formed up again to accompany the bride and groom to their home for the night – the palace made of ice. No other material had been used in its construction – walls and steps, baroque bald columns, even the decorative figurines and window-panes were made of ice. So was the furniture – a huge four-poster bridal bed, chairs, tables, chandeliers, a clock, a commode, a set of playing cards, with the markings coloured in, and a statue of a Cupid. Outside there were other marvels of engineering and the sculptor's art – flowers and trees complete with perching birds, ice cannon which fired real charges, a pair of dolphins which breathed out flames of fire (thanks to a device inside which pumped out naptha), and a life-sized model of an elephant equipped with a machine to squirt out water to a height of two hundred and fifty feet. Everything had been done to excite the eye and astonish the imagination – and all at a cost of only thirty thousand roubles. The Empress accompanied the bridal pair inside, saw them undressed and laid upon their bed of ice. Then she withdrew. From her bedroom she had an excellent view of the Ice Palace, and next morning she saw Golitsyn and his wife emerge apparently none the worse for their experience. The stove installed inside their chilly bedroom, as the scientists of the Academy took careful note, had proved effective.❞

PHILIP LONGWORTH, *THE THREE EMPRESSES*, LONDON, 1972

HISTORY

ASSASSINATIONS

"Under Western Eyes" by Joseph Conrad (1857–1924) describes the fate of a student who is caught up in the Russian Revolution.

❝Mr. de P– was being driven towards the railway station in a two-horse uncovered sleigh with footman and coachman on the box. Snow had been falling all night, making the roadway, uncleared as yet at this early hour, very heavy for the horses. It was still falling thickly. But the sleigh must have been observed and marked down. As it drew over to the left before taking a turn, the footman noticed a peasant walking slowly on the edge of the pavement with his hands in the pockets of his sheepskin coat and his shoulders hunched up to his ears under the falling snow. On being overtaken this peasant suddenly faced about and swung his arm. In an instant there was a terrible shock, a detonation muffled in the multitude of snowflakes; both horses lay dead and mangled on the ground and the coachman, with a shrill cry, had fallen off the box mortally wounded. The footman (who survived) had no time to see the face of the man in the sheepskin coat. After throwing the bomb this last got away, but it is supposed that, seeing a lot of people surging up on all sides of him in the falling snow, and all running towards the scene of the explosion, he thought it safer to turn back with them. In an incredibly short time an excited crowd assembled round the sledge. The Minister-President, getting out unhurt into the deep snow, stood near the groaning coachman and addressed the people repeatedly in his weak, colourless voice. 'I beg of you to keep off. For the love of God, I beg of you good people to keep off.' It was then that a tall young man who had remained standing perfectly still within a carriage gateway, two houses lower down, stepped out into the street and walking up rapidly flung another bomb over the heads of the crowd. It actually struck the Minister-President on the shoulder as he stooped over his dying servant, then falling between his feet exploded with a terrific concentrated violence, striking him dead to the ground, finishing the wounded man and practically annihilating the empty sledge in the twinkling of an eye. With a yell of horror the crowd broke up and fled in all directions, except for those who fell dead or dying where they stood nearest to the Minister-President, and one or two others who did not fall till they had run a little way. The first explosion had brought together a crowd as if by enchantment, the second made as swiftly a solitude in the street for hundreds of yards in each direction. Through the falling snow people looked from afar at the small heap of dead bodies lying upon each other near the carcases of the two horses. Nobody dared to approach till some Cossacks of a street-patrol galloped up and, dismounting, began to turn over the dead. Amongst the innocent victims of the second explosion laid out on the pavement there was a body dressed in peasant's sheepskin coat; but the face was unrecognizable, there was absolutely nothing found in the pockets of its poor clothing, and it was the only one whose identity was never established. 99

JOSEPH CONRAD, *UNDER WESTERN EYES*, EVERYMAN'S LIBRARY, LONDON, AND ALFRED A. KNOPF, NEW YORK, 1992

REVOLUTION

English writer William Gerhardie (1895–1977 was born in St Petersburg and later served in the British Embassy there.

66One morning, as I was about to cross the Troitski Bridge to meet the Admiral, I was stopped by the police and was compelled to go home and change into uniform. When I returned the revolution had already broken out. The Admiral had just witnessed the sacking of the Arsenal by a disorderly crowd. Regiment after regiment was going over to the revolution. Solitary shots, and now and then machine-gun fire, were heared from varius quarters of the city. The Admiral and I stood at the window and watched. Lorry after lorry packed with armed soldiery and workmen, some lying in a 'ready' attitdute along the mudguards, went past us in a kind of wild and dazzling joy ride, waving red flags and revolutionary banners to shouts of 'Hurrah!' from the crowds in the street. The Admiral stood with his hands folded on the window-sill, unable to withhold his enthusiasm. It was a clear, bright day, I think and very cold.

That evening following the outbreak of the revolution was vividly impressed upon my memory. During the day I had listened to innumerable speeches, some of a Liberal loftiness; others of a menacingly proletarian character, threatening death to capital and revolution to the world at large. There was a tendency to flamboyant extravagance and exaggeration. 'Down with Armies and Navies!' shouted one speaker hysterically. 'Down with militarism! Through red terror to peace, freedom and brotherhood!' Therewere placards and banners and processions. 'Land and Liberty!' was a popular watchword. Red was the dominant colour, and the opening bars of the Marseillaise were a kind of recurring *Leitmotiv* in the tumult. Crossing a bridge I passed a company of soldiers newly revolted. They marched alert and joyous to the sound of some old familiar marching song till they came to the words 'for the Czar.' Having sung these words they stopped somewhat abruptly and perplexed. '*How* for the Czar?' one of them asked. '*How* for the Czar?' they repeated, looking at each other sheepishly. Then they marched on without singing. There were peasants who did not know the 'revolution' and thought it was a woman who would supersede the Czar. Others wanted a republic with a czar. And there were others still who interpreted the word republic as 'rezshpublicoo,' thinking that it meant 'cut up the public'.

In the Troitski Square I was stopped by a young enthusiastic Russian officer, who attracted by my British uniform, spoke to me in English, his eyes glittering with excitement. 'Sir,' he said, 'you now will have more vigorous Allies.' And then in the Nevski I passed a procession of Anarchists who are regarded by the Bolsheviks with about the same degree of unmitigated horror as the Bolsheviks are regarded by the *Morning Post*. They marched with a gruesome look about their faces, bearing their horrible colours of black, crested with a human skull and cross-bones. **99**

WILLIAM GERHARDIE, *FUTILITY*,
PUB. DUCKWORTH, LONDON, 1927

AN ARISTOCRATIC REVOLUTIONARY

Prince Peter Kropotkin (1842–1921) was born into the Russian aristocracy but his political beliefs were left-wing extremist. He left the army in 1872 to work for the International Working Man's Association. Arrested and imprisoned in 1874, he escaped to England in 1876, and spent the next forty years in exile, not returning to Russia until the 1917 Revolution.

66One day I received a quite unexpected visit. The Grand Duke Nicholas, brother of Alexander II, who was inspecting the fortress, entered my cell, followed only by his aide-de-camp. The door was shut behind him. He rapidly approached me, saying 'Good-day, Kropótkin.' He knew me personally, and spoke in a familiar, good-natured tone, as to an old acquaintance. 'How is it possible, Kropótkin, that you, a page de chambre, a sergeant of the corps of pages, should be mixed up in this business, and now be here in this horrible casemate?'

'Every one has his own opinions,' was my reply.

'Opinions! So your opinions were that you must stir up a revolution?'

What was I to reply? Yes? Then the construction which would be put upon my answer would be that I, who had refused to give any answers to the gendarmes, 'avowed everything' before the brother of the Tsar. His tone was that of a commander of a military school when trying to obtain 'avowals' from a cadet. Yet I could not say No: it would have been a lie. I did not know what to say, and stood without saying anything.

'You see! You feel ashamed of it now' –

This remark angered me, and I at once said in a rather sharp way, 'I have given my replies to the examining magistrate, and have nothing to add.'

'But understand, Kropótkin, please,' he said then, in the most familiar tone, 'that I don't speak to you as an examining magistrate. I speak quite as a private person, – quite as a private man,' he repeated, lowering his voice.

Thoughts went whirling in my head. To play the part of Marquis Posa? To tell the

Emperor through the grand duke of the desolation of Russia, the ruin of the peasantry, the arbitrariness of the officials, the terrible famines in prospect? To say that we wanted to help the peasants out of their desperate condition, to make them raise their heads, and by all this try to influence Alexander II? These thoughts followed one another in rapid succession, till at last I said to myself: 'Never! Nonsense! They know all that. They are enemies of the nation, and such talk would not change them.'

I replied that he always remained an official person, and that I could not look upon him as a private man.

He then began to ask me indifferent questions. 'Was it not in Siberia, with the Decembrists, that you began to entertain such ideas?'

'No; I knew only one Decembrist, and with him I had no talks worth speaking of.'

'Was it then at St. Petersburg that you got them?'

'I was always the same.'

'Why! Were you such in the corps of pages?' he asked me with terror.

'In the corps I was a boy, and what is indefinite in boyhood grows definite in manhood.'

He asked me some other similar questions, and as he spoke I distinctly saw what he was driving at. He was trying to obtain avowals, and my imagination vividly pictured him saying to his brother: 'All these examining magistrates are imbeciles. He gave them no replies, but I talked to him ten minutes, and he told me everything.' That began to annoy me; and when he said to me something to this effect, 'How could you have anything to do with all these people – peasants and people with no names?' – I sharply turned upon him and said, 'I have told you already that I have given my replies to the examining magistrate.' Then he abruptly left the cell.

Later, the soldiers of the guard made quite a legend of that visit. The person who came in a carriage to carry me away at the time of my escape wore a military cap, and, having sandy whiskers, bore a faint resemblance to the Grand Duke Nicholas. So a tradition grew up amongst the soldiers of the St. Petersburg garrison that it was the grand duke himself who came to rescue me and kidnapped me. Thus are legends created even in times of newspapers and biographical dictionaries.**

PETER KROPOTKIN, *MEMOIRS OF A REVOLUTIONIST*,
PUB. DOVER PUBLICATIONS, INC., NEW YORK, 1971

CAFÉ LIFE

American novelist John Dos Passos (1896–1970) visited St Petersburg in 1928.

**In the evening the café under the Europskaya Hotel seems a great relief. Here's something a guy doesn't have to cudgel his wits to understand. It's like Europe, it's like the East Side of New York. Beer, jingly music, white tablecloths, shoddy whores. You can give your order to the waiter and he politely brings you a breaded cutlet. There are businessmen at the tables, tricky-looking articles who will assist you to buy a genuine antique ikon or a young lady's recumbent halfhour. There are speculators who will change your dollars for rubles in the black market. It's the kingdom of money again, the blessed land of valuta. After a while the nightlife begins to get a stale look, the beer begins to taste sour; best thing to do's to go to bed. It's too drearily obvious that the café's a grimy microcosm of the capitalist world across the Frontier, too obvious to be funny even. I'm no Y.M.C.A. secretary,

but Red Putilov has somehow taken the edge off it. When I ask my Russian friends about it they laugh and say, 'That's the underworld. The police let that place stay open so that they can always know where the criminals are when they want to put their hands on them.' **99**

JOHN DOS PASSOS, *JOURNEYS BETWEEN WARS*,
PUB. HARCOURT BRACE & COMPANY, NEW YORK, 1938

SEASONS

SNOW

English traveler E.D. Clarke (1769–1822) found Russian snow extraordinary.

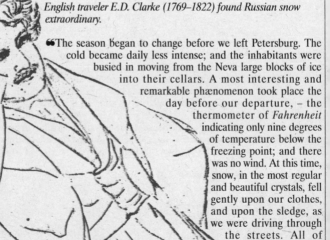

66The season began to change before we left Petersburg. The cold became daily less intense; and the inhabitants were busied in moving from the Neva large blocks of ice into their cellars. A most interesting and remarkable phænomenon took place the day before our departure, – the thermometer of *Fahrenheit* indicating only nine degrees of temperature below the freezing point; and there was no wind. At this time, snow, in the most regular and beautiful crystals, fell gently upon our clothes, and upon the sledge, as we were driving through the streets. All of these crystals possessed exactly the

same figure, and the same dimensions. Every one of them consisted of a wheel or star, with six equal rays, bounded by circumferences of equal diameters; having all the same number of rays branching from a common centre. The size of each of those little stars was equal to the circle presented by the section of a pea, into two equal parts. This appearance continued during three hours, in which time no other snow fell.**

E.D. CLARKE, *TRAVELS IN VARIOUS COUNTRIES OF EUROPE, ASIA AND AFRICA*, PUB. T. CADELL & W. DAVIES, LONDON, 1816

NEVA

Now regarded as one of the major poets of the 20th century, Osip Mandelstam (1891–1938?) fell out of favor with the Soviet regime and died of a heart attack after his second arrest in 1938.

**I'm feeling cold. Transparent springtime is
clothing Petropolis in a green down.
But still the Neva's wave, like a medusa,
inspires in me a slight sense of aversion.
On the embankment of the northern river
the fireflies of the automobiles whirl,
steel dragon-flies and beetles rush along,
the gold pins of the stars are flickering,
but no stars, no stars whatever, will kill
the weightly emerald of the sea's waves.**

OSIP MANDELSTAM, "TRISTIA", FROM *POEMS FROM MANDELSTAM*, TRANS. BY R.H. MORRISON, PUB. ASSOCIATED UNIVERSITY PRESSES, LONDON, 1990

EARLY MORNING

Russian poet and essayist Joseph Brodsky was born in St Petersburg in 1940.

**Once upon a time there was a little boy. He lived in the most unjust country in the world. Which was ruled by creatures who by all human accounts should be considered degenerates. Which never happened.

And there was a city. The most beautiful city on the face of the earth. With an immense gray river that hung over its distant bottom like the immense gray sky over that river. Along that river there stood magnificent palaces with such beautifully elaborated façades that if the little boy was standing on the right bank, the left bank looked like the imprint of a giant mollusk called civilization. Which ceased to exist.

Early in the morning when the sky was still full of stars the little boy would rise and, after having a cup of tea and an egg, accompanied by a radio announcement of a new record in smelted steel, followed by the army choir singing a hymn to the Leader, whose picture was pinned to the wall over the little boy's still warm bed, he would run along the snow-covered granite embankment to school.

The wide river lay white and frozen like a continent's tongue lapsed into silence, and the big bridge arched against the dark blue sky like an iron palate. If the little boy had two extra minutes, he would slide down on the ice and take twenty or thirty steps to the middle. All this time he would be thinking about what the fish were doing under such heavy ice. Then he would stop, turn 180 degrees, and run back, nonstop, right up to the entrance of the school. He would burst into the hall, throw his hat and coat off onto a hook, and fly up the staircase and into his classroom.

It is a big room with three rows of desks, a portrait of the Leader on the wall behind the teacher's chair, a map with two hemispheres, of which only one is legal. The little boy takes his seat, opens his briefcase, puts his pen and notebook on the desk, lifts his face, and prepares himself to hear drivel.**

JOSEPH BRODSKY, *LESS THAN ONE*,
PUB. FARRAR, STRAUS, GIROUX, NEW YORK, 1966

THE TSAR'S MANIFESTO

The ambassador Maurice Paléogue was the only foreigner present at the ceremony, in St George's Gallery in the Winter Palace, when the Tsar proclaimed Russia's entry into the 1914 War.

**After the final prayer the court chaplain read the Tsar's manifesto to his people – a simple recital of the events which have made war inevitable, an eloquent appeal to all the national energies, an invocation to the Most High, and so forth. Then the Tsar went up to the altar and raised his right hand toward the gospel held out to him. He was even more grave and composed, as if he were about to receive the sacrament. In a slow, low voice, which dwelt on every word he made the following declaration.

'Officers of my guard, here present, I greet in you my whole army and give it my blessing. I solemnly swear that I will never make peace so long as one of the enemy is on the soil of the fatherland.'

A mighty outburst of cheering was the answer to this declaration which was copied from the oath taken by the Emperor Alexander I in 1812. For nearly ten minutes there was a frantic tumult in the gallery and it was soon intensified by the cheers of the crowd massed along the Neva.**

MAURICE PALÉOGUE, "AN AMBASSADOR'S MEMOIRS 1914–1917"
FROM *ST PETERSBURG, A TRAVELLERS' COMPANION*,
SELECTED AND INTRODUCED BY LAURENCE KELLY,
PUB. CONSTABLE, LONDON, 1981

ITINERARIES IN ST PETERSBURG

Palace of Pavlovsk ▲   Palace of Tsarskoe Selo and detail of Atlas figure (right) ▼

Winter Palace, Hermitage Museum ▼

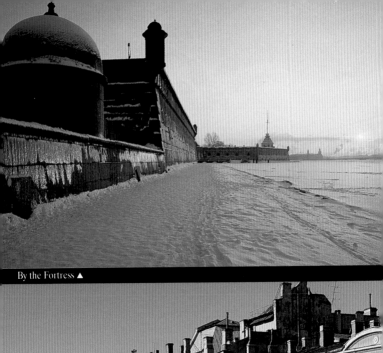

By the Fortress ▲

The Moika Canal ▲ The Sphinx landing stage, University Embankment ▼

Vasilyevsky Island, from the Admiralty Embankment ▲ Palace Embankment and the Hermitage ▼

The frozen Neva and the Peter and Paul Fortress ▼

Palace Bridge ▲

Trinity Bridge (also called Troitsky Bridge) ▼

From the
Peter and Paul Fortress
to the Islands of the Delta

1. PETER AND PAUL FORTRESS 2. PETER AND PAUL CATHEDRAL 3. TRINITY BRIDGE

⊙ Half a day

FROM THE BASTION TO THE MAUSOLEUM CHAPEL

The Peter and Paul Fortress has never been a residential area. Its only inhabitants were the garrison and the clergy attached to the Cathedral. It was, however, the symbolic center of the Russian Empire because successive sovereigns from Peter the Great onward (including the executed Czarevich Alexei ● 36) are buried there.

FORTIFICATIONS

With the coming of the age of artillery a Vauban-style fortress with bastions was planned for the defense of the island. It is likely that Peter the Great was inspired in this by what he had seen in the West (1696–8). After the first earthworks had been raised the walls were continued in stone under the supervision of the architect Trezzini. The bastions bore the name of the princes who were given responsibility for each military sector. Thus, from Peter's (Petrovsky) Gate these are known as the CZAR, NARYSHKIN, TRUBETSKOY, ZOTOV, GULUKIN AND MENSHIKOV BASTIONS. In about 1740 the initial fortifications were doubled around each gate leading to the mainland by a curtain wall with moats; the latter were filled in during the 19th century. As a result it is necessary to pass through St John's Gate in order to reach Peter's Gate. When she built up the Neva embankment Catherine II added a granite dressing to the fortifications in 1779. Although it stands on the Petrograd Side the Arsenal, or Kronverk, complements the ramparts of the fortress and is an integral part of them. In the event, the Peter and Paul Fortress never had to play the defensive role for which it was designed.

THE GATES

PETER'S GATE. The decoration of this gate, with its imperial eagle and wooden bas-relief, refers to the victories of Peter the Great. On either side statues of the goddesses Bellona and Minerva serve as reminders of Peter's military prowess and political sagacity.

NEVA GATE. Built by Lvov between 1784 and 1787, this gate leads to the Fortress' only deep-water landing stage. It is crowned by a triangular pediment and framed by two groups of twin columns, joined by two blocks of facetted stone. The image of SAINT NICHOLAS guards this gate, which serves as the fortress exit toward Vasilyevsky Island, while SAINT BASIL stands sentry over the gate between the Trubetskoy and Zotov bastions.

"The fortress of St Petersburg was built, like all fortresses, to be a visible symbol of the antagonism between the people and its sovereign. No doubt it defends the city, but it threatens it to a far greater extent; no doubt it was built to repel the Swedes, but in practice it has been a prison for Russians."

Alexandre Dumas, *Voyage en Russie*

145

After the annexation by Russia of the mouth of the Neva during the Northern War the first fortress was built, in May 1703. This structure was close to the sea and naturally defended by the Neva itself. The island of Petersburg on which it stood was small enough to be entirely enclosed, leaving no room for enemy forces to gain a foothold. It was the last upstream island of the delta, and no ship could enter the waterway without passing it.

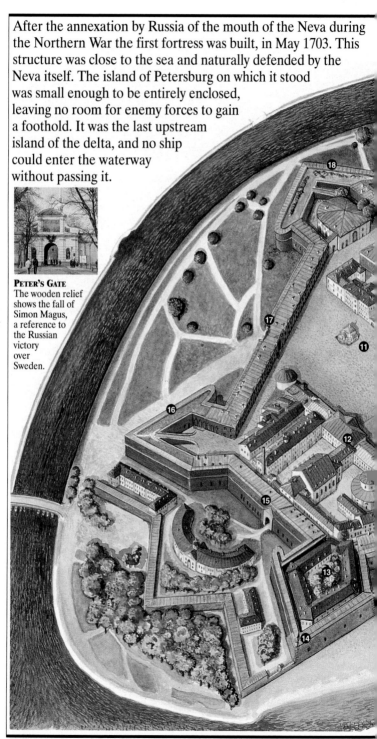

PETER'S GATE
The wooden relief shows the fall of Simon Magus, a reference to the Russian victory over Sweden.

THE CANNON
The cannon-shot which is still fired at noon is the last vestige of the Fortress' military past.

THE PRISON
The Trubetskoy Bastion became a prison in 1872, and held political prisoners and opponents of the Czar. The Czarevich Alexei was tortured in the fortress.

147

IMPERIAL TOMBS
The sobriety of the tombs contrasts with the wealth of the trophies hanging from the walls, as if man's humility were being deliberately juxtaposed with the glory of his acts. The tradition of the mausoleum is once again alive; the last of the Romanovs, who died in France in 1992, is buried here, and it is now planned that the ashes of the last imperial family, shot at Ekaterinburg in 1918, should also be interred here.

PETER AND PAUL CATHEDRAL ★

The first church inside the fortress was built of wood. Its construction began on June 29, 1703, the feast day of Saint Peter and Saint Paul. Later, in 1712, the construction of the present cathedral (PETROPAVLOSKI SOBOR; Петропавлоский собор) was undertaken under the direction of the architect Trezzini, who opted for the Western style of the period. The tower has been struck by lightning and rebuilt a number of times, and the cathedral was reconstructed following a fire in 1753. Its nave is conventional European Baroque, both in its floor plan and its elevation. There is also a pulpit, which is unusual for a Russian Orthodox cathedral.

ICONOSTASIS ● 56. The architectural framework, which is ill-adapted to the Russian ritual, imposed an original solution for the iconostasis; in effect it occupies the entire breadth of the cathedral, and its royal doorway runs the width of the central nave.

CHIMING CLOCK. After 1724 the cathedral was equipped with a Dutch clock, presented by the Czar himself. Its bells, which chime every six hours, originally played a hymn to the Czar on the stroke of noon. For the moment it is silent, not because it has ceased to work but because it has not yet been decided what anthem it should play, the Soviet one being out of fashion.

THE MINT
Peter I decided to move his state mint from Moscow to St Petersburg in 1719. From 1724 onward coins of gold, silver and copper were struck here, along with medals. Although it served as the center of the national money supply under both the imperial and Communist regimes the Mint is now confined to the production of military medals.

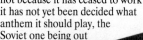

ARTILLERY MUSEUM
The Artillery Museum displays a rich collection of swords, military souvenirs, uniforms and battle paintings. It is devoted to the military engineer corps. Don't miss the collection of tanks in the forecourt.

The political choice is to be made between Bortniansky's "God Save the Czar" (18th century) and a melody written by Glinka (19th century).

THE GOVERNOR'S MAUSOLEUM. Against the east wall of the cathedral is the mausoleum reserved for governors of the Fortress who died during their tenure. Among other duties the governors had to alert the sovereign to the fact that the Neva was once again navigable, by bringing him a goblet of water from the river at winter's end.

THE BOAT HOUSE

THE PAVILION. The Boat House (Botny Dom/Ботный дом), built by the architect Alexander Wist (1761–5) in the Baroque style, is crowned by an allegory of navigation sculpted by David Jensen (1891). Today it is occupied by a luxury souvenir shop.

ST PETERSBURG HISTORY MUSEUM

ENGINEERS' BUILDING. The whole Fortress precinct houses the St Petersburg History Museum; the collections in the Engineers' Building demonstrate certain aspects of daily life, in particular through a series of naive, highly colored shop signs. On the way through to the Commandant's House stands Mikhail Shemyakin's statue of Peter I (1990).

THE COMMANDANT'S HOUSE. Built in the 1740's, this structure contains an exhibition on the history of the Fortress, from its first human occupation to the fall of the monarchy. The naval aspect of its history is especially well represented.

THE OLD ARSENAL

Between 1705 and 1708 the Fortress was protected on the Petrograd Side by the construction of the original Kronverk. Of this auxiliary earthwork nothing remains today but ruins, with a stream at their foot.

MONUMENT TO THE DECEMBRISTS. The execution of the Decembrists ● 42 took place at the Arsenal. The obelisk commemorating the five victims bears a medallion showing their profiles.

ARTILLERY MUSEUM. The Arsenal building is constructed of brick. Its façade is regulated by pilasters; each segment includes a carriage gateway and twinned bays on the second floor. In 1856 the military collections assembled since 1776 were installed in the arsenals of the Kronverk, where they may still be seen today.

THE PRISON
Outside is the sauna bath which the prisoners were allowed to visit once a week. The cells were furnished with an iron bed and a table, both sealed to the wall, and a stool: they were heated turn and turn about by a stove kept in the corridor. From 1872, one corner of the prison was known as the Dance Floor, in reference to a punishment inflicted on malingering soldiers, who were lashed to a stake with their feet resting on pointed sticks. The pain forced them to constantly shift their weight from one foot to the other, so that they looked as though they were dancing.

THE ANCESTOR OF THE RUSSIAN FLEET
For Peter the Great a powerful war fleet was the guarantor of Russia's opening up to the rest of the world. He personally sailed a large Dutch sloop from Moscow, his admirals plying the oars while he himself held the tiller. This vessel, known to this day as the "Grandfather of the Russian Fleet", was placed in the Boat House in 1761; since 1940 it has been in the Naval Museum (Stock Exchange) ▲ 157.

THE FIRST MARKET BUILDING
In the early 18th century the island of Petersburg was the site of the city's food market, the first Gostiny Dvor (right), a restaurant, and the port with its customs house where foreign ships (mostly Dutch) unloaded their cargos. Later the customs houses were moved to Vasilyevsky Island ▲ 156.

MATHILDA KSHESINSKAYA (1872–1971)
A pupil of the choreographer Petipa, Kshesinskaya was one of the ballet stars who trained a new generation of dancers in the Paris schools.

MONUMENT TO THE "STEREGUSHCHY"
Built on a stone plinth, this monument on the corner of Kamennoostrovsky Avenue and the Gorky Prospekt commemorates a destroyer captured by the Japanese in 1907 and scuttled by her two surviving crewmen. The sculptor Karl Isenberg chose to represent his theme on a stele of sheet-metal. On the reverse side is an inscription describing the event and listing the names of the dead.

THE PETROGRAD SIDE

PETERSBURG ISLAND. In the early days of the city this island (known today as the Petrograd Side) was important because it was close to the Fortress. All commercial and social life was concentrated around the old Revolution Square, now renamed TROITSKAYA. It suffered decline with the development of the left bank; by the second half of the 19th century wooden houses without gas or running water were in evidence, just as they were on the right bank.

RAPID MODERNIZATION. At the turn of the 20th century land was cheap and the influx of money into St Petersburg gave a powerful incentive to construction. The Petrograd Side was quickly built up, almost uniformly in the Art Nouveau style ● 90. The construction of the TRINITY BRIDGE (1897–1903) (Troitsky Most) gave the district further cachet by linking it to the grander quarters of the far bank. This bridge replaced a floating one ● 94, which had to be dismantled each year when the ice melted; at this time the Petrograd Side might be cut off from the rest of the city for up to two weeks, or until the Neva had swept away all the ice from Lake Ladoga ■ 18.
MUSEUM OF POLITICAL HISTORY. In 1904, the architect A.I. Hogen built a townhouse ● 92 for Mathilda Kshesinskaya, favorite ballerina of Nicholas II. It was commandeered by the Bolsheviks in March 1917, and later became Museum of the Great October Socialist Revolution. It houses a collection of waxworks of political figures.

ALEXANDER PARK

The Gorkovskaya metro station (Горьковская) is surrounded by an immense park, until recently named after Lenin but

now with its old title of Alexander Park restored. It occupies the old military training grounds around the Kronverk ▲ *149* and is a favorite place for St Petersburgers.

THE ZOOLOGICAL GARDENS. West of the Kronverk is the zoo, converted from a 19th-century private menagerie. It has seen better days; nevertheless, although giraffes and elephants are currently absent, the zoo does have a comprehensive collection of northern animal species, some of them virtually unknown to the Western public. In this zoo children will discover that minks, sables and martens exist in other forms than coats and stoles; they will also be interested by rare animals from Siberia, such as the long-eared hedgehog and the Przewalsky horse. In addition, there is a large aviary of birds of prey, and a number of bears, the emblem of Russia.

THE MOSQUE
(METCHET; мечет) Islam is the second most popular religion in Russia, with about 12 million adherents. Although they were present in St Petersburg from the earliest years, Muslims had no mosque till 1910. Designed by Vasilyev, who took as his model the Gour Emir Mausoleum at Samarkand (15th century), the mosque is thoroughly oriental in style, with an entry porch and two minarets covered in polychrome tiles.

CABIN OF PETER THE GREAT ★

A WOODEN LODGE ● *83*. Facing the Neva is the small cabin occupied by Peter the Great (DOMIK PETRA; домик Петра) in the summer of 1703. The roof is made of wooden slats in the shape of tiles, while the brick imitation of the exterior is reminiscent of a Dutch cottage. One of the two rooms was made into a chapel under Nicholas I; dismantled in 1930, this was replaced by an 18th-century style interior. The stone house built around the cabin also encloses a boat built by Peter the Great himself, along with an exhibition of engravings.

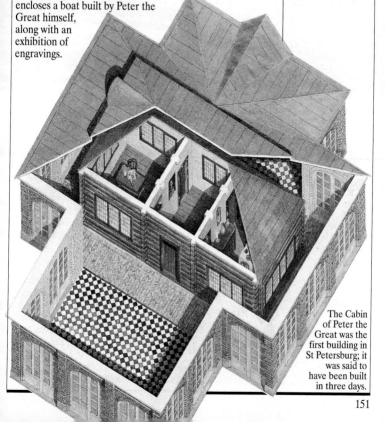

The Cabin of Peter the Great was the first building in St Petersburg; it was said to have been built in three days.

Власть Советам

THE "AURORA"

Built in the city's shipyards, this cruiser inherited the name of a famous fighting frigate of the Crimean War. Moored in front of the Nakhimov Naval Academy since 1948, it is one of the most celebrated symbols of the Revolution.

THE CRUISER "AURORA" ★

The cruiser *Aurora* (KREISSER AVRORA; крейсер Аврора) of the Baltic Fleet was launched in 1903; it became a cadet training vessel after the war with Japan in 1904. The crew, many of whom had progressive ideas, played a key role at the start of the Revolution ● 46; at a signal given from the Fortress, one of the *Aurora*'s guns opened the people's attack on the Winter Palace. It is open to the public as part of the Naval Museum (Stock Exchange).

LENIN SQUARE

In the middle of Lenin Square (PLOSHCHAD LENINA; пл.Ленина) stands a bronze effigy of the great revolutionary sculpted by Sergei Yevseyev. The statue, unveiled in 1926, shows Lenin standing on the turret of an armored vehicle, his right arm thrust out and left thumb grasping his waistcoat. An inscription reads "Long Live the Socialist Revolution throughout the World".

FINLAND STATION. This station, rebuilt in the 1960's, is the boarding point for trains to Finland, Vyborg and the Isthmus of Carelia between Lake Ladoga and the Baltic Sea, and to resorts such as Zelenogorsk, Sosnovo, Repino and Komarovo (the burial place of the poet Anna Akhmatova). At weekends the station is packed with city families heading out of town to their garden plots, returning later with flowers, vegetables, mushrooms and blueberries. A sculpted frieze on the station front depicts the Revolution; Lenin ▲ *248* arrived here on his journey from Finland on April 3, 1917. Locomotive no. 293, which brought him secretly to Finland, was presented to the Soviet Union by the Finnish Railway Company in 1957; it still stands by the platform here, behind glass.

APOTHECARIES' ISLAND

BOTANICAL GARDENS (BOTANICHESKY SAD; Ботанический сад). Apothecaries' Island (APTEKARSKI OSTROV; Аптекарский остров), separated from the island of Petrograd by the river Karpovka, is named after the Botanical Gardens at no. 2 Professor Popov Street. As the successor of the medicinal garden founded by Peter I in 1714, this institution became the Imperial Botanical Garden in 1823. Its collections were enriched over the years by contributions from explorers in Asia, Siberia and Central and South America. At the close of the last century it became a center for agricultural research. The species from temperate climates are distributed around an English-style park (top right) while the greenhouses are reserved for tropical and subtropical plants. This garden is closely associated with the Botanical Museum built up around the vegetable samples collected by Peter the Great for his *cabinet de curiosités* in the Kunstkammer ▲ *160*.

SHALYAPIN HOUSE. In what used to be the house of Shalyapin (Chaliapin), no. 2B Ulitsa Graftio Street, the Museum of Russian Opera has been installed. Here the great singer received the artistic elite of St Petersburg. The exhibition includes recordings of his incomparable voice. Not far away is the *Café Chaliapin*, serving gastronomic specialties inspired by the singer's chef, who was almost as celebrated as his patron.

FYODOR SHALYAPIN (1873–1938)
Shalyapin was one of the great figures of Russian opera. He had a remarkable bass-baritone voice, and was the creator of the character of Boris Godunov in Mussorgsky's eponymous opera.

THE ISLANDS OF THE DELTA

KAMMENY ISLAND (KAMENNY OSTROV; Каменный остров). This island has retained its old name, translated from a Finnish word meaning "stone". In the late 18th century several princely palaces were built here, among them the Stone Island Palace (Kamennoostrovky Dvorets), built (1776–81) by Yuri Felten, with the exception of its façade, attributed to Quarenghi. The Stone Island Palace was commissioned by Catherine II for her son Paul I. It was built on the point of the island, where the Neva divides into two. Its

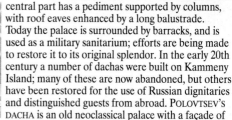

Polovtsev's dacha.

CHURCH OF ST JOHN THE BAPTIST
This church was built on Kammeny Island in 1778 by Felten, to celebrate Catherine II's victory over the Turks.

ELAGIN PARK
The entire island is laid out in the English style, complete with pavilions, stables, landing stage, bandstands and orangeries. Today Elagin Island is St Petersburg's best-loved park.

GOODWILL GAMES
In 1994 the Kirov Stadium was the venue for the Goodwill Games, a quasi-Olympic sporting occasion

designed to anticipate the political thaw between the United States and Russia. This fourth occasion of its kind was broadened to include other countries.

central part has a pediment supported by columns, with roof eaves enhanced by a long balustrade. Today the palace is surrounded by barracks, and is used as a military sanitarium; efforts are being made to restore it to its original splendor. In the early 20th century a number of dachas were built on Kammeny Island; many of these are now abandoned, but others have been restored for the use of Russian dignitaries and distinguished guests from abroad. POLOVTSEV'S DACHA is an old neoclassical palace with a façade of Ionic columns; it was built (1911–16) by Fomin, who modeled it on Russian gentlemen's residences of the 18th century. It has been used as a sanatorium or House of Rest since the October Revolution. By the road out to Elagin Island stands

the Summer Theater, which was built in 1827 by Shustov and altered later by Cavos, in 1844. This theater is entirely constructed of wood, including its frontal colonnade, which gives it the air of a Greek temple. Concerts are occasionally held here.

ELAGIN ISLAND (OSTROV YELAGIN; остров ЕлагинUIN). This island was present to Ivan Elagin by Catherine the Great in 1770. In 1794 it passed to Count Orlov and in 1817 was purchased by Alexander I ● *36*, for his mother Maria Fyodorovna, the widow of Paul I. The transformation of ELAGIN PALACE was Carlo Rossi's ▲ *181* first project in St Petersburg (1818–22). The central feature of the façade overlooking the river is a colonnaded half-rotunda topped by a flat dome, whose upper floor gives access to a roof terrace more appropriate to the climate of Italy than to that of St Petersburg. The interior décor reflects the taste of the time, with a large amount of white and pastel-toned painted stucco as well as much sculpture. This palace was seriously damaged during the last war, since when it has been carefully restored. It now contains a museum of decorative arts of the 19th and early 20th centuries.

KRESTOVSKY ISLAND (KRESTOVSKY OSTROV; Крестовский остров). As they always have done, St Petersburgers still go to the island of Krestovsky to bathe in the waters of the Neva and breathe the sea air, all for the price of a tram ticket. A number of sporting facilities are situated on the island, among them an Olympic Training Institute, and the KIROV STADIUM, which is the largest sporting complex in St Petersburg, having a capacity of 73,000.

Vasilyevsky Island

🕐 Half a day

V asilyevsky Island (VASILYEVSKY OSTROV; Васильевский
остров) is the largest of the various islands in the Neva
Delta. Its street plan was laid out by the architect Jean-
Baptiste Leblond ● 82, whose project was approved by Peter I
on January 1, 1716. Leblond's idea was to divide the island
into a network of streets and canals meeting at right angles.
He also envisaged the excavation of a broad navigable canal,
which would follow the line of the present Bolshoy Prospekt.
Each side of the streets running at right angles to the canal
was called a "line" and bore a number; this system still
operates today. Shortly after Peter I's death the island was
relegated to a secondary role in the development of
St Petersburg, being too frequently subject to flooding, and
the project for a canal network was shelved indefinitely.

HISTORY OF THE RUSSIAN FLEET

The collections of the Naval Museum include over 1,700 model ships, from the oldest (Peter I's small vessel) to the most modern, along with designs and maquettes.

THE POINT (STRELKA)

One of the finest sights on Vasilyevsky Island is the Point (Strelka). Peter the Great intended this site to be the center of his capital, with a broad square and magnificent government buildings.

NAVAL MUSEUM (TSENTRALNY VOENNO-MORSKOY MUZEY; центральный Военно-морской музей). The heart of this architectural ensemble is the old Stock Exchange building ● *87*, rebuilt in 1805–10 by Thomas de Thomon. The Exchange, with its massive granite base, was the place of business to which merchants came on their arrival at the port of St Petersburg ▲ *192*. Since 1940 the building has been allocated to the Naval Museum.

157

RARE SPECIES
The St Petersburg Zoological Museum is one of the largest of its kind in the world. It has examples of over forty thousand different animal species, with about fifteen million specimens in reserve.

MUSEUM OF LITERATURE
(LITERATURNY MUZEY; Литературный музей). The old Customs House was built between 1829 and 1832 under the supervision of Luchini. Since 1927 this building has served as the Institute of Russian Literature (or Pushkin House) and the Museum of Literature. Both establishments were founded after the 1899 exhibition in honor of Pushkin's centenary ● *114.* The archives they possess include over two thousand manuscripts from the 13th to the 18th centuries, along with a number of texts by Tolstoy and Dostoevsky ▲ *207.*

ROSTRAL COLUMNS ★
● *87.* On the square in front of the Exchange are the two rostral columns (the term is derived from the Latin *rostrum,* the bows of a vessel), to which are attached metal ships' prows. These are flanked by colossal statues, which are allegories of the four great rivers of Russia – the Volga, the Dnieper, the Volkhov and the Neva – sculpted in stone from studies by I. Chamberlain and J. Thibaut. For some time beacons, which were fueled by hemp oil, burned on the top of the columns, and these functioned as lighthouses at the entrance to the port.

OLD PORT WAREHOUSES. On either side of the Exchange are port warehouses, built between 1826 and 1832 by the architect Giovanni Luchini. The south building is now the ZOOLOGICAL MUSEUM (ZOOLOGICHESKY MUZEY; Зоологический музей), founded in 1896. This was the former site of the palace of Czarina Prascovia Fyodorovna (1664–1723), the wife of Peter I's half-brother, Czar Ivan Alexeyvich (1666–96) and mother of the future Empress Anna Ivanovna ● *36.* The north warehouse is now the DOKUCHAYEV MUSEUM OF SOIL SCIENCE (TSENTRALNY MUZEY POCHVOVEDENYA IM. V. DOKUCHAYEV; центральный музей Почвоведения им. В. Докучаева),

opened in 1904. This museum is devoted to the study and protection of Russia's soils and to increasing their productiveness.

MAKAROV EMBANKMENT

The granite facing of the Malaya Neva Embankment, as well as the buildings by the Customs House pier (note the broad stairway with its sculpted lions), were built between 1806 and 1809.

LIBRARY OF THE ACADEMY OF SCIENCES (BIBLIOTEKA AKADEMI NAUK; библиотека Академии наук). The main façade of this library (1912–25, architect R. Marfeld) completes the view from the main Neva waterway along the Mendeleev "line", named for the chemist Mendeleev (1834–1907). Founded in 1714, the Library of the Academy of Sciences is one of the oldest scientific establishments in St Petersburg. It contains over seventeen million volumes, as well as collections of engravings, drawings, watercolors, manuscripts, maps and charts.

THE TWELVE COLLEGES (DVENADTSAT KOLLEGUI; Двенадцать Коллегий). Constructed between 1722 and 1742 by Domenico Trezzini ● *83* and Theodore Schwertfeger and now attached to the University of St Petersburg, this complex is made up of twelve identical buildings in an unbroken line, intended for the various government bodies: the Senate, the Synod and the ten "colleges" or ministries. The glazed second floor is now the corridor of the University and is famed for its length. In 1835 all these buildings were handed over to the University authorities, by whom they were partially reconstructed. Visitors are admitted to the museum named after the chemist Mendeleev, who devised the periodic table of chemical elements, and lived and worked here from 1866 to 1890.

STEPAN MAKAROV (1849–1904)
The embankment is named for Admiral Makarov of the Russian Navy, who circumnavigated the world twice.

A CONCENTRATION OF BUILDINGS
The Twelve Colleges constitute the west side of an immense architectural ensemble built in the early 1830's. Apart from the warehouses, it includes the Merchants' Courtyard of the New Exchange (now part of the University) along with an annex of the Museum of the Academy of Sciences, currently used by the St Petersburg department of the Nauka science publishing organization.

UNIVERSITY EMBANKMENT

At the beginning of the University Embankment (UNIVERSITETSKAYA NAB; Университетская наб) are a number of buildings which are linked to the history of the Academy of Sciences.

THE KUNSTKAMMER ★ ▲ 250. The Kunstkammer, Peter the Great's gallery of curiosities, is an interesting example of early Russian Baroque. Built between 1718 and 1734 by the architects G. Mattarnovy, N. Herbel, G. Ciaveri and M. Zemtsov, the Kunstkammer has wings of two stories with a tower between. The Kunstkammer was the first Natural Science Museum in Russia, and it included a library and an observatory. From 1783 to 1796 the Academy was directed by E. Dashkova, a friend of Catherine II and one of the most cultivated women of her time. In 1878 it became the Museum of Anthropology and Ethnology (MUZEY ANTROPOLOGII I ETNOGRAFII IM. PETRA VELIKOVO; музей Антропологии и Этнографии им. Петра Великого). The museum's displays include items which illustrate the daily lives and cultures of many different countries, along with their weapons, clothes and religious objects.

M. LOMONOSOV MUSEUM (MUZEY M. LOMONOSOVA; музей М. Ломоносова). In 1949 the M. Lomonosov Museum ● 53 was installed inside the Kunstkammer, in memory of the great scientist. Among its attractions are Lomonosov's scientific instruments and his writings, in addition to a reconstitution of the Academy of Sciences' conference hall.

ACADEMY OF SCIENCES (AKADEMIYA NAUK; Академия наук). Beside the Kunstkammer, also on the embankment at no. 5 is the main Academy of Sciences building, which was constructed between 1783 and 1789 by Giacomo Quarenghi ● 86. In 1925 the main staircase in the vestibule was embellished with a mosaic panel by Lomonosov, which was entitled *The Battle of Poltava*. In the same year the Academy became known as the Academy of Sciences of the Soviet Union, before its headquarters were transferred to Moscow nine years later, in 1934.

THE GLOBE
At the Lomonosov Museum is a reconstruction of the huge terrestrial globe of the Academy of Sciences. Made in the 1600's for the Duke of Holstein-Gottorp, it was presented as a gift to Peter the Great in 1713.

CABINET OF CURIOSITIES
The collections of monstrosities and curiosities in the Kikin Palace ▲ 250 were amassed by Peter I and transferred to the Kunstkammer in 1727.

MENSHIKOV PALACE (DVORETS MENCHIKOV; дворец Меншикова) ★ ● *82*. At no. 15 on the embankment stands the architectural ensemble of the Menshikov Palace. In the early years of the 18th century Prince Menshikov, who was a close friend of Peter the Great, had his private mansion here. The building has two floors and a mansard roof; it was designed by the architects Giovanni Maria Fontana and Gottfried Schädell. It was here that Peter I organized his lavish assemblies, held celebrations of Russian victories and received foreign embassies. In 1781, two years after Menshikov's death, the palace was the barracks of an elite regiment, the Foot Guards, before it was passed on to the Army's First Cadet Corps. The left wing of the palace was enlarged by the addition of a new building, which was itself enlarged during the 1770's. The works that were begun in 1956 restored the palace's original aspect, which was remarkable for its famously splendid interiors. A spacious vestibule leads to the formal oak staircase, with wrought-iron banisters struck with the monograms of both Peter the Great and Menshikov himself. The stairs in turn lead up to the private apartments of Prince Menshikov and his sister-in-law Varvara Arseneva (who had the responsibility of educating his children); the two areas are separated, however, by formal drawing rooms. The ASSEMBLY ROOM, which is over a thousand square feet in size, is the largest room in the palace. The WALNUT ROOM, with its painted ceiling and boiseries of Persian walnut wood, was Menshikov's favorite room; his BEDROOM (below) is covered with no fewer than 27,811 Delft tiles ● *64*. The palace is now an annex of the Hermitage, which was installed in it for an exhibition on "Russian Culture 1700–30".

ALEXANDER MENSHIKOV (1672–1729)
The son of a baker, Menshikov was a childhood friend of Peter the Great. He wielded immense influence on affairs of state, and distinguished himself in a number of military campaigns (he was promoted to general in 1705). Later he directed part of the construction of St Petersburg. Following the death of Peter the Great, Menshikov, who had become a member of the Secret Supreme Council and had married off his daughter to the future Peter II, was sole master of Russia for over two years. But he aroused the hostility of the nobility and his grip on power ended with his arrest in 1727. All his property was confiscated and he was deported with his family to Siberia, where he died two years later.

MENSHIKOV'S OFFICE
On the walls are portraits of Menshikov's four daughters.

PAINTING, SCULPTURE, ARCHITECTURE
The Academy of the "three noble arts" was founded in 1757, at the instigation of Lomonosov.

ACADEMY OF ARTS (AKADEMIYA KHUDOSHESTV; Академия художеств). Further along the embankment, at no. 17, the building of the Academy of Arts may be found, which was constructed between 1764 and 1768 by the architects Alexander Kokorinov and Jean-Baptiste Vallin de la Mothe ● 86. The traditions of this academy are maintained today by the Repin Institute of Painting, Sculpture and Architecture. Also housed within the building is the Arts Academy of Research, and on the first floor a department exhibiting plaster casts of original artworks from all over the world. The department of architecture displays a variety of designs and projects, together with scale models of Smolny ● 84, St Isaac's Cathedral ● 88, the Engineers' Castle, and the Stock Exchange ● 87.

LIEUTENANT SCHMIDT EMBANKMENT

SPHINX QUAY
(SPUSK SO SPHINXAMI; Спуск со Сфинсами) ★.
This quay was built (1832–4) to a plan by Konstantin Thon. The two sculpted sphinxes on either side of the steps leading down to the river were found at Thebes, the capital of ancient Egypt. Their features are those of the Pharaoh Amenophis III.

LIEUTENANT SCHMIDT BRIDGE. Both the bridge and the embankment are named for Nikolai Schmidt (center), who distinguished himself during the 1905 Revolution ● 44. The Lieutenant Schmidt Bridge (originally named the Nicholas Bridge) was the first permanent bridge across the Neva; it was built between 1847 and 1850 by the engineer S. Kerbedz and the decoration (sea shells and sea horses) is by Bryulov.
THE ACADEMICIANS' HOUSE (DOM AKADEMIKOV; дом Академиков). At no. 1 Lieutenant Schmidt Embankment (NAB LEYTENANTA SCHMIDT; наб. Лейтенанта-Шмидта) stands the Academicians' House, which was constructed in the 1750's by Savva Chevakinsky. The building was completely reshaped in the early 19th century by the architects A. Bezhanov and Andrei Zakharov ● 87. The classical structure of the house is typical of the period; it has twenty-six plaques affixed to its walls, which commemorate the intellectuals who occupied it.

THE FRUNZE NAVAL STAFF COLLEGE (VYCHEE VOENNO-MORSKOYE [UCHILISHCHE] IM. M. FRUNZE; Высшее военно-морское училище им. М. Фрунзе). This imposing building with its Ionic colonnade is the Russian Navy's principal educational institution. It was built between 1796 and 1798 by the architect F. Volkov, and succeeded the Navigation School, which had been founded in 1701 by an edict of Peter the Great. The Navigation School was converted into the Naval Cadet Corps School in 1752.

STATUE OF ADMIRAL KRUSENSTERN (PAMYATNIK ADMIRALU KRUSENCHTERNU; памятник адмиралу Крузенштерну). In front of the Naval Staff College stands the statue of Admiral Krusenstern (1770–1846), which was erected in 1873. Admiral Krusenstern is famous as the commander of the first flotilla of Russian ships to circumnavigate the globe in the early 19th century.

CHURCH OF THE DORMITION (USPENSKAYA TSERKOV; Успенская церковь). The pure lines of the monumental Church of the Dormition stand out clearly on the Neva's skyline. Built between 1893 and 1900 by B. Kosyakov, it stands on the former site of the Pskov Monastery's guest quarters, purchased in the 1880's by the Kiev Monastery ▲ 253.

MINING INSTITUTE (GORNY INSTITUT; Горный институт). Lieutenant Schmidt Embankment ends with the enormous Mining Institute, one of the oldest establishments of its kind in the world. When it was founded in 1773 it was known as the Mining School, later becoming the Mining Corps. The building, with its portico of twelve Doric columns, was built between 1806 and 1811 by Andrei Voronikhin. It houses a museum which contains one of the world's richest collections of minerals, stones and fossils. There are scale models of mines, and the museum also exhibits examples of the tools used in the mining industry.

THE "CHEKUCHI". Beyond the Mining Institute is the industrial and manufacturing quarter, which has always been known as the "Chekuchi" (The Crushers), on account of the mallets which were used to crush the lumps of damp flour piled in the warehouses here. Nowadays the area is a huge naval dockyard which, with its counterpart on the other bank of the Neva, frames the point where the river meets the Gulf of Finland.

PAVLOV (1849–1936)
Since 1949 there has been a museum at the Academicians' House dedicated to the work of the physiologist Pavlov, who lived at apartment no. 18 there from 1918 onward.

MIKHAIL FRUNZE (1885–1925)
This military commander distinguished himself during the Civil War (1918) and in 1924 was named Chief of Staff and Commandant of the Moscow Military Academy.

SMOLENSK CEMETERY ■ *26*
This is made up of three
cemeteries: a Russian orthodox
cemetery, a lutheran cemetery
and an armenian cemetery.

**ST CATHERINE'S
CHURCH**
The Bolshoy Prospekt
begins with St
Catherine's Church,
built (1768–71) by
Yury Felten ● *86* for
the Evangelical
Lutheran community
of Vasilyevksy Island.

BOLSHOY PROSPEKT

The buildings along the BOLSHOY
PROSPEKT (Большой проспект) are
less interesting for their architecture
than for the memories that cling to
them – above all, for the everyday
life of the quarter.

ST ANDREW'S MARKET (ANDREEVSKY
RYNOK; Андреевский рынок). The
area between "lines" five and six is
occupied by St Andrew's Market.
The old part of the building dates
from 1780–90, and its modern section
from 1959.

ST ANDREW'S CATHEDRAL
(ANDREEVSKY SOBOR; Андреевский
собор). The principal Orthodox church
on the island, this building is a
monument of mid-18th century Baroque
architecture (1764–80, architect A. Vist).
The carved iconostasis is a masterpiece
in the genre.

**PEL AND SON'S
PHARMACY** (АРТЕКА
A. PELYA SYNOVEY;
аптека А. Пеля
и сыновей). On the
first floor of a four-
story house nearby was
the original Pharmacy
of A. Pel (1900's).
Pel, a doctor in
chemistry, philosophy
and pharmacology, was
the first in Russia to make preparations based
on organic constituents; he invented a
number of medical compounds which are
still in use today. Since 1983 a museum of
Russian pharmacology has occupied
Pel's old premises, with objects
from the period filling the
old shelves.

PASSENGER PORT
On Naval Glory
Square, fronting the
Gulf of Finland, the
main building is the
Passenger Port
(1977–82), whose
giant 240-foot spire is
topped by a caravel,
similar to the one at
the Admiralty ▲ *190*.

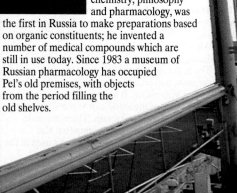

FROM THE HERMITAGE
TO THE SUMMER PALACE

▲ FROM THE HERMITAGE
TO THE SUMMER PALACE

1. THE HERMITAGE
2. PALACE SQUARE
3. ALEXANDER COLUMN
4. ARCH OF THE GENERAL STAFF

⏱ One day

THE HERMITAGE

THE FIRST WINTER PALACES. The Winter Palace, now known as the Hermitage Museum, is the fourth building to have been constructed on this site. After the first "small Dutch-style house" built by Peter the Great it was probably the Italian architect Domenico Trezzini who built the nuptial palace which we consider to have been the first Winter Palace (1711–12). This building was destroyed in 1726. Meantime, the architect Mattarnovy had built a "winter house" next door (1716–19) for Peter I, which was subsequently enlarged and several times altered.

PALACE OF ELIZABETH. This palace, constructed (1754–62) by Bartolomeo Rastrelli, is famous for its lavish Baroque décor. Two orders of composite columns embellish its façades; the upper one is on an enormous scale.

CATHERINE II'S WINTER PALACE. The
interiors were still uncompleted
when Rastrelli was dismissed by
Catherine in August 1762. The director of the Buildings
Chancellery, I. Betsky, called in several foreign architects to
replace him: Jean-Baptiste Vallin de la Mothe, Antonio
Rinaldi and the German Yury Felten. De la Mothe decorated
Catherine II's private apartments (destroyed in the 1837 fire),
the Throne Room, the church, the
apartments of the ladies of honor on the
third floor, and the apartments of Count
Grigory Orlov on the mezzanine floor.
Felten reorganized the Portrait and the
Mirror galleries, and Rinaldi changed
the Throne Room into an oval salon.
Catherine II had ten grandchildren, and
the imperial apartments (including the
theater) were altered to meet their needs
by Giacomo Quarenghi and Ivan Starov.
But the really major changes were to
come with new construction work.

**SUCCESSIVE
EMPRESSES**
In 1732 the Empress
Anna Ivanovna
commissioned from
the Rastrellis (father
and son) a new winter
palace, known as the
Third Winter Palace.
This was completed
in 1736, then
demolished in 1754 to
make way for the
present palace, which
was built by the
younger Rastrelli for
Elizabeth Petrovna.

167

Built by Bartolomeo Rastrelli (1754–62), Elizabeth I's Winter Palace is laid out around an immense closed courtyard with four projecting pavilions at the corners. The main portions of the building facing the Neva and Palace Square are linked by closed lateral galleries with apartments, service areas and staircases giving on to them. The center of the façade giving onto the Neva is barely evident by comparison with the projecting pavilions on either side of it. Although the Palace Square was built much later, the entrance to the courtyard was always by way of the triple arch on the city side.

THE NEW HERMITAGE
The entrance to the palace was from Khalturin (Millionaires') Street, through a monumental portico by ten sculpted Atlas figures.

THE "BENOIS MADONNA"
The great gallery of the Old Hermitage exhibits two famous paintings by Leonardo da Vinci, the *Benois Madonna* (1478) and the *Litta Madonna* (early 1480's).

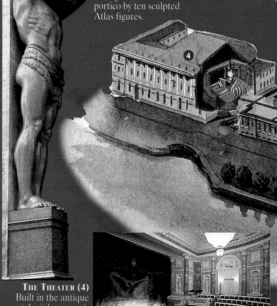

THE THEATER (4)
Built in the antique style, it has a semi-circular auditorium and décor inspired by the Olympic Theater at Vicenza (Italy).

"La Musique"

The Hermitage's collection of paintings by Matisse (1869–1954) is one of the largest in Europe, constituting a veritable museum within a museum. In all there are thirty-seven paintings by this master, among them *La Danse* and *La Musique*.

"Composition VI"

The work of Vasily Kandinsky is on the third floor of the south wing, after the Fauvist section. This painting, *Composition VI*, is an example of the artist's Abstract period.

The Large Hermitage (3)

Built in two stages, the Large Hermitage was the work of Yury Felten (1771–87). It occupies a site between the palace and the Winter Canal excavated by Peter the Great between the Neva and the Moika. Its name was changed in the 19th century to the Old Hermitage.

The New Hermitage (5)

The imperial collections were saved from the fire which devastated the Winter Palace in December 1837. With a view to housing them adequately and displaying them to the general public, it was decided in 1839 that a New Hermitage should be built. The museum was opened by Nicholas I in 1852.

The Revolution
Guards at the Winter Palace, October 24, 1917.

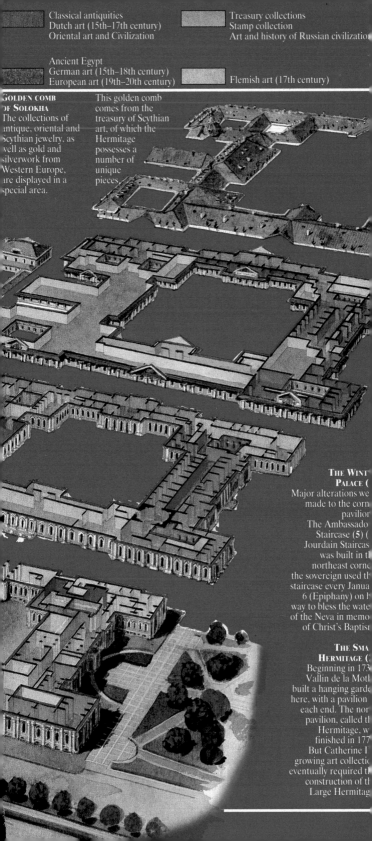

Classical antiquities
Dutch art (15th–17th century)
Oriental art and Civilization

Treasury collections
Stamp collection
Art and history of Russian civilization

Ancient Egypt
German art (15th–18th century)
European art (19th–20th century)

Flemish art (17th century)

GOLDEN COMB OF SOLOKHA
The collections of antique, oriental and Scythian jewelry, as well as gold and silverwork from Western Europe, are displayed in a special area.

This golden comb comes from the treasury of Scythian art, of which the Hermitage possesses a number of unique pieces.

THE WINTER PALACE (
Major alterations were made to the corner pavilion. The Ambassador Staircase (5) (Jourdain Staircase) was built in the northeast corner the sovereign used this staircase every January 6 (Epiphany) on his way to bless the water of the Neva in memory of Christ's Baptism.

THE SMALL HERMITAGE (
Beginning in 173 Vallin de la Mothe built a hanging garden here, with a pavilion each end. The north pavilion, called the Hermitage, was finished in 177 But Catherine I growing art collection eventually required the construction of the Large Hermitage

"Saskia as Flora"
This painting by Rembrandt dates from the first years of his marriage to Saskia van Uylenborch, shown here as a goddess of Roman mythology.

THE STATE RECEPTION ROOMS

After the 1837 fire Stasov rebuilt the Ambassadors' Staircase (**6**). He also restored the curve of the stairs, recreated the fanciful golden moldings against their white background, and reinstated the trompe l'oeil windows with their mirrors. The War of 1812 Gallery (**2**) still bears the stamp of Rossi, its decorator. Here are displayed the portraits of the Russian generals who took part in the war against Napoleon. The Alexander Hall (**1**) contains a medallion with the profile of Alexander I, and moldings of warlike themes symbolizing the Czar's victory (in the war of 1812–14). Bryulov decorated this with clusters of Gothic columns, two-headed eagles and classical medallions. The Hall of St George (**3**) is decorated with Carrara marble columns with gilded bronze capitals. The Throne, now installed in the Hall of Peter I, formerly stood below the bas-relief of Saint George and the Dragon. In the Pavilion Hall (**4**) copies of mosaics from Roman spas are set in the floor. This hall also contains reproductions of the Fountain of Tears from the Bakhtchisarai Palace in the Crimea. On the orders of Catherine II Quarenghi painted a reproduction of Raphael's *Loggia* (**5**) at the Vatican along the Winter Canal side of this room (1783–92).

The history of the Hermitage as a museum began with Peter the Great, who himself bought a number of works of art – among them *David and Goliath* by Rembrandt and the *Tauride Venus*. In the reign of Catherine II the imperial collections occupied rooms in the Hermitage of the Winter Palace, which gave its name to the museum. The museum is considered to have been officially born in 1764, when the Berlin dealer Gotzkowski sent the Empress of Russia 225 paintings intended for Frederick II of Prussia, in payment of a debt. Later, on the advice of Diderot among others, Catherine bought many more works of art (and above all complete collections) in Paris, Dresden and London.

DUTCH PAINTING IN THE 15TH AND 17TH CENTURIES
The most remarkable works in this collection are Campin's diptych, *The Trinity* and the *Virgin at the Hearth, Saint Luke Painting the Virgin* by Van der Weyden, *The Healing of the Blind Man at Jericho* by Van Leyden, and *The Adoration of the Magi* by Van der Goes. All 17th-century genres and great masters are represented, except for Vermeer. There are two portraits by Hals, landscapes by Van Goyen and Van Ruisdael, and pictures by Van Ostade, Steen, de Hooch and Ter Borch. In the Rembrandt Room are twenty-five pictures spanning the painter's entire career, from *The Sacrifice of Abraham* (1635) (right) and *The Descent from the Cross* (1634) to *David and Uriah* and *The Return of the Prodigal Son* (mid-1660's).

VENETIAN PAINTERS

The series of galleries at the Old Hermitage includes works such as *Judith* (right) and *Madonna and Child* by Giorgione, and eight paintings by Titian, among them *Danaë*, *Mary Magdalen*, *Portrait of a Woman*, *The Transportation of the Cross* and *Saint Sebastian*.

17TH–18TH CENTURY SPANISH PAINTINGS

Among these are works by El Greco, Velasquez, De Ribera, Zurbaran, Murillo and (right) Goya's *Portrait of Antonia Sarate*.

17TH CENTURY FLEMISH PAINTINGS

The section includes twenty-six pictures by van Dyck including the *Portrait of Charles I*. Of the forty works by Rubens the most notable are *Christ with Crown of Thorns* (below), *The Alliance of Earth and Water* and *Perseus and Andromeda*.

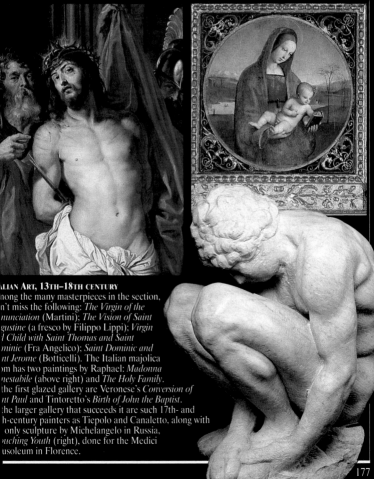

ITALIAN ART, 13TH–18TH CENTURY

Among the many masterpieces in the section, don't miss the following: *The Virgin of the Annunciation* (Martini); *The Vision of Saint Augustine* (a fresco by Filippo Lippi); *Virgin and Child with Saint Thomas and Saint Dominic* (Fra Angelico); *Saint Dominic and Saint Jerome* (Botticelli). The Italian majolica room has two paintings by Raphael: *Madonna Conestabile* (above right) and *The Holy Family*. In the first glazed gallery are Veronese's *Conversion of Saint Paul* and Tintoretto's *Birth of John the Baptist*. In the larger gallery that succeeds it are such 17th- and 18th-century painters as Tiepolo and Canaletto, along with the only sculpture by Michelangelo in Russia, *Crouching Youth* (right), done for the Medici Mausoleum in Florence.

7TH–19TH CENTURY ENGLISH PAINTING

This section of the museum comes after the room in which works by Fragonard and Greuze are exhibited. Note in particular *The Infant Hercules Killing the Serpents* (right, by Reynolds); and *The Duchess of Beaufort* by Gainsborough).

15TH–18TH CENTURY FRENCH PAINTING

This collection is a worthy rival to that of the Louvre itself. The major works are Le Nain's *The Milkmaid's Family*; *Tancredi and Hermine* and *Landscape with Polyphemus* (Poussin); *The Little Savoyard* and *The Awkward Proposal* (Watteau); and *Stolen Kiss* (Fragonard, right).

19TH-CENTURY FRENCH ART

Among the works dating from the first half of the 19th century are *Bonaparte at the Bridge of Arcole* (Gros); *Morphée* (Guérin, left); *Portrait of Count Guriev* (Ingres); *Lion Hunt in Morocco* and *Arabs Saddling a Horse* (Delacroix).

Mainly assembled by the Muscovite collectors Morozov and Shchukin at the beginning of this century, this collection is one of the finest in the world. It includes six paintings by Renoir (among them *Portrait of Jeanne Savary* and *Young Woman with a Fan*), five pastels by Degas, including *Young Woman at her Toilet* (below, left); eight landscapes by Monet, eleven Cézannes, four van Goghs (*The Bush*, left), fifteen Gauguins from the artist's Tahiti period (above), eight paintings and thirteen panels by Denis, eight canvases and triptychs by Bonnard, two Vuillards and six Vallotons. The Fauvists are represented by nine Marquets, five Vlamincks, fourteen Derains and five Van Dongens. Finally among the thirty-seven paintings by Picasso is *Absinthe* (below).

PALACE SQUARE

AN IMPERIAL ESPLANADE. Even though the entrance to the courtyard of the Winter Palace ▲ *168* was originally planned not for the Neva side but for the city side of the building, Palace Square (DVORTSOVAYA PLOSHCHAD; Дворцовая площадь) was laid out at a relatively late date. The architect Bartolomeo Rastrelli ● *84* had proposed a semicircular colonnade to transform the area into a gigantic courtyard and provide a counterpoint to the Baroque façade of the Winter Palace. But Empress Elizabeth died

The police fired on the crowd; the resultant carnage created an unbridgeable gulf between the Czar and his people and provided the impetus for revolution.

before the completion of the project and Catherine II dismissed Rastrelli when she ascended the throne. All this time the square was no more than a huge field; but in 1772 the architect Starov resurrected the idea of a colonnade which Catherine had rejected, although the semicircular plan appealed to her. Finally, in 1779 the Arts Academy launched a competition which was won by Yury Felten ▲ *162*. Opposite the palace he built a half-circle of houses with identical façades. Still, the ensemble lacked real grandeur, and Carlo Rossi ● *86* was commissioned in 1819 to lay out a more regular square.

THE GENERAL STAFF HEADQUARTERS. The main function of the buildings fronting the square was to provide a general headquarters for the Army's main staff. In 1819 it was decided that Russia's administrative center should also be moved here, concentrating the Ministry of Finance and the Foreign Ministry in the same place. Carlo Rossi went back to the old semicircular layout as defined by the existing buildings, and put all of them behind a single façade, the center of which was pierced by a huge triumphal arch, the ARCH OF THE GENERAL STAFF. The skill with which this was accomplished is famous in the annals of architecture. The arch, sited directly on the axis of the main palace entrance, had to link the square with the curved street coming from the

PALACE SQUARE
The Winter Palace, Admiralty Gardens, former headquarters of the General Staff, and the Guards' former headquarters bound this huge area.

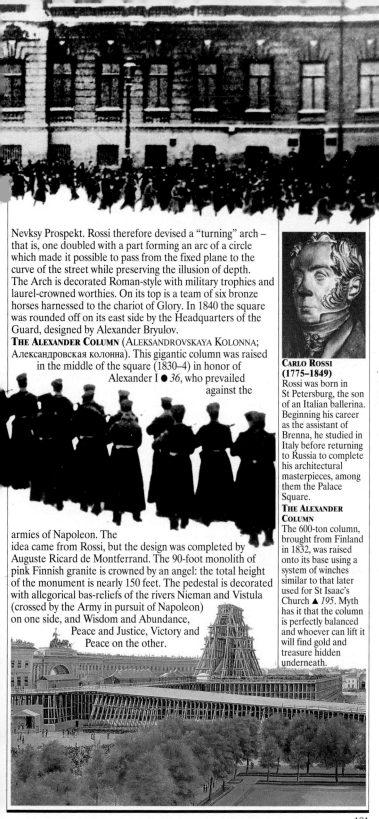

Nevksy Prospekt. Rossi therefore devised a "turning" arch – that is, one doubled with a part forming an arc of a circle which made it possible to pass from the fixed plane to the curve of the street while preserving the illusion of depth. The Arch is decorated Roman-style with military trophies and laurel-crowned worthies. On its top is a team of six bronze horses harnessed to the chariot of Glory. In 1840 the square was rounded off on its east side by the Headquarters of the Guard, designed by Alexander Bryulov.

THE ALEXANDER COLUMN (ALEKSANDROVSKAYA KOLONNA; Александровская колонна). This gigantic column was raised in the middle of the square (1830–4) in honor of Alexander I ● *36*, who prevailed against the armies of Napoleon. The idea came from Rossi, but the design was completed by Auguste Ricard de Montferrand. The 90-foot monolith of pink Finnish granite is crowned by an angel: the total height of the monument is nearly 150 feet. The pedestal is decorated with allegorical bas-reliefs of the rivers Nieman and Vistula (crossed by the Army in pursuit of Napoleon) on one side, and Wisdom and Abundance, Peace and Justice, Victory and Peace on the other.

CARLO ROSSI (1775–1849)
Rossi was born in St Petersburg, the son of an Italian ballerina. Beginning his career as the assistant of Brenna, he studied in Italy before returning to Russia to complete his architectural masterpieces, among them the Palace Square.

THE ALEXANDER COLUMN
The 600-ton column, brought from Finland in 1832, was raised onto its base using a system of winches similar to that later used for St Isaac's Church ▲ *195*. Myth has it that the column is perfectly balanced and whoever can lift it will find gold and treasure hidden underneath.

PUSHKIN'S HOUSE
The poet's study and
his 4,000-book library
(above) have been
carefully preserved as
they were when the
Pushkin family lived
here. Pushkin died in
this house on January
29, 1837 ● *117*.

Arms of the
Volkonsky Family.

"The Neva, with its
bridges and piers, is
the true glory of
St Petersburg. The
prospect of it is so
immense that
everything else is tiny
by comparison. The
Neva is a basin filled
to the brim; its banks
merge with the water,
which seems about
to overflow on every
side. Venice and
Amsterdam seem to
me much better
defended against
the sea than is
St Petersburg.**"**
Astolphe de Custine,
La Russie en 1839

THE MOIKA EMBANKMENT

CAPELLA ● *72.* The original Capella
(no. 20), known as the Glinka Singing
Academy in this century, was founded
by Peter the Great; the present school
was built in 1880 by the architect
Leonty Benois at the end of a courtyard.
The auditorium is separated from the
street by high cast-iron railings which
link two identical buildings. The
Capella ensemble is a fine example
of eclectic late 19th-century décor.

DLT STORE (Dom Leningradskoi Torgovli). This store backs
on to the Moika Embankment (NAB. REKI MOIKI; наб. реки
Мойки), although its main entrance is at no. 21 Bolshaya
Konninchenaya. Built by the architect E.V. Virrich (1908–10),
it is important in the history of St Petersburg architecture as
one of the first metal-and-glass structures in the city. The
huge salerooms were patterned on the Parisian *grands
magasins* built at the turn of the century.

PUSHKIN MUSEUM (MUZEY-KVARTIRA PUSHKINA; музей-
квартира Пушкина). An earlier house on this site (no. 12,
built in the 1730's) belonged to the Volkonsky family. This
mansion was replaced in 1770 by another in the classical
Russian style, and subsequently altered extensively. Six fluted
Corinthian pilasters distinguish the projecting central section,
of the height of two floors, with a curved façade reflecting the
bend in the river. On the courtyard side are broad arches
(now glassed in) which still incorporate elements of the
original building. The Pushkin family rented the second floor
here in 1836.

IMPERIAL STABLES. The first imperial stables were
built in 1720 for Peter the Great, by the architect
N.F. Gerbel. The buildings were laid out around a
polygonal courtyard. Although entirely
reconstructed on the same site by Vasily Stasov
between 1816 and 1823, they have retained their
original form, specifically the curve imposed by the
Moika. The CHURCH is contained in the square central
portion of the façade giving on to the square. This
somewhat complex ensemble included not only the stables
and the riding ring, but also several warehouses, the
administrative offices (the master of the stables was an

important figure in the imperial service), the lodgings of the staff and the church.

PALACE EMBANKMENT

THE WINTER CANAL BRIDGE. The Winter Canal meets the Neva by the Old Hermitage. The bridge which spans it is characteristic of those built by Yury Felten in the 1770's as part of the works carried out on the banks of the Neva, its tributaries and the various canals.

THE FORMER / NEW MIKHAIL PALACE. Built by Shtakenshneider (1857–61) for Mikhail Nicolayevich, son of Nicholas I ● *36*, this palace (no. 18) occupies a site bordered on one side by the Palace Embankment (DVORTSOVAYA NAB.; Дворцовая наб.) and on the other by Millionaires' Street. It follows the alignment of the other houses, blending well with the other private mansions of the quarter, although its lower level is notable for its French Renaissance-style panels and pilasters. The rear façade, however, is much more modest, and was reserved for the Grand Duke's domestic servants and staff. The dimensions of the palace are impressive, and it is said that one of the Grand Duke's sons would borrow a bicycle to visit his sister-in-law, whose quarters were located in another part of the palace.

Left to right: The galleried bridge across the Winter Canal, built by Yury Felten to link the Winter Palace with the theater ▲ *168*; the façade of the Hermitage ▲ *168* on the Neva side; finally, a detail of the façade of the Academicians' House. This former palace at no. 26 Palace Embankment, built by Alexander Rezanov (1867–71), illustrates the style of Shtakenshneider, characterized by its Italian Renaissance and Baroque elements. The red sandstone façade is itself strongly reminiscent of Florence.

BESIDE THE NEVA
The Palace Embankment owes its name to the residence of the Czars, today's Hermitage Museum ▲ *168*. The consolidation of the river banks with granite was undertaken over fifteen years, beginning in 1763, with the architect Yury Felten playing an important role.

183

THE MARBLE PALACE

FLOOR PLAN OF THE MARBLE PALACE ·
This follows the traditional U-design of urban palaces, with a courtyard fronting the main entrance.

A GIFT OF THE EMPRESS. For nearly twelve years Catherine II was the mistress of Count Grigory Orlov (1734–83). During this time she presented him with the Marble Palace (MRAMORNY DVORETS; Мраморный дворец). Orlov, with his brothers Alexei and Fyodor, led the conspiracy against Peter III which placed Catherine II on the Russian throne. The palace was built by the architect Antonio Rinaldi (1768–85) on a site between the Palace Embankment and Millionaires' Street. The main façade is decorated with four Corinthian columns at its center. The original entrance was by way of the Red Canal, which ran along the east side of Marsovo Pole. This canal was filled in during the 19th century, at which time a service wing was built and a new main entrance was built in the courtyard at the side of the palace.

GRANITE AND MARBLE. The contrast between the rough

granite of the first floor and the refined marble of the upper levels, from which its name derives, gives the Marble Palace an original if somewhat severe aspect. Its roof was formerly covered in copper sheeting, while the window frames of the *piano nobile* were of gilded bronze, with polished glass panes. Marble was as much in evidence inside the building as outside. The main FORMAL STAIRCASE and the MARBLE ROOM (left) are still in their original state. From 1937 to 1991 the Marble Palace was the home of the Lenin Museum; today it contains a permanent exhibition on the Romanov family ● *36*.

THE FIELD OF MARS

A RECENT ARRIVAL
In the courtyard of the Marble Palace stands an equestrian statue of Alexander III, which replaced Lenin's armored car in November 1994. The statue, originally erected on Insurrection Square (Pl. Vostaniya) ▲ *244*, was brought from the Russian Museum, its home since 1937.

MARSOVO POLE (MARSOVO POLE; Марсово поле). With the Summer Garden to eastward, the Moika to the south, the Red Canal to the west and the Neva to the north, this broad area was not given its final form until 1817–19, when the architect Vasily Stasov (1769–1848) built the Pavlovsky barracks at the same time as Carlo Rossi was completing the Mikhail Palace. Their joint efforts led to a definitive project for the quarter, and the layout of the various green spaces was dictated by the architecture they designed.

BARRACKS OF THE PAVLOVSKY GUARDS REGIMENT (KAZARMY PAVLOVSKOVO POLKA; казармы Павловского полка). The west side of the square is entirely occupied by this gigantic building. At the center of its long yellow façade are twelve Doric columns, crowned by a monumental pediment

decorated with the usual trophies, weapons and winged victories. There are pavilions on either side in front of the building topped by a triangular pediment, which is echoed by a similar arrangement fronting Millionaires' Street. In the middle of Marsovo Pole, now laid out as a park, stands the Liberty Monument (right), formerly known as the Monument to Revolutionary Fighters. On the Neva side the quadrilateral ends at Suvorov Square; and in the center is a statue of General Suvorov ▲ 252.

ADAMINI HOUSE. On the southwest side of Marsovo Pole, the corner house (no. 7) with a semicircular colonnade was built by the architect D. Adamini (1823–7) in the later classical style ● 86. The basement of this building was a meeting-place during World War One and the Revolution for Russian artists like Vsevolod Meyerhold, Alexander Blok, Anna Akhmatova,

Mikhail Kuzmin, Vladimir Mayakovsky and Anatoly Lunacharsky.

SALTYKOV AND BETSKY HOUSES. On the north side, fronting the waters of the Neva, Giacomo Quarenghi built the Saltykov House (1784–8); in 1820 it became the Austrian Embassy. It was celebrated for the salon over which presided the ambassador's wife, the grand-daughter of Marshal Kutuzov.

▲ FROM THE HERMITAGE TO THE SUMMER PALACE

The *Tauride Venus*.

SUMMER GARDEN (LETNY SAD; Летний сад)

A GARDEN IN THE FRENCH STYLE. In 1704 Peter the Great made a rough sketch of a Western-style garden, with rare plant species brought from Siberia, the Urals, Holland and Kiev. The French model won the Czar's favor after his visit to Versailles in 1717, and as a result the gardens, which extend between the Neva to the north, the Fontanka to the east and the Moika to the south, are regular and symmetrical. The gardens were divided into quadrilaterals which were planted with trees and (in the old days) shrubs and flowers. There were also cunningly devised fountains and sculptures.

STATUES FROM ITALY. Most of the statuary in the Summer Garden was bought in Italy, according to the vogue of the early 18th century. Subjects from Greek mythology include

GATES OF THE SUMMER GARDEN
After the consolidation of the Neva's banks Felten was entrusted with the stretch of the Embankment in front of the gardens and the Summer Palace, as well as with the design and manufacture of a wrought-iron gate. Finished in 1784, this gate was so pure in form and so beautifully made that it was considered one of the finest works of its kind of the period.

Cupid and Psyche, and the *Tauride Venus*, excavated at Rome; while real-life history is represented by the busts of Agrippina, Christina of Sweden and Jean Sobiesky. The *Venus*, transported with the utmost care from Italy, was Peter the Great's favorite piece. He placed it in the gallery at the entrance to the garden, but moved it later to the grotto, where he had it guarded by a sentinel for fear that it would be damaged. Today the *Venus* is in the Hermitage Museum ▲ *168*.

PLEASURE GARDENS. Pavilions, a grotto, an aviary, a menagerie and an orangery were installed in the Summer Garden, as Peter directed. Thirty-six granite monoliths, with alternating urns and vases as amortizements, frame the elements of the wrought-iron railing with its gilded points. In 1777 serious flooding destroyed the machinery, the channels and all the fountains, which were never repaired. Finally, Carlo Rossi built a COFFEE HOUSE (1826) and Louis Charlemagne a TEA HOUSE (1827) in the park. In 1855 a monument by Piotr Klodt was raised to Ivan Krylov, the "Russian Aesop".

SUMMER PALACE

PETER I'S PROPERTY. In 1711 Peter the Great built his Summer Palace ● *83* (LETNY DVORETS; Летний дворец) at the juncture of the Fontanka and the Neva beside his Summer Garden. The construction was based on the "model house" commissioned from the architect Domenico Trezzini ● *83*. In 1713 the German Andreas Schlüter doubled the size of the Summer Palace and completed the building's decoration, making bay windows in the pale yellow brick-and-staff walls. Between the windows he placed terracotta bas-reliefs; these were inspired by various mythological themes which could be seen to reflect Russia's military victories.

THE ROOMS. The interior of the Summer Palace is arranged in the Dutch style, with tall faience stoves and furniture which is simple in style. The walls of the vestibule are lined with beautifully carved panels, and also feature a relief depicting Minerva, who was the goddess of wisdom and of war.

> "I saw the Czarina approaching, preceded by Count Grigory Orlov and followed by two ladies . . . as soon as she drew level, she enquired with a smile whether the beauty of these statues had interested me. I answered, keeping pace with her, that I thought they had been placed there either to impress fools, or else to provoke the mirth of those who happened to know a little history."
>
> J.-J. Casanova

SUMMER PALACE
To reach Peter the Great's Palace on the northeast side of the Summer Garden, turn off the Main Avenue in the direction of the Fontanka.

A WALK IN THE SUMMER GARDEN
In the 19th century the trees in the gardens were allowed to grow unpruned, in the English manner, and its shady avenues became famous. Pushkin, who lived nearby, often came here to read in the mornings, wearing his dressing gown.

Fontanka Embankment

Law School. The houses which ran along the Fontanka Embankment (Nab. Reki Fontanki; наб. реки Фонтанки) in the 18th century were mostly rebuilt in 1835 by Melnikov, who adapted them for a new purpose. The Law School (no. 6) has two floors above a tall stylobate. A colonnade occupies the center and domes stand at the corners; the interior was completed by Vasily Stasov.

The Church of St Panteleimon (Tserkov Sv. Panteleimona; церковь св. Пантелеймона). This church is the last remaining vestige of the old merchant shipyards, which occupied this quarter after 1739, and to which the salt warehouses were added at the end of the 18th century. It was dedicated to Saint Panteleimon, to commemorate the Russian fleet's victory over the Swedes in 1714 in Hangö Bay on St Panteleimon's Day. The church, which has a dome on an octagonal drum, is completed by a Baroque bell tower.

Museum of Decorative and Applied Arts (Muzey Dekorativno- Prikladovo Iskustva; музей декоративно-прикладого Искусства). The glass cupola visible from the Fontanka Embankment is that of an art school (no. 12, Solyanka Street) founded by Baron Stieglitz and built (1879–81) at his expense by the architects Krakau and Hedich. Within the complex is the museum, built (1885–96) by the architect Mesmacher for the students.

From the Admiralty to the Haymarket

🕐 One day

In the early years of St Petersburg the smartest residential quarters extended over what is now the Petrograd Side ▲ *148* and Vasilyevsky Island ▲ *156*. By contrast, those of the Admiralty were purely utilitarian, occupied by craftsmen and soldiers in their barracks. With the closure of the Admiralty's naval dockyards an altogether grander kind of house began appearing on the far side of the Neva.

THE ADMIRALTY

THE NAVAL DOCKYARDS. The Admiralty (ADMIRALTEISTVO; Адмиралтейство) is a focal point of the city: three major thoroughfares converge on it, and its spire is one of the great landmarks of St Petersburg. The first Admiralty building marked the edge of the dockyards and gave onto the Neva. It was protected by a line of fortifications, with moats and bastions. After it was rebuilt in brick in 1738 the Admiralty was made up of two major constructions separated by an

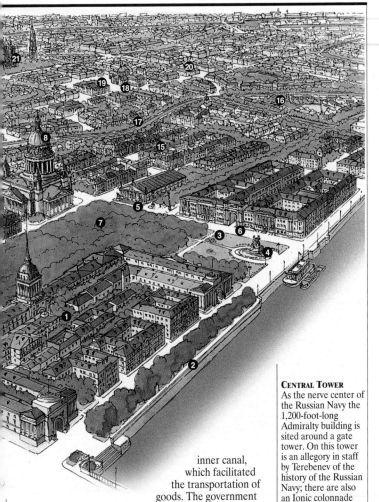

CENTRAL TOWER
As the nerve center of the Russian Navy the 1,200-foot-long Admiralty building is sited around a gate tower. On this tower is an allegory in staff by Terebenev of the history of the Russian Navy; there are also an Ionic colonnade and various statues.

inner canal, which facilitated the transportation of goods. The government occupied the first building, while the second contained the carpentry shops, the forges, the cordwainers' shops, the general workshops and the reserve supplies needed for each body of craftsmen.

HEADQUARTERS OF THE GENERAL STAFF. In 1718 the Admiralty became the Headquarters of Peter I's General Staff. For a while after this the porches of the pavilions at its ends were fronted by a canal on its way to the Neva, which was not filled in until the mid-19th century. In the old days red flags would be hoisted on the roofs of these pavilions to warn the people of impending floods. Later a complex of buildings was erected on the site of the old dockyards between the Neva and the two wings, effectively concealing the Admiralty from passers-by on the embankment. It is now a military zone, closed to the public with the exception of the central tower.

191

▲ NAVAL CONSTRUCTIONS

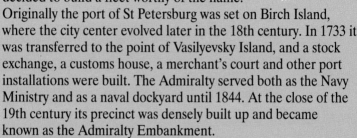

THE "POLTAVA"
The keel of the first Russian ship of the line, the *Poltava*, was laid in December 1709.

Confronted by the naval power of Sweden Peter the Great, the "Father of the Russian Navy", decided to build a fleet worthy of the name. Originally the port of St Petersburg was set on Birch Island, where the city center evolved later in the 18th century. In 1733 it was transferred to the point of Vasilyevsky Island, and a stock exchange, a customs house, a merchant's court and other port installations were built. The Admiralty served both as the Navy Ministry and as a naval dockyard until 1844. At the close of the 19th century its precinct was densely built up and became known as the Admiralty Embankment.

KRONSTADT
From the 18th century onward Kronstadt was Russia's principal naval base; but after the appearance of steamships in the 1850's merchant cargoes began to be unloaded there, for transportation to St Petersburg on lighters. According to a popular saying of the period, "The voyage from London to Kronstadt is much shorter than the voyage from Kronstadt to the point of Vasilyevsky Island." In 1885 the port was moved to Gutuyevsky Island.

THE "GRANDFATHER OF THE RUSSIAN FLEET"
This was the name given to Peter the Great's first ship ▲ *149*, in which he learned to navigate.

THE ADMIRALTY

Toward 1738 the Admiralty was rebuilt. Its initial floor plan remained the same, but stone now replaced the original wood and clay materials. The Tower was raised to a height of over 200 feet. In 1823, after reconstruction works undertaken by the architect Andrei Zakharov, the building assumed its present appearance. Even before the completion of the works in 1829 the Navy Ministry was transferred here from Moscow, and a bureau was set up for the use of Czar Alexander I.

THE GALLEYS

In Russia the word "galley" was applied to any warship with oars. The crews of these vessels were made up of soldiers and sailors in the pay of the Army. The construction and repair of the galleys was carried out at the dockyards of Galley Island, west of the Admiralty.

THE FIRST DOCKYARDS

The construction of the first factory in St Petersburg, the Admiralty's naval dockyard, began on November 5, 1704. Peter I noted in his diary: "This day we laid the foundations of the Admiralty amid great joy and celebration. The building is to be 200 sagens in length and 100 sagens broad [1 sagen = 6½ feet]."

THE EMBLEM OF THE CITY

A spire was added to the Admiralty Tower in 1719, with a golden apple and a weathercock in the form of a caravel.

193

MONUMENT
ÉLEVÉ À LA GLOIRE
DE PIERRE-LE-GRAND.

On either side of the
entrance stairway are
statues of the
Dioscuri mastering
their horses. This
riding school,
formerly used for
dressage and
exercising in periods
of bad weather, now
houses temporary art
exhibitions.

PETER THE GREAT
Peter the Great
surveys the city he
founded from
horseback, in the
pose imagined for
him by the French
sculptor Etienne
Falconet, who won a
competition arranged
by Catherine II in
1765. The sculpture
was not completed
until 1778; it
represents the Czar
ascending a rock and
trampling a serpent
(symbolizing the
Swedes) underfoot.
This statue was the
inspiration for one of
Pushkin's most
celebrated poems,
The Bronze Horseman
● 118.

DECEMBRISTS SQUARE

DECEMBRISTS SQUARE (PL. DEKEMBRISTOV; пл. Декабристов)
owes its name to the protagonists of one of the more painful
episodes in the history of St Petersburg and Russia ● 42.
EQUESTRIAN STATUE OF PETER I. Contrary to the fashion of
the day, the Czar is represented neither as a Roman emperor
nor as a prince of his own time. Instead he wears a long robe,
a mantle, soft leather boots and a simple sword at his side –
the garb of an ordinary Russian prince. Only the crown of
laurels on his head, sculpted by a pupil of Falconet's,
Anne-Marie Collot, reminds us of his rank. On either side of
the plinth are four words, which translate: "To Peter I,
Catherine II".
THE RIDING SCHOOL. Designed by Quarenghi
(1804–7), with sculpted décor by Paolo Triscorni,
the Riding School is a low quadrangular building
not unlike a Greek temple, with a double
colonnade and pediment.
VICTORY COLUMNS. Following the disappearance
of the Admiralty dockyards the canal
connecting the site with the New Holland
district was covered by a brick arch which
became the Horseguards Boulevard. On a
granite pedestal here are winged Victory
figures in bronze, modeled by Christian
Rauch (1845–6) and presented to the Czar
by the King of Prussia in commemoration of
their joint victory over Napoleon.
SENATE AND SYNOD. By creating new
institutions for Russia Peter the Great
managed to disarm those of his
opponents who were obstructing his
reforms. He suppressed the
Patriarchate which had
hitherto wielded absolute
power over the Church, and
replaced it by a Synod,
with authority to settle all
religious questions.
Likewise in 1711 he
outmaneuvered the
Duma of the Boyars by
setting up a nine-
member Senate to
manage affairs of
state in his
absence. The
architects
Rossi and
Stasov
designed twin
buildings for
these
institutions

(1829–34), which were connected by an arch spanning Galernaya Street. The columns are set forward, with a heavy entablature decorated with statues of angels. A frieze in bas-relief emphasizes the attic, in the center of which is a sculpted group featuring allegories of Probity and Justice. In the direction of the Neva, the Senate building is distinguished by a colonnade which curves round to meet the embankment. Today the Senate and Synod buildings contain historical archives; they also incorporate the Palace of Count Laval, whose daughter followed her husband, the Decembrist Trubetskoy, into exile in Siberia.

ALEXANDER GARDEN. The Alexander Garden (ALEKSANDROVSKY SAD; Александровский сад) was planted for the two-hundredth anniversary of the birth of Peter the Great, and covers the fortifications and moats which formerly defended the Admiralty. The statues here are mostly copies of antique originals made in the 18th century, along with busts of famous Russians like Gogol, Lermontov, Glinka and Zhukovsky.

St Isaac's Cathedral

St Isaac's Cathedral had difficult beginnings. Between the first church, built of wood on the present site of the Senate, and the project of Rinaldi, inherited by Renna and rejected by Montferrand, nearly a dozen architects seem to have tried to build this cathedral on its sodden, unstable site.

MONUMENT TO PREZVALSKY
This statue in the Alexander Garden, sculpted by Schroeder in 1882, celebrates the explorer Przevalsky (1839–88), who went out to discover Asia on behalf of the Imperial Geographical Society. In his account of his travels Przevalsky described the wild camel whose image now graces his statue's plinth, along with the rare Siberian horse species which was named after him ▲ 151.

THE FIRST ST ISAAC'S CHURCH
Wishing to honor the saint on whose feast day he was born, Peter I dedicated what was later to become St Petersburg's largest place of worship to an obscure Dalmatian monk.

Montferrand left an album of watercolors showing the different stages of the cathedral's construction, from the transportation of the columns to their erection.

ST ISAAC'S CATHEDRAL
The upper parts of the building are classical in style, with a huge dome, four smaller bell towers, and abundant statuary on the roof.

A TECHNICAL EXPLOIT. The architect Auguste Ricard de Montferrand, who designed the cathedral as we know it (1818–58), gave it a Byzantine floor plan, somewhat lengthened. He solved the problem of the unstable foundations by setting the 300,000-ton building on 11,000 pilings, reconciled the dictates of the disposition of the square and the orientation of the Christian sanctuaries, and added deep porches with double rows of columns to the north and south façades. These monolithic columns, made of Vyborg granite brought by sea from Finland, are over 50 feet high and weigh 114 tons each. Before constructing the main dome Montferrand made a study of similar European buildings; his greatest innovation was his use of cast iron for the rafters.

REALISTIC DÉCOR. To give his monstrous brainchild at least a veneer of lightness, the architect used materials of contrasting colors: for example, the gray granite of the walls offsets the pink columns, while the bronze of the pediments, statues, monumental doors and capitals echoes the gold of the domes. The décor of the interior ● *88* is extremely lavish; the central door of the white marble iconostasis ● *56* is paneled with lapis lazuli, while all the inside columns are covered in malachite.

ST ISAAC'S SQUARE ★

Conceived as a whole and remodeled by Montferrand as part of the work on the cathedral, St Isaac's Square (ISAAKIEVSKAYA PL.; Исаакиевская пл.) was no more than a huge building site at the time when Rossi was busy with the Senate and the Synod.

MONUMENT TO NICHOLAS I. This equestrian statue (1859), the work of the sculptor Piotr Klodt, represents the Czar in the uniform of the Horse Guards. The pedestal is decorated with four bronze bas-reliefs of the principal episodes of his reign.

Between the motifs are allegorical statues of Justice, Strength, Faith and Wisdom, which have the features of the Empress and the daughters of the Czar, who together commissioned the monument.

MUSEUM OF MUSICAL INSTRUMENTS ★. The collection of musical instruments exhibited at the Zubovsky house (no. 5) includes a number of interesting pieces, including a bone flute dating from the second millennium BC, and the pianos of great composers. The museum is shortly to be moved to the Fountains House ▲ *236*.

MARIINSKY PALACE (MARIINSKY DVORETS; Мариинский дворец). This palace, built (1839–44) by Shtakenshneider, is the final element of the square. Intended for the Grand Duchess Maria, daughter of Nicholas I, it replaced an older construction of Vallin de la Mothe. It was purchased by the State in 1884 and was used thereafter by the Council of the Czar's Ministers. After the Revolution it became the seat of the Provisional Government of the Russian Republic; today it is the headquarters of the St Petersburg Municipal Council.

BOLSHAYA MORSKAYA

This main thoroughfare (once Herzen Street) begins at the Arch of the General Staff ▲ *180* and intersects Nevsky Prospekt ▲ *214* and St Isaac's Square.

ASTORIA HOTEL. The Astoria (neoclassical and Art Nouveau) was designed by the architect Lidval in 1911. The first and second floors are faced with granite decorated with medallions, garlands and mascarons, while the façades are punctuated with pilasters. In 1917 the Astoria was a focus of resistance to the Revolution, which was invested on November 7 by Red Guards and sailors. In the first years of the Soviet regime it was the headquarters of the Petrosoviet. In 1990 it was merged with the neighboring Angliya Hotel (where the poet Sergei Esenin committed suicide in 1925) and entirely renovated.

LOBONOV-ROSTOVSKY MANSION
This majestic private mansion on the corner of Decembrists Square and the Voznesensky Prospekt occupies a three-cornered site. It was built by the architect of St Isaac's Cathedral, Auguste Ricard de Montferrand (1817–20).

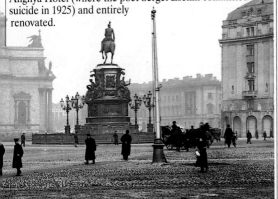

DEMIDOV MANSION. This building (no. 43) bears the name of an industrialist whose family made a fortune from mines in the Urals. Constructed between 1836 and 1840, it was inspired by Italian Renaissance architecture and is laid out around an inner courtyard. Formerly it had a hall that was entirely covered in malachite taken from its owner's mines, and this served as the model for the one in the Winter Palace ▲ *172*.

NABOKOV'S HOUSE. Vladimir Nabokov (below) was born in St Petersburg in 1899 and grew up in no. 47. The scion of a liberal aristocratic family, Nabokov was a privileged child and idolized by his mother; he recalls his happy youth in his memoir, *Other Shores*. Following the October Revolution the Nabokovs left Russia for Europe; the writer then emigrated to the United States in 1940, adopting that country's citizenship.

POLOVTSEV MANSION. This lavish townhouse (no. 52), also called the Architects' House, was built by Pel (1835–6). The Senator A. Polovtsev, who acquired it in 1860, was also the president of the Russian Historical Society. The interior is notable for its neo-Gothic library, a gilded hall and a salon decorated with malachite and bronze. The restaurant here, which was once used exclusively by architects, is now open to all.

DEMIDOV MANSION
The gateway here is flanked by Atlas figures and caryatids supporting a richly sculpted balcony. At the turn of the century Demidov Mansion was the Italian Embassy; today it is a machine-tool training institute.

CENTRAL POST OFFICE

The first post office, or Postamt, founded by Peter I in 1714, was on Suvorov Square ▲ *186*. It was later transferred to larger premises on the present Millionaires' Street; and in 1782 Catherine II moved it to the present site. This was the departure point for the post coaches which criss-crossed the Russian Empire; all the milestones in the nation indicated their exact distance

GAGARIN HOUSE
The pavilion at no. 45, next door to Demidov Mansion, was built in the 1840's. It is now the Composers' House.

from the Postamt. In 1859, when the Post Office was in need of more space, it expanded to the other side of Postamt Street and a covered gallery was built in the form of an archway to connect the two buildings. Clocks were hung here, showing the time in the major foreign capitals. Today the Postamt still fulfills its original function and is open twenty-four hours a day.

NOVAYA GOLLANDIYA (NEW HOLLAND DISTRICT)

THE FORMER TIMBER STORES. The Novaya Gollandiya district covers an area that was once a Navy storage depot constructed on an artificial island skirted by the Admiralty, Kryukov and Moika canals. Before the depot was built the timber used for shipbuilding was kept at the Admiralty ▲ *190*, in close proximity to the yards, where it was seasoned in the Dutch fashion; for this reason the wood store was known as "New Holland". The immense building with its rounded corners is characteristic of the work of the architect Vallin de la Mothe, who was commissioned to construct the market galleries. The bare brick edifice which ultimately resulted is virtually blind on its exterior, with nothing but small-paned bay windows on the corners.

THE ARCH ● *88*. A large pool stands at the center of the store area, which can be reached by boat through an archway high enough to admit fairly substantial superstructures. This arch is classical in design, framed by two columns bearing a Doric frieze. The arch itself rests on smaller columns. The austerity of the architectural design is relieved to some extent by the colors of the brick walls and the metopes, which contrast with the gray granite columns and triglyphs. The district of Novaya Gollandiya has been associated with the Russian Navy for as long as it has been in existence; today it remains a military zone, and is not open to the public. In the 19th century it was used as a prison. In more recent times it has been suggested that the Novaya Gollandiya district should be converted into a cultural center, or a tourist area which would incorporate hotels and boutiques. A third project has been proposed that would move the Naval Museum into the precinct, as this institution is at the moment somewhat cramped in its present building at the Stock Exchange ▲ *157*.

"My mother's boudoir had an overhanging window, which was convenient for looking outside, since it had a view across Morskaya Street toward Mariya Square . . . from this window, a few years later, at the start of the Revolution, I observed more than one skirmish, and for the first time in my life I saw a dead man."

Vladimir Nabokov

APARTMENT OF ALEXANDER BLOK
The apartment in which the writer spent a few months (no. 57, Decembrists Square) is now a museum displaying mementos of his life, amid the sober surroundings he favored.

199

From the 18th century onward the Mariinsky was the imperial ballet theater. Among the five theaters maintained by the court (two in Moscow and three in St Petersburg) it was especially favored from the time of Nicholas I. Nothing was too lavish for the ballets of the Imperial Theater, which was endowed with sumptuous décors created by court artists such as Roller and (later) Golovin and Benois. Known as the Kirov under the Soviet regime, the Mariinsky reverted to its original name in 1992.

MARIUS PETIPA (1818–1910)
A world-renowned choreographic genius, Petipa was ballet master at the Mariinsky from 1869 to 1903. He put on more than sixty performances and was one of the architects of academic ballet.

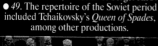

THE KIROV BALLET
From 1935 the Mariinsky Ballet was known as the Kirov Ballet, in honor of Sergei Kirov ● *49*. The repertoire of the Soviet period included Tchaikovsky's *Queen of Spades*, among other productions.

PAVLOVA (1881–1931)

No choreographer before Petipa had celebrated the ballerina with so much brio. His ballets brought a whole constellation of dancers to the fore, including Mathilda Kshesinskaya, O. Presbrazhenskaya and Anna Pavlova.

THE CORPS DE BALLET

The genius of Petipa reached its climax in his collaboration with the composers Tchaikovsky and Glazunov. With *The Sleeping Beauty* (1890), *Swan Lake* (1895) and *Raymonda* (1898) Petipa created a style in which the *corps de ballet* became an essential component of the choreographic language.

YUSUPOV PALACE

Built by Vallin de la Mothe in the 1760's, the Yusupov Palace (YUSUPOVSKY DVORETS; Юсуповский дворец) was converted at the end of the 19th century for Princess Zenaida Yusupov. Seriously damaged during World War Two, it has since been heavily restored and its magnificent art collection moved to the Hermitage. The interior decoration of the palace testifies to its former brilliance; the formal salon, the MOORISH SALON, and the Buffet Room (where the acoustics are extraordinary) in particular. So as not to overload the slender vaulting of the BALLROOM, which was not strong enough to support crystal or gilded bronze, the chandeliers were fashioned of gilt papier-maché so that they resembled metal. An Italianate THEATER (above) is situated in the North Wing of the building.

THE DEATH OF RASPUTIN. On the first floor of the Moika side of the building a concealed entrance leads to a salon in which exclusive parties were given; it was in this salon that Rasputin ● *37*, the hypnotic monk who oscillated between spirituality and debauchery, met his horrible end. In the uneasy atmosphere of the period Rasputin's mesmeric gift had given him enormous power over the Empress and her entourage. To rid the court of this inconvenient character Prince Felix Yusupov plotted his murder, in which the Grand Duke Dmitry also had a hand. Felix Yusupov died in Paris in 1967.

HE POISONING F RASPUTIN

the basement of e Yusupov Palace ere is a waxwork hich recreates the cor and mosphere of asputin's gruesome urder.

THEATER SQUARE ★

Theater Square (TEATRALNAYA PL.; Театральная пл.) contains, in close proximity, two of the main institutions of the musical life of St Petersburg.

THE MARIINSKY THEATER ▲ *200*. The first permanent theater in St Petersburg was built in 1783. At the turn of the 19th century, a time when a distinctive national school of composers was taking shape in Russia, this theater mounted the first performances of Russian operas. In 1803 the ballet and opera companies separated from the theater company, and in 1836 the theater, rebuilt by the architect Kavos, opened its season with *A Life for the Czar*, the work by Glinka which signaled the birth of classical Russian opera. Later, supplanted by an Italian company, the Russian actors were transferred to Moscow in

1845, and it was not until the 1850's that the national troupe returned to St Petersburg. In 1860 the building, which had been entirely reconstructed following a fire, was rechristened the Imperial Mariinsky Theater. It was nationalized in 1917, and became known as the Kirov Ballet from 1935 to 1993, but has now it has reverted to its original name. During the Soviet era it continued to mount operas and ballets by both foreign composers and native Russian ones such as Prokofiev and Shostakovich. Nowadays the theater is under the direction of V. Gergiev, whose primary objective is to revive the great masterpieces of Russian opera. The ballet company, whose fame is universal, continues to tour the world's great capitals.

THE CONSERVATOIRE. Fronted by statues of Glinka and Rimsky-Korsakov, the St Petersburg Conservatoire was founded in 1862 on the initiative of Anton Rubinstein. It was the first advanced music school in Russia, teaching seven disciplines; these were musical theory and composition; choir and orchestra conducting; singing; orchestral instruments; piano and organ; ballet and opera direction; and lastly, traditional instruments. The Conservatoire has two auditoriums: in the larger of the two, pupils give public performances; the smaller one, which has magnificent acoustics, a painted ceiling and a gallery of portraits of musicians, is used for Russian and international festivals and competitions.

Statue of Nikolai Rimsky-Korsakov ▲ *239* in front of the Conservatoire.

SYNAGOGUE
The Jewish community of St Petersburg was heavily repressed prior to the reforms of Alexander II ● *36*. In 1893 the construction of a synagogue and cultural center confirmed these reforms; the synagogue, at no. 2 Lermontov Street, is built in the Moorish style.

In an area once overwhelmingly inhabited by sailors, this cathedral was understandably dedicated to their patron, Saint Nicholas. With its blue, white and gold exterior, St Nicholas' Cathedral is similar in many ways to Smolny, which was built by Rastrelli; indeed Chevakinsky, the architect of St Nicholas, was a pupil of the Italian. A remarkable illustration of religious Baroque, this church remained open throughout the Soviet era.

BESIDE THE KRYUKOV CANAL

The cathedral is built to the classic Greek cross plan, with a central cupola and four turrets at each corner, topped by onion domes ● 57. On the exterior the composition is punctuated by columns backed against the walls. The lower church (there is no crypt, because of likely flooding) supports a richly embellished upper one. Services are held on the upper level, where the décor is especially lavish because of the largesse of Catherine II, who presented ten gold-covered icons to commemorate ten naval victories. The equally gold-laden iconostasis ● 57, of carved wood, was executed between 1755 and 1760. The bell tower is separate from the church proper ● 85, standing at the entrance to the cathedral precinct, where it is reflected in the Kryukov Canal ▲ 210.

1. Main entrance
2. Secondary entrance
3. Lower church
4. Stairs leading to upper church
5. Iconostasis
6. Portal
7. Altars
8. Central cupola
9. Onion-domed corner turret

SENNAYA PLOSHCHAD
In Dostoevsky's time the crowded and filthy Haymarket was known for its low dives, taverns, cabarets, brothels and prostitutes' hotels. The district exercised a deep fascination on Raskolnikov, the hero of *Crime and Punishment*: at the close of the novel, visiting the Haymarket for the last time, "...he let himself fall to the ground ... on his knees in the center of the square, he bent and kissed the muddy stones with ecstasy and delight ... then he straightened, and prostrated himself a second time."

HAYMARKET SQUARE

From St Nicholas' Cathedral, Sadovaya Street (SADOVAY UL.; Садовая ул), typical of 19th-century St Petersburg, leads through to Haymarket Square (SENNAYA PL.; Сенная пл.). At the end of the 18th century there was a huge market here where hay, oats and straw were sold, hence the name. The Haymarket area was once one of the worst slums of St Petersburg, but today the old buildings have been replaced by buildings constructed after World War Two. The only original edifice still standing is the Police Station, with its four-columned classical portico.

THE CHURCH OF THE ASSUMPTION IN HAYMARKET SQUARE, now demolished, was built in the mid-18th century to a project by A. Kvasov, in which Rastrelli had a hand. It was the architectural focus of the square. Closed in 1938, the church was knocked down in 1961 to make way for the Sennaya metro station.

DOSTOEVSKY DISTRICT ★

A HERMETIC SPACE. Dostoevsky never had a house of his own in St Petersburg; instead he was constantly on the move,

> ## "FEW PLACES EXERCISE ON THE HUMAN SPIRIT SO SOMBER, VIOLENT, AND STRANGE AN INFLUENCE . . ."
>
> FYODOR DOSTOEVSKY

changing his domicile a score of times in the eight years he lived in the city center. As a rule he chose buildings that faced churches. Whether large and spacious or narrow and closed off, a room for Dostoevsky had a profound underlying meaning. Time and again the image of the oppressive, constricting bedroom appears in his books. This hermetic space, bounded by a corner, a wall, a palisade or an alleyway, is a frequent characteristic of his work; it has the value of a symbol, expressing the inner life of the hero and his state of mind.

CUT OFF FROM THE WORLD. Dreamers, "men of the underworld" with ravaged consciences, the heroes of Dostoevsky always live in "corners"; they flee the reality that surrounds them. The writer himself nearly always lived on street-corner houses, which made him feel even more isolated from the rest of the world than he actually was. He had a clear preference for Vladimir Square ▲ *238* and the Haymarket. It was here that he set his characters, who walked the same streets as he did and saw the same buildings and scenes from their windows as he saw. The lives of both Dostoevsky and his heroes are seamlessly blended with the life of St Petersburg itself. Indeed, this may be one reason why Dostoevsky moved with such regularity: once he had completed a novel, he became impatient to leave the places which his art and his imagination had transformed into fiction.

A CITY REINVENTED
Dostoevsky's St Petersburg has two dimensions, one real, the other imaginary. On the one hand, there is the city which really existed, with real people and locations; and on the other, there is the imagined metropolis, peopled by invented characters, which is such a strong characteristic of his work. Dostoevsky loved his city, where he had grown up and made his literary career. St Petersburg is present in about twenty of his thirty novels, sometimes as a background but more often as a character in its own right.

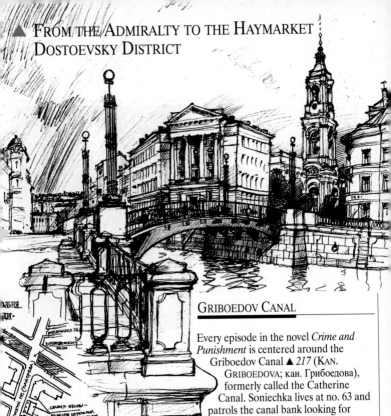

GRIBOEDOV CANAL

Every episode in the novel *Crime and Punishment* is centered around the Griboedov Canal ▲ *217* (КАН. ГРИБОЕDОВА; кан. Грибоедова), formerly called the Catherine Canal. Soniechka lives at no. 63 and patrols the canal bank looking for clients. On the far side of the canal stands the building occupied by the moneylender Alena Ivanovna, the old woman whom Raskolnikov robs and kills with an axe. No. 65 was the old Police Station to which Raskolnikov is summoned, and which Dostoevsky himself visited.

PRZEVALSKY STREET

RASKOLNIKOV'S HOUSE. The corner house here, no. 5, is thought to be the model for Raskolnikov's. In the mid-19th century this three-story building belonged to a man called Joachim. If you turn right after entering the porch you will see in the corner the door which gives onto the staircase described in the novel. Dostoevsky gives an exact account of Raskolnikov's comings and goings, and his hero's fate is decided by a series of coincidences. Thus Raskolnikov, who has carefully thought out everything he needs to do before he commits his crime, finally forgets to bring an axe with which he intends to do the deed.

ASCENSION BRIDGE
"Raskolnikov went straight to X Bridge, stopped in the middle of it, leaned his elbows on the parapet, and looked down . . . with his head craned over the water, he began mechanically to contemplate the last pink rays of the setting sun … Eventually red circles emerged before his eyes, and the houses, passers-by, quays, coaches and everything else began spinning and dancing around him."

Crime and Punishment

TREASURY STREET

Dostoevsky occupied three different houses in Treasury Street (KAZNECHEYSKAYA UL.; Казначейская ул.), close by the Haymarket, known as Petit Bourgeois Street until the turn of the century. The writer, who was already famous, lodged in one of the most wretched slums in St Petersburg; not

> **"**He hadn't the least desire to go into the street like that. And as for going home, that would be even worse. 'A beautiful opportunity, lost forever!' he muttered, standing with dangling arms under the porch just in front of the concierge's tiny lodge, which was also open. Suddenly he gave a start. Within the lodge two steps away, something was shining on the bench, just to the right.**"**
> *Crime and Punishment*

because he liked the romantic, meandering Catherine Canal, or because he wanted to study the sordid existence of the tenants of the surrounding buildings, but because he simply did not have the means to live elsewhere. Considering that "the mind is narrowed by small lodgings", he preferred to have two spacious rooms, a luxury which was very expensive in the grander districts of the city.

OLONKIN HOUSE. This house (no. 7), on the corner of Treasury and Przevalsky streets (the latter used to be called Carpenters' Lane), was Dostoevsky's home from August 1864 to January 1867. It was here that he wrote *Crime and Punishment* and received his second wife, Anna Grigorievna Snitkina, for the first time. The two also worked together for the first time at this house, when Anna (whom he had engaged to help him finish a novel, *The Gambler*, in double-quick time) took down his dictated text in twenty-six days. The building contained a wine-shop and tavern kept by a tradesman, Efimov; and although the district was noisy at all hours Dostoevsky mostly worked at night.

THE "TIMES". Dostoevsky's elder brother also lived on Petit Bourgeois Street; together they edited and published the *Times* and *Epoch* reviews.

ASCENSION PROSPEKT

Ascension Prospekt (VOZNESENSKY PR.; Вознесенский пр.) features in nearly every one of Dostoevsky's novels set in St Petersburg. He lived there himself between 1847 and 1849, and again in 1867. In the 1860's one of his friends, Apollo Grigoriev, also lived in the street, which appears often on the itineraries of Raskolnikov, of Arkady Dolgoruky in *Raw Youth*, and of the characters in *Insulted and Injured* and *The Eternal Husband*.

THE CHIL HOUSE. Dostoevsky lived here, at nos. 8–23, from spring 1847 to April 23, 1849 while he was writing *White Nights*, *The Landlady* and *Netoshka Nezvanova*. And it was here, also, that he was arrested, in the night of April 22–3, 1849.

> **"**With his heart failing him, trembling with nerves, he approached an enormous house, one side of which backed on to the canal, with the other overlooking X Street. This building was divided into a crowd of small apartments, whose tenants were artisans of every kind: tailors, locksmiths, cooks, Germans, prostitutes, petty functionaries, etcetera. People went in and out through the two carriage entrances.**"**
> *Crime and Punishment*

TRINITY CHURCH
This five-domed building, constructed by Stasov (1828–30), supplanted an 18th-century wooden church.

KRYUKOV CANAL

Beside the Kryukov Canal stands the clock tower of St Nicholas' Cathedral ▲ *204*, a fine three-story building of harmonious proportions. This is one of the most romantic corners of St Petersburg, and it was not for nothing that Dostoevsky set perhaps his most poetic novel, *White Nights*, around the Kryukov and Catherine canals.

2ND ISMAILOV BATTALION STREET

From this street, where he lived in 1872 and 1873, Dostoevsky could see the Trinity Church, which was where he was married to Anna Grigorievna Snitkina in 1867.

PIONEERS' SQUARE

"We, the Petrachevtsi, heard out our sentence of death standing on the scaffold without a trace of remorse. I cannot speak for all of us, but I do not think I am mistaken when I affirm that at that instant, in that minute, the majority among us were very close to dishonoring themselves by forsaking their convictions."
Journal of an Author

It was on Pioneers' Square (PIONERSKAYA PL.; Пионерская пл.), formerly known as Semenovsky Square, that the members of the Semenovsky circle were led to believe they had been condemned to death (December 22, 1848). Those who had been present at the meetings of this literary and political group, at which Vissarion Bielinsky's letter was read out ▲ *237*, appeared before a military tribunal, who condemned them to death after eight months' imprisonment in the Peter and Paul Fortress ▲ *146*. At the last moment the sentence was commuted to deportation to a labor camp. Afterward Dostoevsky recorded in *The Idiot* Prince Myshkin's description of the minutes they spent in the full expectation of death.

Around the Nevsky Prospekt

▲ NEVSKY PROSPEKT

The buildings along Nevsky Prospekt recount the history of this main thoroughfare of St Petersburg, laid down through the forest in the decade following 1710. The road was originally laid with tree-trunks; gradually houses and palaces began to be built along its length, the most beautiful structures concentrated between Palace Square and the Fontanka (the original limit of the city). In the mid-18th century it was baptized Nevsky Prospekt, after the monastery to which it led. This avenue, over 2½ miles long, is "at once the most elegant street and the chief shopping area of St Petersburg . . . being an original blend of shops, palaces and churches; on the signs gleam the beautiful characters of the Russian alphabet." (Théophile Gautier)

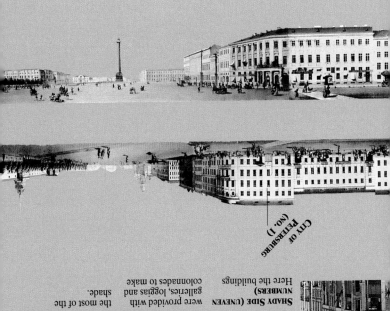

CITY OF PETERSBURG (NO. 1)

SHADY SIDE (UNEVEN NUMBERS)
Here the buildings were provided with galleries, loggias and colonnades to make the most of the shade.

CITY OF PETERSBURG (NO. 1)
This late 18th-century building was altered between 1910 and 1912 by Ziedler, on behalf of the Commercial Bank of Petersburg.

KARL BRYULOV (NO. 6)
The painter Karl Bryulov stayed at this address in 1836, where Nikolai Gogol visited him several times to pose for his portrait.

SUNNY SIDE (EVEN NUMBERS)
Despite their diversity the façades of the buildings along the sunny side of the Prospekt give an overall sense of elegance and unity.

KARL BRYULOV (NO. 6)

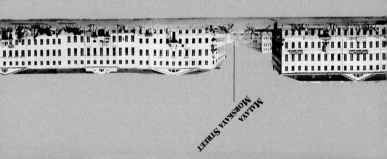

MALAYA MORSKAYA STREET

MALAYA MORSKAYA STREET
From 1902 to 1992 this street bore the name of one of its most famous residents, Nikolai Gogol, who lived in an apartment at no. 17 between 1833 and 1836. He wrote *Taras Bulba* here.

213

DURING THE SIEGE

At no. 14 there is a moving reminder of the siege of Leningrad: a plaque reads, "Comrades! In the event of artillery fire, this side of the street is the most dangerous."

BOLSHAYA MORSKAYA STREET

Before reverting to its original name Bolshaya Morskaya Street was rebaptized Herzen Street, after the writer who lived at no. 14. Bolshaya Morskaya Street cuts directly across Nevsky Prospekt. The even street numbers end at the Arch of the General Staff. At nos. 3–5 the former Azovsko-Donskoy bank (1908–9)

provides another example of the luxurious tastes of the old financiers. This building has now been converted into a telephone exchange.

"WOLFF AND BÉRANGER" (NO. 18)

Pushkin met his second, Danzas, at this pastry-shop on January 27, 1837, before his final duel ● *116*. The literary café here opened in 1985.

NO. 14

BOLSHAYA MORSKAYA STREET

CHICHERIN PALACE (NO. 15)

POLICE BRIDGE

The rearrangement of the banks of the Moika took place earlier than that of the other canals. Nevertheless it was only in the years 1798–1810 that these were completely reconstructed in granite. The People's Bridge, which spans the Moika, used to be called the Police Bridge on account of its proximity to the Chicherin Palace (no. 15) and the central police building.

DUTCH CHURCH (NO. 20)

The central part of this long building (1830–3, designed by Paul Jacot) had a massive portico behind which the church was situated; the wings contained the residences of the pastor and the members of the Dutch mission. In the 19th century the offices of the Society for the Encouragement of Painters occupied the first floor.

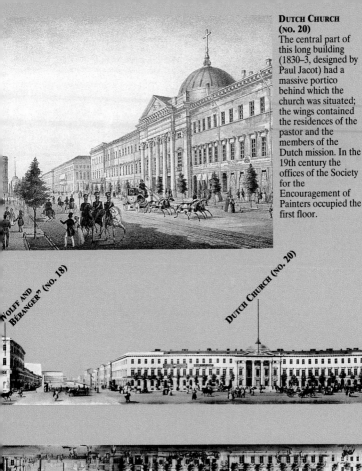

"WOLFF AND BÉRANGER" (NO. 18)

DUTCH CHURCH (NO. 20)

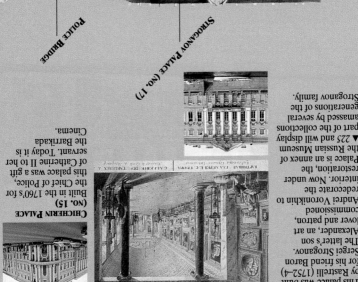

CHICHERIN PALACE

POLICE BRIDGE

STROGANOV PALACE (NO. 17)

STROGANOV PALACE (NO. 17)

This palace was built by Rastrelli (1752–4) for his friend Baron Sergei Stroganov. The latter's son Alexander, an art lover and patron, commissioned Andrei Voronikhin to redecorate the interior. Now under restoration, the Palace is an annex of the Russian Museum ▲ 225 and will display part of the collections amassed by several generations of the Stroganov family.

CHICHERIN PALACE (NO. 15)

Built in the 1760's for the Chief of Police, this palace was a gift of Catherine II to her servant. Today it is the Barrikada Cinema.

215

"DOMINIQUE" (NO. 24) Before the Revolution no. 24 was the famous restaurant *Dominique* where the young Dostoevsky habitually dined in the 1840's. Later the interior was sketched by the painter Repin.

SMYRDIN PUBLISHING HOUSE (NO. 22) Formerly the bookseller A. Smyrdin, the publisher of Pushkin and Gogol, occupied the right wing of the Lutheran church building.

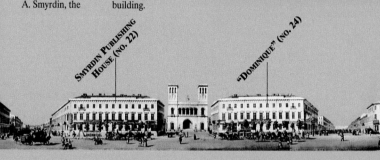

SMYRDIN PUBLISHING HOUSE (NO. 22)

"DOMINIQUE" (NO. 24)

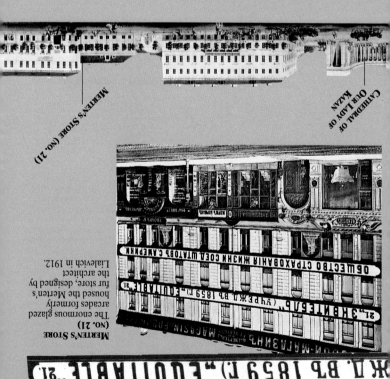

MERTEN'S STORE (NO. 21)

CATHEDRAL OF OUR LADY OF KAZAN

MERTEN'S STORE (NO. 21) The enormous glazed arcades formerly housed the Merten's fur store, designed by the architect Lialevich in 1912.

GRIBOEDOV CANAL

This waterway was cut between 1764 and 1790 to avoid flooding. Hilarion Kutuzov, the father of Marshal Kutuzov, originally proposed this idea to Elizabeth I.

DOM KNIGI BOOKSTORE (NO. 28)

The Singer Sewing Machine Company wanted to build a ten-story building on this site and, despite the opposition of the municipality, constructed in 1907 what is now St Petersburg's largest bookstore, with a glass globe on its dome.

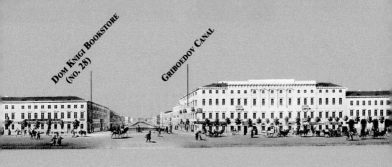

DOM KNIGI BOOKSTORE (NO. 28)

GRIBOEDOV CANAL

KAZAN SQUARE

CATHEDRAL OF OUR LADY OF KAZAN

Designed by Voronikhin and built between 1801 and 1811, this cathedral reflects both Russian and Western styles. While it respects the Orthodox canon of an altar facing east, its lateral colonnade (like that of St Peter's in Rome) is very striking. The Soviet authorities converted it into a museum of the history of religion and atheism.

KAZAN SQUARE

The cathedral of Kazan, with its semicircular colonnade of ninety-six columns, forms one of St Petersburg's most majestic squares.

The tomb of Marshal Kutuzov (1745–1813) is preserved in the cathedral.

KAZAN SQUARE

ST CATHERINE'S CHURCH (NOS. 32–4)
The refined Baroque elegance of St Catherine's (1763–83, Vallin de la Mothe) contrasts strongly with the massive buildings around it.

ST CATHERINE'S CHURCH (NOS. 32–4)

"GRAND HOTEL EUROPE" (NO. 36)

ARTS SQUARE

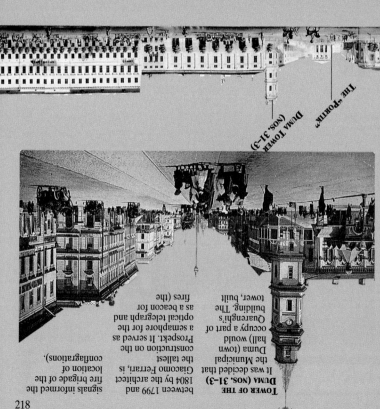

THE "PORTIK"

DUMA TOWER (NOS. 31–3)

TOWER OF THE DUMA (NOS. 31–3)
It was decided that the Municipal Duma (town hall) would occupy a part of Quarenghi's building. The tower, built between 1799 and 1804 by the architect Giacomo Ferrari, is the tallest construction on the Prospekt. It served as a semaphore for the optical telegraph and as a beacon for fires (the signals informed the fire brigade of the location of conflagrations).

GRAND HOTEL EUROPE (NO. 36)

Beyond the Grand Hotel Europe, now restored by European investors to its pre-Revolutionary glory, cross Mikhailovskaya Street, to reach the Arts Square.

ARMENIAN CHURCH

This wonderful little church was built by Yury Felten in 1780 and restored between 1835 and 1837 by the architect A. Melnikov.

MEETING PLACE OF THE DECEMBRISTS (NO. 42)

The Decembrist Gavril Batenkov (1793–1863) lived at no. 42, where he entertained other conspirators such as Kondraty, Ryleyev, Trubetskoy and Bestuzhev (left).

ARMENIAN CHURCH

No. 42

GOSTINY DVOR (NO. 35)

GOSTINY DVOR (NO. 35)

After a series of fires and lootings the tradespeople of Nevsky Prospekt decided to finance the construction of a stone galleried market by Vallin de la Mothe. Behind these façades, which have a total length of more than half a mile, is the largest store in the city. Maintenance work on the gallery in 1965 brought to light over 300 lbs of gold hidden by merchants.

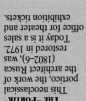

The "PORTIK"

This neoclassical portico, the work of the architect Rusca (1802–6), was restored in 1972. Today it is a sales office for theater and exhibition tickets.

THE "PASSAGE" (NO. 48)

This 180-yard gallery, built in 1846, was commissioned by Count Essen-Stenbock from the architect R. Zheliazevich as a site for shops, a concert hall and a *salon de thé*. The façade, which the tradesmen thought too modest, was altered in 1902 by the engineer Kozlov.

THE "PASSAGE" (NO. 48)

SADOVAYA STREET

SCHROEDER PIANO WORKS (NO. 52)

SALTYKOV-SHCHEDRIN LIBRARY (NO. 37)

▲ 231.

documents and autographs of Peter the Great and Mozart

▲ A MAJOR RESERVE
In addition to a large stock of French books (among them the 7,000 books of Voltaire's library) are a number of other treasures, notably rare 11th- and 12th-century manuscripts such as the *Ostromir Gospels* (1056),

К.М. ШРЕДЕР

SCHROEDER PIANOS (NO. 52)
No. 52 belonged to K. Schroeder, the piano manufacturer. Today it is a bookshop.

SADOVAYA STREET
The "Street of the Gardens" (left) leads through to the Michael Garden, the Summer Garden and the Engineers' Castle.

ELISEEV STORE (NO. 56)
This foodshop (don't miss its magnificent Art Nouveau interior) was built in 1907 by G. Baranovsky for the Eliseev brothers.

НЕВСКИЙ ПРОСПЕКТ 56

ELISEEV STORE (NO. 56)

OSTROVSKY SQUARE

SALTYKOV-SHCHEDRIN LIBRARY (NO. 37)
The curving façade giving onto Nevsky Prospekt is the work of the architect Sokolov (1796–1801); the rectilinear colonnade was added by Rossi thirty years later, when the Library (inaugurated 1814) needed to be enlarged. It is named for the Russian writer Saltykov-Shchedrin (1826–89).

Many well known figures, including Tolstoy, Gorky, Mendeleev, Pavlov, Plekhanov and Lenin all frequented the Saltykov-Shchedrin Library.

ANICHKOV BRIDGE
The four horses and their tamers (all different) on the Anichkov Bridge were sculpted by Klodt in 1849 and 1850.

APARTMENT BLOCKS (NOS. 64–6)

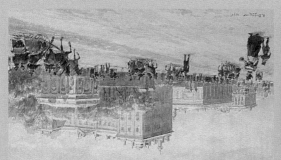

ANICHKOV PALACE (NO. 39)
This palace, completed by Rastrelli in 1751 after a project by Zemtsov, was frequently altered prior to the 19th century. First of all it was given by Elizabeth I to her morganatic husband Alexei Razumovsky. Later Catherine II gave it to Prince Potemkin, on two occasions: the first time in 1776, then a second time after he had sold it to pay his debts. Potemkin gave lavish balls here.

FONTANKA

The Fontanka, named for the fountains of the Summer Garden which it fed with water, was only a muddy watercourse when Elizabeth ordered it to be dredged and reinforced, first with wood and later with granite.

ANICHKOV BRIDGE

ANICHKOV PALACE (NO. 39)

"A PERPETUAL STREAM OF CARRIAGES GOES BY AT FULL SPEED, AND CROSSING THE PROSPEKT IS NO LESS PERILOUS AN UNDERTAKING THAN CUTTING OVER THE BOULEVARD FROM RUE DROUOT AND RUE DE RICHELIEU IN PARIS."

THÉOPHILE GAUTIER

THE HEIRS OF THE PIONEERS
After 1817 the Anichkov Palace became the residence of the heirs to the Russian throne. Alexander III liked it so much that he remained there after his coronation, filling the house with his art collections, which were later to be exhibited at the Russian Museum ▼ 225. In 1935 the Anichkov buildings became the Palace of the Pioneers, where the red-scarfed pioneers came to spend their free time.

223

⊕ Half a day

STATUE OF PUSHKIN
Sculpted in 1957 by Mikhail Anikushin, this monument is the first thing you arrive when you arrive from the Mikhail Street side.

The former Mikhail Square thoroughly deserved its new name of Arts Square (PL. ISKUSSTV; площадь Искусств) since institutions of music, literature, painting and sculpture are all concentrated here behind Carlo Rossi's façades, on a site which was no more than a swamp at the beginning of the 19th century. In the center of the square is a statue of the poet Pushkin ● *114*, whose imperious gesture seems to invite you to begin your visit on the left hand side of the square.

BRODSKY MUSEUM

The painter Isaac Brodsky (1883–1939), after whom Mikhail Street was named during the Soviet era, lived between 1924 and 1939 at no. 3, which was a building constructed in the early 19th century according to plans by Rossi. Those who admire socialist realism will look for Brodsky's edifying canvases, such as *Lenin's Speech at the Putilov Factory Workers' Meeting* (1929) and *Lenin at Smolny* (1930) ▲ *248*. Others, however, may prefer his comprehensive collection of 19th- and 20th-century paintings, which includes works by Repin, Surikov and Serov.

LITTLE THEATER OF OPERA AND BALLET

THE FORMER MIKHAILOVSKY THEATER

● *68.* At no. 1 Arts Square is the old
Mikhailovsky Theater (now called the
Little Theater of Opera and Ballet, Maly
Theater or Mussorgsky Theater), built by
the architect Alexander Bryulov, partly to
plans by Rossi (1831–3). "Certain
productions have their premieres in
St Petersburg almost at the same time as
in Paris. We may be forgiven a certain
pride at seeing, some six or seven
hundred leagues from Paris, at a latitude
of sixty degrees, that our language is
sufficiently widely spoken to maintain full
houses in an exclusively French theater."
Thus Théophile Gautier described the

The auditorium of
the Little Theater of
Opera and Ballet.

"French Theater of St Petersburg" as it was sometimes known
at that time; it is now a mecca for ballets and musical
productions.

RUSSIAN MUSEUM ★

MIKHAIL PALACE (RUSSKY MUZEY/MIKHAILOVSKY DVORETS;
Михайловский дворец). The central building of the Russian
Museum, with its Corinthian façade, was built for the Grand
Duke Mikhail, brother of Alexander I, by Carlo Rossi
(1819–25). This architect, who laid out Mikhail Square in its
entirety, also arranged the interior details of the palace. All
that survives of this today is the vestibule and main staircase,
along with the White Room (where visitors can see sculptures
by Mikhail Kozlovsky, bas-reliefs by Stepan Pimenov and
murals by Vighi).
FIRST RUSSIAN MUSEUM. In 1898 Nicholas II transformed the
Palace into the Russian Museum of Alexander III, bringing in
some of the paintings and art objects earlier assembled by his
father at the Anichkov Palace ▲ *223*. Works from private
collections, from the Hermitage ▲ *168* and from the Fine Arts
Academy ▲ *162* were added to these, leading to the
construction of a west wing in the direction of the
Griboedov Canal, by Leonty Benois (1914–16). The
nationalization of private property in 1917
also greatly enriched the
museum.

MIKHAIL PALACE
After the death of the
Grand Duke Mikhail
his widow organized
brilliant musical
evenings with the aid
of the composer
Anton Rubinstein.
The latter, with the
backing of the Grand
Duchess, founded
both the St
Petersburg and
Moscow music
conservatories.

Created by an *ukaze* of the Emperor Alexander III, the Russian Museum opened its doors on March 7, 1889 in Carlo Rossi's Mikhail Palace. Today it is one of the largest museums in the world, with reserves of over 380,000 paintings and *objets d'art*. The purpose of the museum is to exhibit Russian works of art that range in date from the 10th century to our own time; among them is an extraordinary collection of some six thousand icons.

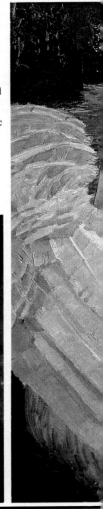

"THE SWAN PRINCESS" (1900)
Superb and disquieting, *The Swan Princess* by Mikhail Vrubel (1856–1911) illustrates Pushkin's story *The Czar Saltan*.

"EVGRAV DAVYDOV" (1809)
Since the creation of the Academy of Arts of St Petersburg the teaching reflected mainly French art. The Russia of the early 19th century did not escape the vogue for Romanticism, fueled by the patriotic war of 1812, as this portrait of Evgrav Davydov by Orest Kiprensky (1782–1836) shows.

"THE DINNER" (1902)
The collections of the museum reflect the artistic and cultural blossoming of Russia on the eve of the Revolution. One of the movements of the period, the World of Art, adopted an esthetic which was simultaneously predominant in Berlin, Vienna and Paris. Leon Bakst (1868–1924) went to the French capital; a lover of 18th-century painting and the poetry of the French Symbolists, he knew how to pay homage to them without compromising any of the essentially Russian character of his art.

"THE ZAPOROG COSSACKS" (1891)
National traditions have been a constant source of inspiration to Russian art, and historical episodes, legends and tales supplied many of the favorite themes of the 19th century.

"THE PROMENADE" (1917)
Marc Chagall, who was initially influenced by the World of Art movement, later looked for a means of escape into the world of fantasy.

"ANNA IVANOVNA" (1741)
Artists whose destinies were closely linked to that of Russia were also represented: left, the Empress Anna Ivanovna and her servant, by Rastrelli.

Details of the façade of the Church of the Resurrection, representing the arms of all the regions of Russia.

ETHNOGRAPHIC MUSEUM

The Mikhail Palace is flanked, on its left, by a wing built (1900–11) by Vasily Svinin to house the ethnographic section of the National Museum (MUZEY ETNOGRAFII; Государственный музей Этнографии). Founded in 1901, it was not opened to the public until 1923; it became a separate museum in its own right in 1934. The richness of its collection makes it far and away Russia's most important ethnographic museum. All the peoples of the former Soviet Union are represented: for example, Moldavians and Bielorussians, Azeris and Turkmens, Evenks and Nenets.

MARBLE HALL. The great entry hall of the museum is sumptuous: Svinin had its walls covered with delicate pink Carelian marble, while the sculptor Kharlamov executed a 300-foot frieze representing all the peoples of the former Russian Empire.

SHOSTAKOVICH PHILHARMONIA

The building constructed by Paul Jacot in 1839 for the Assembly of the Nobility was the scene of major concerts organized by the St Petersburg Philharmonic Society; here, in the Great Hall, Tchaikovsky, Berlioz and Wagner came to conduct their own works, and Isadora Duncan danced. After the Revolution the Great Hall and auditorium became the property of the Philharmonic Society (founded in 1921); a year after the death of Shostakovich (left) in 1976 it was renamed for him. The Philharmonia building projects into the ITALIANSKAYA with two further theaters, the MUSICAL COMEDY THEATER

(no. 13) and the KOMISSARZHEVSKAYA THEATER (no. 19). The latter opened in October 1942, hence its nickname the "Blockade Theater".

THE "LENINGRADSKAYA". On the evening of August 9, 1942, the date that had been fixed by Hitler for the fall of Leningrad, the Philharmonia gave the city's first performance of Shostakovich's *Leningrad Symphony*, or *7th Symphony*, which was broadcast from the Great Hall by all the nation's radio stations. Some of the members of the orchestra were still in uniform, having been recalled from the front for the occasion. Others wore the traditional white tie and tails.

CHURCH OF THE RESURRECTION ★

THE NEO-RUSSIAN STYLE ● 89. The twisted onion domes, proliferating mosaics and asymmetry of the Church of the Resurrection (KHRAM VOSKRESENIYA KHRISTOVA; храм Воскресения Христова) come as a surprise in this city known for its Baroque curves and classical rigor. The mosaics have just been restored and are magnificent.

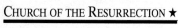

Alfred Parland, who built the church (1883–1907), won the competition set up by Alexander III, which stipulated that it had to be in the "purely Russian style of the 17th century".

ENGINEERS' CASTLE ★

A walk through the MIKHAILOVSKY GARDEN will take you past the rear façade of the Mikhail Palace to the Engineers' Castle (INZHENERNY ZAMOK; Инженерный замок).

STATUE OF PETER THE GREAT. Bartolomeo Carlo Rastrelli, the father of the architect, began this equestrian statue of Peter I while the Czar was still alive, and ultimately used his death-mask as a model. In 1800 Paul I placed the statue in front of the Castle's main entrance, with the inscription: "To the great-grandfather, the great-grandson."

MIKHAIL CASTLE. Paul I decided to build a secure fortress on the site of Empress Elizabeth's Summer Palace. The castle was inaugurated on November 8, 1800, St Mikhail's Day in the Orthodox calendar. The name Mikhailovsky, contrary to that of Arts Square or the Russian Museum, has nothing to do with the Grand Duke Mikhail; instead it refers to the Archangel Mikhail, who, according to Paul I, appeared and commanded him to build a chapel bearing his name on this site. This inspiration, which obliged the architect Brennan to design each of his four façades completely differently, did not mitigate the castle's frowning, military aspect.

SCHOOL OF ENGINEERING. Alexander I abandoned the castle, with its sinister associations. Subsequently it became the barracks of a squadron of the Imperial Guard, the headquarters of an institute for the blind, and the Chancellery of the Ministry of Instruction and Religious Affairs. In 1822 the Military Engineering School moved here, and it assumed the name of Engineers' Castle. Fyodor Dostoevsky ▲ 207 was a student at the school in 1838, occupying a corner room on the third floor overlooking the Fontanka, where he liked to read and work.

MIKHAIL CASTLE
Designed by Bazhenov, this massive building was constructed by Brenna to a medieval plan. The castle was surrounded by water (the Fontanka, the Moika and two other canals, now running underground), and was linked to the city by drawbridges, which were raised every evening.

ASSASSINATION OF PAUL I
In the night of March 11, 1801, supporters of Alexander murdered Paul I in the Mikhail Castle, where he had resided for only forty days. The secret rooms and passages Paul I (justifiably paranoid) had devised stopped many of the plotters from reaching the murder scene.

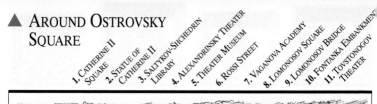

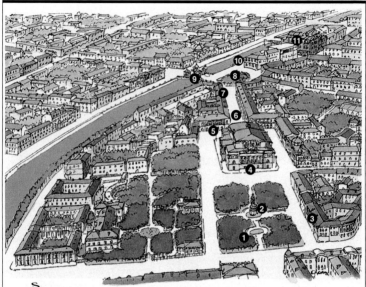

🕒 Three hours

"If God did not exist, it would be necessary to invent him." One of the famous Voltaire manuscripts in the Public Library.

OSTROVSKY SQUARE (PL. OSTROVSKOVO; площадь Гстровского) is bordered on one side by Rossi's Saltykov-Shchedrin Library ▲ *221*, and on the other by the pavilions of the Anichkov Palace ▲ *223* and its gardens. This square, even more than Arts Square, is an example of the architectural ensemble of balanced proportions and restrained ornamentation for which Rossi was famous ▲ *181*. Formerly it bore the name of the wife of Nicholas I, Alexandra; in 1923 this was changed in honor of the celebrated Russian dramatist Alexander Ostrovsky, whose most famous works were *Poverty No Vice* (1854), *The Storm* (1860) and *Snegurochka* (1873), which had been performed at the Alexandrinsky Theater.

CATHERINE II SQUARE

STATUE OF THE EMPRESS. This massive monument (over 40 feet tall) standing in the center of the square was sculpted in 1873 by Matvei Chizhov and Alexander Opekuchin, after a project by Mikhail Mikeshin. Catherine the Great is shown in her state robes, while around the plinth cluster sundry favorites and personalities of the period: the officers Suvorov ▲ *252*, Rumantsev, Orlov ▲ *184* and Chichagov, the statesmen Potyomkin ▲ *251*, Bezborodko and Betskoy, the poet Derzhavin and Princess Dashkova, President of the Academy of Sciences.

ALEXANDRINSKY THEATER ★

Known as the Pushkin Theater during the Soviet era, the Alexandrinsky Theater (ALEXANDRINSKY THEATR; Александринский театр) was built in 1832, to a project by Carlo Rossi in the Russian classical style ● *86*. It was named in honor of the Empress Alexandra Fyodorovna. The troupe at this theater, one of the oldest in Russia, was founded in 1756 during the reign of Elizabeth I ● *36*. In 1836 it staged the first production of Gogol's *The Government Inspector*.

RUSSIAN DRAMA. The history and development of theatrical genres in Russia (classicism, Romanticism, Realism) are linked to the evolution of this theater, which became the *de facto* national dramatic academy. The repertoire during the second half of the 18th century included the works of Russian authors such as Alexander Sumarokov, Iakov Kniazhnin, Vasily Kapnist and Ivan Krylov, as well as such French masters as Corneille, Racine, Molière and

Beaumarchais. At the dawn of the 20th century the Imperial Alexandrinsky Theater turned to the new drama of Anton Chekhov, whose *Seagull* flopped badly in 1896. After the 1917 Revolution the theater actively promoted new Soviet-style plays, and today it remains one of the most popular with the St Petersburg public. Its repertoire is a blend of Russian and Western classics, along with contemporary plays. The leading actors of 1950–80, who used the title of "Artists of the People of the USSR" (Boris Freindlikh is their principal representative), are mostly still working today.

THEATER MUSEUM ★

This museum, founded in 1918, was established on the premises of the former Management of the Imperial Theaters of Russia. Its reserve was assembled from the imperial archives and from the private collections of theater personalities; today it includes over 420,000 items, all exhibited, which retrace 250 years of Russian music and theater. Among these are Bakst's sketches ● *170*. One of

the exhibits housed by the museum is a reconstruction (half its actual size) of a Constructivist stage set designed in the early 1920's for the Moscow Theater.

ORIENTAL MANUSCRIPTS
The Saltykov-Shchedrin Library possesses, among its oriental treasures, this manuscript of the *Bhagavad-Gita*.

Another special jewel of the Theater Museum is its collection of ballet shoes, which gives an idea of the technical evolution of the ballerina's art.

AGRIPPINA VAGANOVA (1879–1951)

From 1921 until her death Agrippina Vaganova reigned supreme over the dance school which was named after her in 1957. A former pupil of O. Presbrazhenskaya, E. Vazem and P. Gerst, she became the star dancer of the Mariinsky Theater ▲ *200*. Nicknamed the "Czarina of Variations", she described her teaching system in her book *The Foundations of Classical Dance* (1934). According to Vaganova all the expressive power of dance derives from the assimilation of technique combined with a rigorous mastery of the body and of the positioning of the feet and hands.

COLLECTIONS. The museum also displays the personal archives of Marius Petipa, Maria Savina and Fyodor Shalyapin (including the jeweled robe that he wore as Boris Godunov), along with the autographed musical scores of Nikolai Rimsky-Korsakov, letters of Piotr Tchaikovsky and projects for costumes and décors of many different periods throughout the history of Russian theatrical production. The museum's collection of costumes is one of the world's largest, and includes, among others, those of SLEEPING BEAUTY (1890).

FOR MUSIC LOVERS. In the evenings people crowd into the museum's small concert hall. The piano on which Tchaikovsky once played bursts into sound; recordings of former stars are played; contemporary artists perform, and videos of the greatest ballets and operas are screened.

ROSSI STREET

VAGANOVA CHOREOGRAPHIC SCHOOL. In 1737 the dance teacher of St Petersburg's Polish aristocracy, the Frenchman Jean-Baptiste Landet, who had danced professionally in Paris and Dresden and had been master of ballet in Stockholm, suggested to the Empress Anna Ivanovna that a dance school should be founded to train the leading dancers of the imperial court's ballet troupe. In 1738 Her Majesty's Dance School was inaugurated, exclusively for children of Russian families of modest means. The first class was made up of twelve girls and twelve boys. The best pupils of this first generation (1742) soon demonstrated a mastery of their art which astonished everyone. In the 19th century the director Charles Didelot ● 71 was replaced by Marius Petipa ▲ 200, who formed a strong pedagogical team. Since that time the school has regularly sent its pupils on to glittering careers on the Russian stage. The School of St Petersburg has exercised a very powerful influence on the development of European and American ballet; indeed the ballet of the 20th century would have been considerably the poorer had it not been for such figures as George Balanchine, Rudolph Nureyev, Natalia Makarova, Anna Pavlova, Tamara Karsavina and Mikhail Baryshnikov, brilliant choreographers and dancers who were trained at the Vaganova Choreographic School.

ROSSI STREET
The height of the buildings and the width of Rossi Street are exactly equal (66 feet), while the length of it (660 feet) is exactly ten times this. It was laid out by Carlo Rossi between 1828 and 1834, and was originally known as Theater Street.

LOMONOSOV SQUARE

Rossi Street leads on to another of that architect's projects, Lomonosov Square (PL. LOMONOSOV; пл. ломоносова). The austerity of the buildings here accorded well with the use that was made of them, prior to the Revolution, by the Ministry of Public Instruction and the Interior Ministry. At that time the square was named after Peter the Great's companion-in-arms, Chernyshev. In the middle of the square stands a bust of Mikhail Lomonosov ● 53 by Sabello (1892).

TOVSTONOGOV THEATER
The Tovstonogov was one of the first post-Revolutionary theaters in the city. Its inaugural play, performed in 1919, was Schiller's Don Carlos; later its repertoire included contemporary pieces such as Mayakovsky's The Bedbug and The Bath-House (both 1929). The theater originally bore the name of one of its founders, Maxim Gorky, before adopting that of Tovstonogov, the director who ran it from 1956 onward.

LOMONOSOV BRIDGE ● 90. Formerly the turrets of this bridge concealed the chains used for raising and lowering its ramp. Today the turrets are purely ornamental. The Lomonosov Bridge was identical to another bridge further along the Fontanka, opposite the Anichkov Palace, before the latter was reconstructed and provided with its celebrated horses ▲ 222.

FONTANKA EMBANKMENT

To the right, on the way down the Fontanka Embankment (NAB. REKI FONTANKI; наб. реки юнтанки), is the Press Building, the offices of several newspapers and at one time the *Leningrad Pravda*'s nerve center. Beside it stands the Tovstonogov Theater ● 69.

Details of the various bridges spanning
St Petersburg's canals.

FROM THE FONTANKA TO INSURRECTION SQUARE

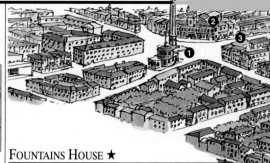

🕐 Half a day

FOUNTAINS HOUSE ★

On the Fontanka Embankment the regularity of the 19th-century façades is broken by a green park, at the end of which is Fountains House (no. 34) (FONTANNY DOM; Фонтанный дом).

SHEREMETEV PALACE. In 1712 Marshal Sheremetev was allotted a large building site beside the river, where he erected a wooden country house. This was replaced in the 1730's by a stone house. In 1750–5 the architect Argunov, who came from a family of serfs famous for their artistic talents, added a floor to the palace and transformed its façades, giving it its present aspect. The central façade of the main building was heightened by the addition of a mezzanine and a semicircular pediment.

MUSIC AND CULTURE. Many famous writers, artists and intellectuals have lived and worked in Fountains House, beginning with the actress Prascovia Kovaleva (Zhemchugova), who married Nikolai Sheremetev in 1801. From the mid-18th century to the 1870's the house was the venue for the concerts of the Sheremetevs' Capella, which was one of the best private choirs in Russia and greatly admired by such figures as Glinka, Liszt and Berlioz. After the Revolution the house was used by a series of different organizations and its interior was much altered. A few years ago it was reallocated to the State Museum of Theater and Music, which is currently restoring the prestige of this former center of musical and cultural life. For the moment an exhibition on "The Sheremetev Family and St Petersburg's Musical Culture" occupies two rooms here.

AKHMATOVA MUSEUM. (MUZEY ANNY AKHMATOVOI; музей Анны Ахматовой). The poet Anna Akhmatova lived from 1924 to 1952 in the apartment on the third floor of the south wing, overlooking the courtyard. During the 1920's this place was frequented by poets, painters and writers, among them Mayakovsky, Tatlin, Lebeder and Tyrssa. Akhmatova's rooms were made into a museum in 1989; one of them has been redecorated to look as it would have appeared between 1938 and 1941. Here Akhmatova's husband and later her son were arrested. In the other room a display of her poetry explains how she won so important a place in the history of Russian society, culture and literature between 1910 and 1960. There is also a portrait of the poet by Modigliani, executed during a visit to Paris in 1911.

HOUSE OF LETTERS

The house that was situated at the intersection of Nevsky Prospekt and the Fontanka Embankment (nos. 40–60) was entirely destroyed during the siege of World War Two ● *50* but subsequently rebuilt. The critic Vissarion Bielinsky lived here from 1842, in what was known during the 19th century as the "House of Letters". Bielinsky was an influential journalist, and had a powerful effect on the younger generation of writers. He gathered around him a circle of Russia's intellectual avant-garde which included the writers Nekrasov, Turgenev, Grigorovich and Dostoevsky. Today the house is used by the regional tax office.

VISSARION BIELINSKY (1811–48)
Bielinsky's ideas about the condition of the people and the role of Russian writers are expressed in his letter to Gogol, which was clandestinely circulated among the intelligentsia. Dostoevsky spent four years in a labor camp and six years in exile in Siberia, partly because he had read this letter.

237

BELOSELSKY-BELOZERSKY PALACE

In the mid-18th century the house of Prince Shakhoskoy was bought by Myatlev, the head of the Assignat bank. It was subsequently altered by the classical architect Thomas de Thomon and became the palace of Prince Beloselsky-Belozersky. The new owners were wealthy and famous, members of a family which went back to Vladimir Monomachus, the great Kievan prince. Their double-barrelled name originated in 1798, when Paul I gave Beloselsky the right to use the name of Belozersky, in recognition of his ancestors' services to Russia. The palace was rebuilt between 1846 and 1848 by the architect Shtakenshneider ▲ *183*. From 1898 to 1917 it belonged to the imperial family; one of its last owners was the son of Alexander II, Prince Sergei Alexandrovich, who took part in the assassination of Rasputin. Following the Revolution, the palace became the headquarters of a local branch of the Communist Party, but it is now a business center, and also holds exhibitions. Its Rococo exterior and red façade make the palace one of the most striking buildings on the Nevsky Prospekt. Two houses along from the Palace can be found the Galitzine Memorial Library, the Mayakovsky Library of Foreign Literature, the Goethe Institute and the British Council.

MUNICIPAL CULTURE CENTER
After the Revolution the Beloselsky Palace was occupied for a while by the Communist Party's regional committee. Today it is the Municipal Culture Center. The Hall of Mirrors and the Oak Room (the former private theater of the palace) are used for plays and concerts, while other parts of the building provide exhibition areas for classical and contemporary art.

VLADIMIR SQUARE
Vladimir Prospekt leads to the square of the same name, whose buildings form a circle around the Vladimir Church (dedicated to the Virgin and Saint John of Damascus).

VLADIMIR PROSPEKT

OPEN THEATER (OTKRYTY TEATR; Открытый театр). This single-story building (no. 2) has a striking façade with an eight-column portico, Ionic pilasters and masks. It was built in the 1820's by the architect Mikhailov as a mansion for the Korsakov family. After the Revolution it was occupied by a number of different theatrical institutions. Today it is the Open Theater of St Petersburg, under the direction of Igor Vladimirov.
LITTLE (MALY) DRAMATIC THEATER ● *69*. At no. 18 Rubinshteina Street is the Little

Theater (MALY DRAMATICHESKY TEATR), which has gained worldwide fame under the direction of Lev Dodin.

VLADIMIR SQUARE (VLADIMIRSKAYA PL.; Владимирская пл). The first church in the center of this square was built in 1747 and replaced in 1761 by a stone building. The anonymous architect may have been Trezzini, who worked under Rastrelli. In 1783 a two-story bell tower was erected alongside it by Quarenghi; in 1848 the architect Ruska added two further stories. Closed since 1932, the Vladimir Church has been reopened by the Russian Orthodox authorities.

RIMSKY-KORSAKOV MUSEUM

The famous composer lived for the last fifteen years of his life at no. 28 Zagorodny Prospekt. In 1971 his apartment was transformed into a museum (MUSEY-KVARTIRA RIMSKOVO-KORSAKOVA; музей-квартира Римского-Корсакова). The vestibule, study, salon and dining room here recreate the atmosphere of what was one of the centers of St Petersburg culture, where Rimsky-Korsakov held his musical evenings, the "Korsakov Wednesdays". Glazunov, Lyadov, Rachmaninov, Teneyev and Shalyapin all attended these events. Today an entire room is devoted to musical life in St Petersburg in the late 19th and early 20th centuries, and every Wednesday meetings of singers and musicians are once more held in the concert room. In this apartment Rimsky-Korsakov wrote over forty romances, in addition to his *Principles of Orchestration*, *Chronicle of My Musical Life* and the operas *Sadko*, *The Czar Saltan*, *The Czar's Bethrothed* and *Kashtshey the Immortal*.

"LOUSE EXCHANGE"
The intersection of Nevsky Prospekt, Vladimir Prospekt and Liteiny Prospekt used to be known as the "Louse Exchange"; porters and craftsmen looking for work used to gather here, along with itinerant barbers who sat their clients on stools to cut their hair.

RIMSKY-KORSAKOV (1844–1908)
● 72. The composer's name is closely linked with the Conservatoire, where he taught the composition class.

DOSTOEVSKY MUSEUM ★

This museum (MUSEY-KVARTIRA F.M.
DOSTOYEVSKOVO; музей-квартира Ф.
М. Достоевского) was opened in 1971,
ninety years after the death of Dostoevsky
▲ 206. The apartment had to be
reconstituted, but its atmosphere remains
faithful to the personality of the master and
to the spirit of his time.

A WRITER'S PRIVACY. Dostoevsky lived in this
apartment on two occasions (for a few months in 1846,
and during the last years of his life) with his wife Anna
Grigorievna and their two children, Lyuba and Fedya. Here
he wrote his celebrated *Discourse on Pushkin*, as well as *The
Brothers Karamazov*. Dostoevsky liked his study (above)
because it was spacious and isolated from the rest of the
apartment. The place was austere and ascetic. Above the sofa
on which he slept is a reproduction of Raphael's *Virgin of
Saint Sixtus*, a painting he especially loved. Beyond the
windows are the domes of the Vladimir Church, of which he
was a parishioner. The streets and the passers-by in this
district still compose the same ". . . inexhaustible, magnificent
almanac, which one can leaf through in one's spare moments,
when one is bored, after a meal . . .".

MARATA STREET

MUSEUM OF THE ARCTIC AND ANTARCTIC (MUZEY ARKTIKI I
ANTARKTIKI; музей Арктики и Антарктики). The former
St Nicholas Church is the only building of the United
Schismatics (a branch of the Old Believers ● 56) which
remains intact at St Petersburg; it was closed in 1932 to make
way, in 1937, for the Museum of the Arctic and Antarctic,
which houses, among other exhibits, stuffed polar wildlife and
items from expeditions. Today there is a project to return the
church to the Old Believers and move the museum elsewhere.

NEVSKY PROSPEKT

On the section of Nevsky Prospekt between Liteiny and
Vladimir prospekts and Marata Street is a series of apartment
blocks dating from the second half of the 19th century and
early 20th century. At no. 60 lived the satirical writer Mikhail
Saltykov-Shchedrin ▲ 221; in 1815 Vladimir Zhukovsky, the
translator of English, French and German poetry, lived at
no. 82.

**RADISHCHEV
(1749–1802)**
This celebrated
writer, the first
thoroughgoing
Russian dissident,
lived at no. 14 Marata
Street from 1775 to
1790. He was
arrested, imprisoned
at the Peter and Paul
Fortress, and sent to
Siberia on the orders
of Catherine II for his
revolutionary *Voyage
from Petersburg to
Moscow*. Freed in
1796 by Paul I, he was
amnestied in 1801 by
Alexander I, but
killed himself in 1802.

ACTORS' HOUSE. This building (no. 86), with its white-columned portico, is known in St Petersburg as the Actors' House. It unites several theatrical associations, such as the Union of Theater Workers, the Russian Theater Society and the Stanislavsky Palace of the Arts. Built in the 18th century as a private mansion, then reconstructed between 1820 and 1830 by the architects Ovsianikov and Fossati, it belonged in the 19th century to the Yusupov family, who organized concerts and exhibitions there. Today the Actors' House still mounts soirées, seminars, conferences, and exhibitions of theater décor as well as international festivals and competitions.

"NEVSKY PALACE". No. 57, opposite the Actors' House, was built in 1861 by the architect Langé and belonged to the craft school of Czarevich Nicholas ● *36*. It was formerly the Renommée Hotel, which rented furnished rooms, before it became the Hermès and finally the Baltic Hotel at the end of World War Two. It was restored in 1993, and is today a luxury establishment.

SAMOILOV MUSEUM. In the same block as the Nevsky Palace, on the Groom Street side, is the Samoilov family museum which was opened 1994. From 1869 onward a number of famous actors, composers, painters and writers frequented this house.

PUSHKIN STREET

On a square halfway down Pushkin Street (PUSHKINSKAYA UL.; Пушкинскя ул.) is a statue of the writer, which was the first to be erected to him in St Petersburg. It is the work of the sculptor Opekushin, who was also responsible for the Moscow statue of Pushkin (1880), this monument was unveiled in 1884.

NO. 10 PUSHKIN STREET. Today a number of artists inhabit this derelict house. As representatives of alternative culture in St Petersburg they organize exhibitions, entertainments and concerts in the courtyards of the building and in the street outside. The creative drive behind this unusual center is currently a popular phenomenon in St Petersburg.

St Petersburg
IN THE MOVIES

THE LAST YEARS OF THE EMPIRE
The first Russian production company was founded in 1907. St Petersburg at that time appears (with the help of Czarist censors) as a 19th-century city, a sumptuous décor perfect for adaptations such as *The Queen of Spades* (1916) by Iakov Protozanov, the greatest director of the early Russian cinema.

MAX LINDER AT ST PETERSBURG
Max Linder, immensely popular in Russia, came to St Petersburg in 1913. The public flocked to see his movie, which ended with a ballooning scene. Then the theater lights came on, and Linder himself appeared on the end of a rope, as if he had come in through the roof.

St Petersburg's first cinema was established on the Nevsky Prospekt, on the initiative of the Lumière brothers. Although Moscow was the cinematic capital of Russia under the Czars, St Petersburg was an inspiration to a number of directors and developed a distinct cinema tradition of its own. Today directors no longer seem threatened by censors, but the new economic situation of the Russian cinema is making movie production extraordinarily difficult.

FILMING LENINGRAD
Certain Soviet directors rapidly established their "Leningrad" credentials, notably Kozintzev and Trauberg. Ermler (with Johanson) was mainly concerned to film a city transformed by socialism (*Ruins of Empire*, 1929).

THE FIRST MOVIE SHOWING
This was held on May 4, 1896 at the Aquarium Theater, and was organized by the Lumière brothers.

HOLLYWOOD'S ST PETERSBURG

In 1927 Greta Garbo played Anna Karenina in Goulding's movie. Seven years later Marlene Dietrich marched through Sternberg's unreal Peterhof (*The Scarlet Empress*). More recently American stars have ventured into revolutionary Petrograd (Warren Beatty in *Reds*).

John **GILBERT**

Greta Garbo in **LOVE**

An Edmund Goulding PRODUCTION
from the novel
AnnaKarenina *by* Lyof N.Tolstoi

A Metro-Goldwyn-Mayer PICTURE

FAR FROM ST PETERSBURG

With the Russian vogue of the 1930's pasteboard Petersburgs sprang up like mushrooms. Harry Borg played a disquieting Rasputin in the French movie *La Tragédie Impériale* (1938).

LENFILM

The recasting of the Leningrad studios under the name of Lenfilm in 1936 (the name has survived to this day) sounded the death-knell of their creative insolence. Experimentation was definitely out of favor when Heifitz and Zarkhy filmed *The Baltic Deputy* (1936).

THE CITY OF REVOLUTION

For its epics the Soviet cinema often used the streets of Leningrad. Crowds of extras, directed by Eisenstein, flooded past in his theoretical and disturbing *October* (1927).

INSURRECTION SQUARE
In 1909 a statue of Alexander III by Trubetskoy was erected in the center of the square; at the time this monumental sculpture ▲ *184* was nicknamed "The Scarecrow".

LIGOVSKY PROSPEKT

Nevsky Prospekt intersects Ligovsky Prospekt (LIGOVSKI PR.; Лиговский пр.), laid out in the late 19th century on a part of the canal of that name, now filled in, which fed the fountains in the Summer Garden ▲ *186*. In the 18th and 19th centuries this street was famous for its queues of carriages, its supply of drinks, its tea-rooms, taverns and cheap hotels.

OCTOBER CONCERT HALL. At the head of the Prospekt there used to be a remarkable Greek Orthodox church. This was built between 1861 and 1866 in a Byzantine style that was highly unusual for St Petersburg. Closed down in the late 1930's, it was demolished in 1961 and replaced by the October Concert Hall (1967).

INSURRECTION SQUARE

BREAD MUSEUM
At no. 73 Nevsky Prospekt is an industrial bakery; on the fourth floor is the Bread Museum. The exhibition here traces the history of breadmaking from the foundation of St Petersburg, and describes the various uses to which bread has been put over the centuries.

INSURRECTION SQUARE (PL. VOSTANIYA; пл. Восстания) was the original terminal point of Nevsky Prospekt before it was extended to the Alexander Nevsky Monastery ▲ *253*. It was the scene of some of the most violent encounters between police and demonstrators during the February Revolution.

FROM THE CHURCH TO THE METRO. Until 1918 this square was called Our Lady of the Sign, after the church built here by Elizabeth I in 1767. At the close of the 18th century it was decided that the original wooden church should be replaced by a stone one, whose foundations were laid in 1794; thereafter the works took ten years to complete. The result was a five-domed church dominating the square. It remained in use until 1938 but was demolished in 1940. Today its place is taken by the Ploshchad Vostaniya metro station.

MOSCOW STATION (MOSKOVSKY VOKZAL; Московский вокзал). The inauguration on November 1, 1851 of the railway linking St Petersburg with Moscow was a momentous event in the life of the capital. The original Nicholas Station was designed by Thon. The central part of its grand green and white façade was decorated on two levels, with Corinthian columns, and now this is all that remains of the old building, as it has now been completely modernized inside. In 1967 a bust of Lenin was placed in the main hall on a monumental pedestal, and on its walls were inscribed the decree of the second Party Congress of 1924 which changed Petrograd to Leningrad ● *33*. Now that the city has reassumed its original name the bust of Lenin has been replaced by that of Peter the Great. For St Petersburg's statues "musical chairs" has always been the norm.

FROM SMOLNY
TO THE ALEXANDER NEVSKY
MONASTERY

SMOLNY

Suvorov Avenue leads to the remarkable Smolny architectural complex. Behind the Dictatorship of the Proletariat Gardens rises the austere yellow and white façade of the Smolny Institute, while to the left, behind the trees, rise the Baroque domes of the Cathedral and Monastery. The origin of the name Smolny goes back to the time of Peter the Great. Until 1723 this site was occupied by the Smolny Dvor (tar depot), where tar was prepared and stored for caulking ships' timbers ▲ *192*.

DICTATORSHIP OF THE PROLETARIAT SQUARE (PL. PROLETARSKOY; пл. Пролетарской Диктатуры Diktatury). The access to the Smolny Institute, which played so prominent a role in the Revolution, had to be on a par with its symbolic importance; this, at any rate, is what the architects Vladimir Shchuko and Vladimir Guelfreikh must have thought when they erected their massive neoclassical propylaea ● *88* (1923–4) on either side of the main thoroughfare, and complemented them ten years later with a rectilinear garden. In the garden the architects installed busts of Karl Marx and Friedrich Engels, sculpted by Sergei Yevseyev.

SMOLNY MONASTERY AND CATHEDRAL (SBOR SMOLNOVO-MONASTYRIA; собор Смольного-Монастыря) ★. A convent at Smolny was first founded by the Empress Elizabeth I ● *36*, who decided to take the veil toward the end of her life. The project (a maquette of it is on display at the Academy of Arts ▲ *162*), which was designed by Rastrelli and begun in 1748, originally allowed for a 420-foot bell tower. Catherine II, once she was on the throne, sacked the Italian architect in 1764 and founded a school for young ladies in the convent.

⏲ One day

A LAVISH CATHEDRAL ● *85*
The cathedral as completed by Vasily Stasov in 1835 preserves the style of Rastrelli, in which the ornamental exuberance of Baroque includes purely Russian elements such as the five onion domes.

247

▲ LENIN AND THE REVOLUTION

For taking part in an illegal political meeting the
seventeen-year-old student Vladimir Ilyich
Ulyanov was arrested, banned from the
University and exiled to a distant village in
Kazan. Thus began Lenin's life as a dedicated
revolutionary. By 1916 he was living in Zurich
and had despaired of any revolution in his
lifetime; the spontaneous rising of the Russian
masses in October 1917 came as a total surprise
to him.

A CLANDESTINE EXISTENCE
Lenin lived clandestinely in
St Petersburg during the 1905–7
Revolution ● *44* and in the same
city (by then named Petrograd)
under the Kerensky regime from
July 5 to October 25, 1917. Left,
Lenin disguised as a worker, under
the name of K. Ivanov.

APRIL 1917
Lenin outlined his
program at the Tauride
Palace in April 1917. He
declared the "Tasks of
the Proletariat" to be of
the utmost urgency; and
to the astonishment of
his listeners he proposed
an immediate end to the
war, the overthrow of
the government, and the
handing over of all
political power to the
soviets.

**LENIN AT THE
SMOLNY INSTITUTE**
Lenin arrived at the
headquarters of the
Petrograd Soviet, the
Smolny Institute, on
the evening of
October 24, 1917 to
direct the coup d'état.
He stayed there until
the government left
for Moscow on March
11, 1918. He ran the
Council of People's
Commissars within
the Palace, wrote, and
received delegations
and journalists;
among the latter was
J. Reed, author of a
celebrated account of
the October
Revolution, *Ten Days
that Shook the World*.

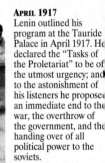

POWER TO THE BOLSHEVIKS

On October 25, 1917, at 10.40pm, even as the attack on the Winter Palace ● *44* was under way, the Second Pan-Russian Congress of Soviets opened at Smolny. The Mensheviks and right-wing Socialist Revolutionaries disapproved of Lenin's coup d'état. They proposed to open talks with the Provisional Government, with a view to setting up a democracy. After a short, violent debate they walked out in a body, abandoning the field to the Bolsheviks.

BACK IN PETROGRAD

In July 1920 Lenin took part in the Second Congress of the Komintern at the Tauride Palace. The same month he sent a message to Stalin, then fighting at Kharkov: "The situation in the Komintern is excellent. Zinoviev, Bukharin and I believe that we should immediately encourage the Revolution in Italy. In my view, we should first Sovietize Hungary and perhaps the Czech state and Romania. This requires mature consideration. Let us know your conclusion."

LENIN'S TRAGEDY

On May 25, 1922 Lenin fell ill, with a paralyzed right arm and leg and acute aphasia. He returned to work in October, but by December was once more confined to his bed. His health declined progressively thereafter, and he was cut off from the levers of power within the Kremlin.

THE DEIFICATION OF LENIN

Krupskaya, Lenin's wife, entreated the Politburo in vain not to embalm his body but to bury it as he had wished.

249

NIKOLAI KARAMZIN (1766–1826)
The great historian and writer Nikolai Karamzin spent the final years of his life at the Tauride Palace.

SMOLNY INSTITUTE (SMOLNY INSTITUT; Смольный институт) ★. This long neoclassical building, built by Quarenghi in 1806–8, was a school for young ladies until August 1917, at which time the Soviet of Workers' and Soldiers' Deputies of Petrograd ● *46* was installed there. On October 24, 1917, in the evening, Lenin arrived to seize control of the insurrection. The long corridors of the Institute swarmed with Red Guards, soldiers, sailors and factory delegates seeking weapons, tracts or newspapers. On October 25, while the fighting was still going on, the Second Pan-Russian Congress of Soviets opened, at 10.40pm in the Lecture Hall. At 3.10am the delegates greeted the news of the fall of the Winter Palace with wild cheering. That evening they ratified the decrees proposed by Lenin on peace and land ownership, as well as on the formation of the Council of People's Commissars. The Council, headed by Lenin, operated from Smolny until it was moved to Moscow in March 1918. Since 1991 the Institute has housed the offices of the Mayor of St Petersburg, but one can still visit the historic Lecture Hall, Lenin's study and the bedroom he occupied with his wife, Nadezhda Krupskaya. There is also a permanent exhibition about the Institute as it was at the time of Catherine II.

THE FIRST KUNSTKAMMER
After Kikin's death his palace was used for the Kunstkammer, Peter the Great's assemblage of curiosities. Here was displayed a collection bought from the Dutch anatomist Frederik Ruysch (1717), a specialist in embalming. In 1727 the Kunstkammer was transferred to Vasilyevsky Island ▲ *160*.

KIKIN PALACE

At the Stavropol intersection stands one of the oldest buildings in St Petersburg, the palace of the Boyar Alexander Kikin. Kikin was an opponent of Peter the Great's policies who supported the Czarevich Alexei in his doomed attempt to overthrow the Emperor ● *39*. After fleeing to Austria on the advice of Kikin the Czarevich returned to Russia in January 1718 and was condemned to death a few months later. Most of the people he denounced as his accomplices, among them Kikin, were executed. Nowadays the Kikin Palace building houses a music school.

TAURIDE PALACE

Nearby, on the left-hand side of Shpalernaya Street, runs the 760-foot yellow façade of the Tauride Palace (TAVRICHESKY DVORETS; Таврический дворец), which has a stark Doric pediment crowned by a green dome. Constructed between 1783 and 1789, this was one of the first classical buildings in Russia ● 86.

POTEMKIN'S REWARD. Catherine II was much given to showering palaces on her favorite, Prince Potemkin. After presenting him with the Anichkov Palace ▲ 222 she had the Tauride Palace built for him, modeled on the Pantheon in Rome. Scarcely was it finished than she offered to buy it back for 460,000 roubles; Potemkin, a notorious spendthrift, was always heavily in debt and needed the money. In February 1791, on his return from Iasi, the former capital of Moldavia, where he had negotiated an advantageous peace with the Turks, Catherine gave the palace to Potemkin a second time. He used it to throw parties of legendary extravagance.

OTHER OCCUPANTS. After Prince Potemkin's death the Tauride in 1792 was decreed an imperial palace. When the Empress died Paul I revenged himself on his mother and her favorite by stripping the place bare and converting it into a

barracks. The Column Room was converted into a stable, and its furnishings and works of art were moved to the Mikhail Castle ▲ 229. Alexander I had the palace restored by Luigi Rusca (1802–4).

FROM THE DUMA TO THE SOVIETS. After the February Revolution ● 46 the left wing of the palace was occupied by the Soviet of the Workers and Soldiers of Petrograd, while the right wing was used by the Committee of the Duma which formed the Provisional Government. The Tauride Palace was later used as the Leningrad Higher Party School before becoming the seat of the local parliaments.

TAURIDE GARDENS. (TAURICHESKI SAD; Таврический сад). Although probably not as luxuriant today as in Potemkin's time these gardens are still a pleasant place to walk. In winter its avenues are used by cross-country skiers.

POTEMKIN, PRINCE OF THE TAURIDE
The Greeks called the Crimea the Tauride; they believed that its barbarian inhabitants were in the habit of burning foreigners on sight (Euripides states this categorically in his *Iphigenia*). When the Crimea was annexed to Russia in 1783 it reverted to its original name; and Potemkin, who led the campaign against the Ottomans, was named Prince of the Tauride by Catherine II. His palace, built at this time, was given the same name.

THE ASSEMBLY
Between 1906 and 1917 the Palace became the seat of the Duma ● 46.

A MAJESTIC FAÇADE
The stylistic restraint shown by the architect Starov in his design for the palace provoked the enthusiasm of the poet Gavril Derzhavin: "Its exterior is distinguished neither for its sculptures, nor its gilding ... old-fashioned, elegant good taste is the true source of its dignity and majesty."

ALEXANDER SUVOROV (1729–1800)
Alexander Suvorov was born in Moscow. His father was a general who had fought with Peter the Great. During the Russo-Turkish War (1787–91) Catherine II conferred on him the rank of Field Marshal after he crushed the Polish uprising (1794).

SUVOROV MUSEUM

The popularity of Field Marshal Alexander Suvorov made possible a nationwide subscription toward the Suvorov Military History Museum (Voenna-Istorichesky Muzey Suvorova/военно-исторический музей А. В. Суворова). In 1904 the architects Guerman Grimm and Alexander Gogen completed this building, with its enormous panels of mosaic illustrating the principal events in Suvorov's life. Inside, a selection of the general's possessions is on display, together with maps, weapons and various other items that have survived from his campaigns.

TOWARD THE MONASTERY

SUVOROV AVENUE (SUVOROVSKY PROSPEKT; Суворовский проспект). This broad thoroughfare, which leads to the Smolny District, used to be known as Elephant Avenue. In the early 18th century the Persian shahs were in the habit of sending elephants as gifts to the Russian emperors (indeed, in 1741 Nadir Shah gave a total of fourteen elephants). One of the special stables constructed for these somewhat cumbersome offerings stood by the side of today's Suvorov Avenue; it was by this route that the elephants would travel

on their way to drink from the waters of the river Neva.

NEVSKY PROSPEKT. The section of the Nevsky Prospekt ▲ 212 which leads to the Alexander Nevsky Monastery was built shortly after the foundation of the monastery; the idea behind its construction was to give the monks access to the road to Novgorod, where the metropolitan resided. Close by what has now become Insurrection Square ▲ 244 the monks' route joined with the road linking the dockyards of the Admiralty to this same Novgorod road. It was during the reign of Anna Ivanovna – in fact on April 20, 1738 – that it was finally decreed that "the great thoroughfare from the Admiralty to the Nevsky Monastery should be called the Nevsky Prospekt".

ALEXANDER NEVSKY
The battle that took place beside the Neva in 1240 won its victor the sobriquet of Alexander Nevsky.

ALEXANDER NEVSKY MONASTERY

BY PETER'S WILL. In 1710 Peter the Great built the Alexander Nevsky Monastery (ALEKSANDRO-NEVSKY LAVRA; Александро-Невская Лавра) in honor of Prince Alexander Novgorod, on the site of his victory over the Swedes in 1240. The construction work began in 1712, and by the following year a wooden church had been consecrated and monks had moved in. After the death of Peter the Great the works continued, but the building was not completed until the last years of the 18th century, during the reign of Catherine II. In addition to the St Petersburg monastery there are other *lavras* (great monasteries) at Pechersky (Kiev, Ukraine), Trinity-St-Sergei (Zagorsk) and Pochaevsky-Uspensk (Volhynia, Ukraine).

TOURING THE MONASTERY. In the recess of the curving monastery wall rises the dome of the main entrance, built between 1783 and 1785 by the architect Ivan Starov. Once through the gateway arch you will see beyond the walls surrounding them the Lazarus cemetery (on the left) and the Tikhvin cemetery (on the right). Some of the tombstones here are the work of famous sculptors, such as Ivan Martos and Mikhail Kozlovsky, and the graves of many of the country's most famous composers, including Tchaikovsky, Borodin, Glinka and Rimsky-Korsakov, are located in Tikhvin Cemetery.

LAZARUS CEMETERY (LAZAREVSKAYE KLADBISHCHE; Лазаревское кладбище). The Lazarus Cemetery is the oldest cemetery in St Petersburg. It was inaugurated in 1716 with the burial of Natalia Alexeyevna, who was the much-loved sister of Peter the Great. Later it was mainly used for the deceased of the great aristocratic families, but it also harbors the remains of such luminaries as the encyclopedist Mikhail Lomonosov (1711–65), the architects Adrian Zakharov (1761–1811), Carlo Rossi ▲ *181*, Giacomo Quarenghi (1744–1817), Andrei Voronikhin (1759–1814), as well as Thomas de Thomon ● *87*, who had been appointed court architect in 1802.

🕓 Two hours

TIKHVIN CEMETERY (Tikvinskoye Kladbishche; Тихвинское кладбище). Also called the Artists' Necropolis. A number of major Russian artists are buried here, including Dostoevsky ▲ *207*.

RELICS OF ALEXANDER NEVSKY
In 1742 Peter the Great decided to move the relics of Alexander Nevsky (then in the town of Vladimir) to St Petersburg. To begin with they were displayed at the Church of the Annunciation, and then transferred to Trinity Cathedral in 1790, where they were placed in a silver sarcophagus (now at the Hermitage).

CHURCH OF THE ANNUNCIATION
(BLAGOVESHCHENSKAYA TSERKOV; Благовещенская церковь). The avenue between the two cemeteries crosses a small canal (which joins the Obvodny "lateral" canal, built between 1805 and 1834, to the southward) and leads on to the Monastery entrance.

The Church of the Annunciation, which lies immediately to the left, is the oldest in the Monastery. Built between 1717 and 1725 by Domenico Trezzini, it was from the start used as a burial place for major figures such as Vasily Dolgoruky, who traveled to Europe with Peter the Great; Alexei Razumovsky, the morganatic husband of the Empress Elizabeth; Ivan Shuvalov (who was another celebrated favorite of the Czarina's); and the great strategist Field Marshal Alexander Suvorov ▲ 252. At Suvorov's funeral on December 6, 1800, his coffin appeared to be too wide to be able to pass through the door, but one of the soldiers carrying the bier gave the order: "Forward! Nothing ever stopped Suvarov!" and somehow they managed to force it through. Today the church contains a part of the collection belonging to the Sculpture Museum, which was installed in the Monastery during the Soviet era. Among the items on display are maquettes of a variety of different monuments and statues of St Petersburg (including the Alexander Column ▲ 181 and the Monument to Peter I ▲ 194).

LAVISH DECORATION
The interior décor of Trinity Cathedral contains an altar of marble and agate, and walls covered in copies of works by Guercino, Van Dyck, Rubens and such Russian painters and other masters as Grigory Ugriumov, Marcin Bielsky and Nikolai Utkin.

TRINITY CATHEDRAL (TROITSKY SOBOV; Троицкий собор). A church built by Schwertfeger originally stood on this site, but its walls were so fissured that in 1753 Elizabeth Petrovna ● 37 ordered its demolition. The stones were reused to pave Nevsky Prospekt; and the subsequent cathedral was built by Ivan Starov (1778–90) with a restrained pediment, colonnade and single dome, in the classical style. It is the only place of worship in the Monastery precinct still open for services. Behind it stretches the St Nicholas Cemetery (NIKOLSKOYE), where many prominent personalities from the Soviet era are buried.

FEDOROVSKAYA CHURCH (FEDOROVSKAYA TSERKOV; Федоровская церковь). This church (right), built between 1742 and 1750 by Trezzini, to the south of Trinity Cathedral, was also used as a mausoleum for the last kings and princes of Georgia.

PALACES ON THE OUTSKIRTS OF ST PETERSBURG

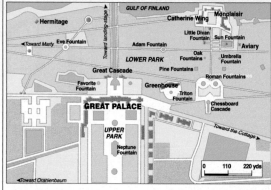

Half a day

STRELNA
On the way to Peterhof note (on the right) Strelna Palace (early 18th century), along with the grand-ducal residences of Mikhailovka and Znamenka, built for the sons of Nicholas I.

Peterhof (Петергоф), one of the oldest summer palaces in the St Petersburg region, is perhaps the most exotic of all because of its seaside situation. Like the city 20 miles away it is named for the first Emperor of Russia (Peterhof means "Peter's Court"). Peter the Great built a preliminary residence here in 1710, on a raised site overlooking the Gulf of Finland. Then, in place of this small wooden building, in which he habitually stayed on his way to Kronstadt ▲ *192*, he proceeded to construct a far bigger palace (1714), broadly sketched out by himself for the benefit of his architect Johann Braunstein.

UPPER PARK

The Upper Park (VERKHNY SAD; Верхний сад) "... is no less beautiful than that of the King of France" according to the archives. This area served as a front courtyard to the main residence of Peterhof. It was to this great palace that Peter I summoned the entire diplomatic corps to celebrate the official inauguration of what became known as the "Russian Versailles".

GREAT PALACE ★

As we see it now the Great Palace (BOLSHOY DVORETS; Большой дворец) still has the exterior planned by the Empress Elizabeth I ● *36*. After 1745 she had the initial building altered by the architect Bartolomeo Rastrelli ● 84, who, after enlarging Peter I's original palace, added to it a couple of single-floor galleries, each ending with a pavilion (a church on the east side and an armorial pavilion of the west side). He also surrounded the Upper Park with a long railing punctuated by broad pillars, later designing a formal enfilade in the purest Baroque style.

PORCELAIN EXHIBITION. The permanent exhibition of porcelain (which is mostly Russian) located on the first floor is a testament to the high level of technical mastery achieved by the imperial works at St Petersburg between 1750 and 1800.

BAROQUE STAIRCASE
The grand staircase was entirely restored in 1985.

FORMAL STAIRCASE. The stairway to the second floor is typical of the Russian Baroque period. Its décor, designed by Rastrelli in about 1750, combines richly carved and gilded elements in wood (mostly limewood) with numerous trompe l'oeil features.

CHESME HALL. Contiguous with the ballroom (recently restored) is a large space dedicated to the naval victory of Chesme (1770); this was altered by Yury Felten ● 86 to house major commemorative paintings by Hackert (1737–1807).

THRONE ROOM. In the Throne Room, alongside portraits of Russian sovereigns, is a canvas by the Danish painter Vigilius Erichsen of Catherine II on her horse Brilliant. There are also four pictures of the Battle of Chesme by Joseph Wright of Derby. The Audience Chamber, with its décor by Rastrelli, offers an interesting collection of Russian marquetry gaming tables which date from the latter part of the 18th century.

WHITE DINING ROOM ★. The table set in the White Dining Room, whose neoclassical décor was redesigned by Felten toward 1775, displays a complete set of Wedgwood china delivered from England in 1768.

CHINESE ROOMS. On either side of the Portrait Hall are extravagant Chinese Rooms decorated by Vallin de la Mothe with walls set with lacquer screens and exotic marquetry floors.

LAVISH STUCCO
The walls of the White Dining Room are decorated with white stucco bas-reliefs.

FOUNTAINS AT PETERHOF

The wide variety of fountains at Peterhof is the principal feature of the park. Elsewhere (notably at Versailles) all the surviving fountains are classical in design; not so at Peterhof, where their extravagance and sheer playfulness give us a vivid idea of the atmosphere that must have reigned in a park of this kind during the early 18th century. The Great Cascade, with its Samson Fountain, is the most impressive of all.

GREAT CASCADE
On the slope between the upper and lower terraces, the Great Cascade is a major feature of Peterhof. The statue of *Samson and the Lion* symbolizes the Russian victory over the Swedes at Poltava (1709).

PINE AND OAK FOUNTAINS
Here the technical skills of fountain construction are applied to living trees.

MARLY CASCADE
▲ *260*. Also called the "Golden Mountain", the Marly Cascade is made of white marble and plaques of gilded copper, which cover its successive levels.

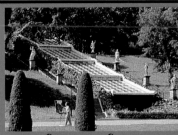

CHECKERBOARD CASCADE
The water spouts from the jaws of fierce dragons above giant sloping checkerboards.

THE SUN
The perpetually spinning sun and its silvery rays.

ROMAN FOUNTAINS
Erected in 1739 at the foot of the Checkerboard Cascade, these statues are reminiscent of those by the fountains of St Peter's in Rome. They were reconstituted in 1792; gilded bronze masks spout water from their plinths.

PORTRAIT HALL. In 1764 the Portrait Hall in the central part of the Palace was decorated by the architect Vallin de la Mothe ● *86* with a rare ensemble of 368 portraits of women painted by Count Pietro Rotari.

PARTRIDGE ROOM. The adjoining Partridge Room takes its name from its partridge-design hangings. These hangings were woven in Lyons, France, after cartoons by Philippe de la Salle.

DIVAN ROOM. In this room, whose walls are covered with Chinese silk, there stands an enormous sofa framed by a balustrade in the Turkish manner.

OAK STUDY
This room, with its carved oak boiseries after drawings by Nicolas Pineau (1684–1754), contains assorted personal possessions of Peter I.

CROWN ROOM. The Crown Room is also covered in 17th-century Chinese silk. During the 18th century the imperial crown was kept in this room when the Court was residing at Peterhof .

LOWER PARK

LOWER PARK (NIZHNY PARK; Нижний парк) was originally planted with lime trees, oaks, elms and maples from Holland, Germany, Estonia and the regions of Moscow and Novgorod. The geometrical parterres are crowded with the sculptures and fountains that were then deemed to be the essential features of any princely park. At the ends of the domain's various prospects there are pavilions designed for the pleasures of the Russian sovereigns and their courtiers.

HERMITAGE PAVILION (PAVILION ERMITAZH; павильон Эрмитаж). In the main room of the Hermitage Pavilion, used for dining, there is a mechanism which lifts the central section of the table, loaded with the dishes ordered by guests, from the first floor straight to the second floor.

MARLY PALACE (DVORETS MARLY; дворец Марли). Marly Palace, a favorite of Peter the Great, is furnished according to his own simple taste.

MONPLAISIR ★ (MONPLEZIR; Монплезир). At the far end of the Lower Park, which was surrounded by an earth dyke to protect it from flooding, the small palace of Monplaisir has a ceiling painted after drawings by Philippe Pillement (1684–1730); Monplaisir palace also has a collection of Dutch and Flemish pictures of battle scenes.

A SEA VIEW
Monplaisir, on the seafront, was a favorite with Peter the Great, who liked to spend several months out of every year there. William Coxe, visiting the palace in 1784, wrote: "We can form an idea of the austere simplicity in which this sovereign was accustomed to live . . .".

BENOIS MUSEUM
East of the Palace are former court buildings which now contain a museum dedicated to the Benois family ● 104.

CATHERINE WING (EKATERININSKY KORPUS; Екатерининский корпус). In the Catherine Wing, added to Monplaisir in the 1740's, there is a remarkable china service on display, which was made at the imperial St Petersburg works between 1809 and 1817. It is known as the Guriev Service, after the director of the factory. The gilded chandeliers in the Yellow Salon, of pasteboard and carved wood, are remarkable for their quality.

ALEXANDRIA PARK

IMPERIAL STABLES (TSARSKIE KONIUCHNI; Царские конюшни). Beyond the Benois Museum the huge former imperial stables (which are now a rest home and closed to the public) are situated. These stables are the work of the architect Nikolai Benois (1856–1928). The extraordinary neo-Gothic architecture of these buildings bears witness to the Czar Nicholas I's pronounced taste for this style.

Nicholas I's study.

GOTHIC CHAPEL (KAPELLA; капелла). By continuing toward the east through the gates of the Alexandria Park you will reach the imperial family's private oratory, a Gothic chapel built (1831–3) to a design by the Berlin architect Karl Schinkel (1781–1841).

COTTAGE (KOTTEDJ; Коттедж)★. You can reach this small pavilion (right) either by walking through Alexandria Park or by car. The cottage was constructed by the architect Adam Menelaws between 1826 and 1829, and it has now been carefully restored to display collections of objects and furniture, along with Russian porcelain and crystal in the dining room. The original stairway leads to the study of Nicholas I, from which he communicated with his fleet by semaphore. The Czarina's study has a stained-glass screen and a remarkable frieze around the bay window. Another interesting feature is the intricate star-burst ceiling of the Grand Drawing Room next door to the Czarina's study.

NEO-GOTHIC STATION. To the north of Alexandria Park stands the picturesque neo-Gothic railway station, which was built by Nikolai Benois.

❝[The Cottage] is a small house built in the new Gothic style currently fashionable in England.❞
Astolphe de Custine

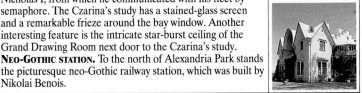

261

COURTYARD/GARDEN
Like Peterhof the Great Palace is fronted by a huge courtyard/garden surrounded by open land. Two levels of terraces and steps link it to a lower garden area.

CHINESE STUDY
The fine marquetry floors and boiseries of the Chinese Study illustrate large exotic scenes. All are by Russian master cabinet-makers.

About 25 miles from St Petersburg, not far from Peterhof ▲ *256*, is the Oranienbaum estate, which occupies a comparable sloping site and dates from exactly the same period. Originally given by Peter the Great to his companion-in-arms Alexander Menshikov ▲ *161*, it soon reverted to the Crown and was regularly embellished in the 18th century. Until recently foreign tourists were excluded from Oranienbaum, which stands directly opposite the Kronstadt Naval Base ▲ *192*. Nevertheless, it is one of the very few residences around St Petersburg which did not suffer heavily during World War Two, and has more or less remained in its original state.

GREAT PALACE

Giovanni Maria Fontana began the building works in 1710. The Great Palace (BOLSHOY DVORETS; Большой дворец) takes full advantage of its elevated position, with a central section and two single-story galleries curving round on either side to domed pavilions (a chapel to the west and a Japanese pavilion to the east). Long occupied by government bodies, the Great Palace is currently under restoration although part of the palace is now open to the public. The Japanese Pavilion has been restored.

CHINESE PALACE ★

The stucco walls and ceilings of the Chinese Palace (KITAISKY DVORETS; Китайский дворец), built by Rinaldi ● *86* in 1762, provide the background for frescos and oil paintings by Italian artists. The interior is Rococo in style, and the external architecture is of a less flamboyant Baroque.

GLASS STUDY. On the floor, once of glass, are two extraordinary "smalt" marquetry tables.

CHINESE KITCHEN. In the Chinese Kitchen and the Cavalry House, both nearby, are objects from the Far East and 17th- and 18th-century paintings.

Detail of the Glass Study in the Chinese Palace.

PETER III'S PALACE

Near the Great Palace is the Palace of Peter III (DVORETS PETRA III; дворец Петра III), to which Oranienbaum devolved in 1743. Peter III, nephew of Empress Elizabeth I ● *36* and a monarch of rabid military bent, built a fortress here called Peterstadt, where he had Russian troops parade about in German uniforms. Nothing remains of it but this small, two-story palace, constructed by Antonio Rinaldi ● *86* and decorated in Chinese style with silk hangings, lacquer paintings and dress cabinets. The Picture Hall houses Italian and Flemish paintings.

"SLIDING HILL" ★

Heading toward the sea, you come to "Sliding Hill" (PAVILION KATALNOY GORKY; павильон Катальной горки), also designed by Rinaldi (1762–74). Built on a helical plan, until the early 19th century it had an extension in the form of a 1,500-foot wooden colonnade, in the middle of which was a *montagne russe* ▲ *185* for the diversion of the court (a model of this is displayed on the first floor). From the second-floor windows you can see the island of Kronstadt, and notably the dome of its huge Byzantine-style cathedral (1902–13).

ROUND ROOM. The central salon, or Round Room, still has its original *scagliola* floor, made of powdered marble mixed to imitate colored marble marquetry.

PEARL GLASS
The Glass Study in the Chinese Palace, a masterpiece of extravagance, has eleven panels and two door lintels in pearl glass made in the workshops of the great Russian scientist and writer Mikhail Lomonosov, after whom Oranienbaum was renamed in 1948.

MEISSEN PORCELAIN
In the Porcelain Room is a rare series of Meissen figurines, which symbolize the prestige of the Russian Empire.

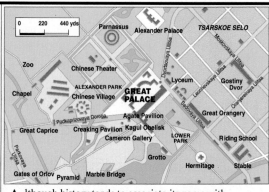

Although history tends to associate its name with Catherine the Great the palace of Tsarskoe Selo (TSARSKOÏE SELO; Царское Село) was built at the beginning of the 18th century. In 1710 Peter the Great gave his second wife, Catherine, a small property 15 miles south of St Petersburg. When Elizabeth, Catherine's daughter, came to the throne in 1741 she found the house too small; and in 1743 she commissioned Mikhail Zemtsov ● 84 to enlarge it. This he did by adding two wings, linked to the main building by single-story galleries leading to pavilions. The finished

ensemble, however, lacked unity, and in 1752 Bartolomeo Rastrelli ▲ 84 was asked to entirely redesign it. The building we see today is the result of his work, is a surprising 900 feet in breadth.

CATHERINE PALACE ★

FAÇADE. The columns, with composite capitals, are themselves supported by massive Atlas figures; they punctuate most of the bays in the façade of the Catherine Palace (BOLSHOY EKATERININSKY DVORETS; Большой Екатерининский дворец), which incorporates no fewer than five projecting and pedimented buildings. The series of diverse rooms within, restored in the 1960's, gives an idea of the development of the Russian interior through three very different epochs.

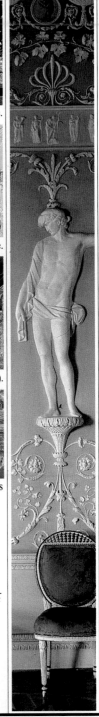

STATE STAIRCASE.
This was installed between 1860 and 1864 by Hippolyte Monighetti (1819–78) in the center of the palace. On the upper landing are folding chairs with the monogram of Elizabeth I, made in the workshops of Tula ● 60.

Catherine Palace.

GREAT HALL. Decorated in a generous Baroque style, with a painted ceiling representing "The Triumph of Russia", this immense room is the focal point of the palace as it was redesigned by Rastrelli in the late 18th century.

State Staircase.

KNIGHTS' BANQUETING HALL. In this hall the table is set with china that was made to order for Catherine II by the Gardner works in Moscow. The banqueting hall was formerly heated by a pair of enormous Dutch faience stoves.

Great Hall (detail below).

PICTURE GALLERY.
The paintings exhibited in this gallery are mostly by Flemish, Italian and French artists of the 17th and 18th centuries.

There are just under 120 works altogether, by painters such as Luca Giordano, David Teniers and Jean-Marc Nattier, which hang here side by side in the decorative spirit of the 18th century.

AMBER ROOM. The Amber Room, whose tall panels were presented to Peter the Great by the King of Prussia in 1716, is currently under restoration and is not open to the public.

FIRST APARTMENT. The rooms of the first apartment, converted by the Scottish architect Charles Cameron ● 86 for the heir to the throne Czarevich Paul Petrovich ● 37, are decorated in the neoclassical style, Catherine II's favorite. In the GREEN DINING ROOM ★ (details on the left and right of these pages) the accent is deliberately innovative; on the ceiling, which is bare of ornamentation, are ample white stucco figures in relief, alternating with tall matching antique tripods. The BEDROOM is even more surprising, with its multiple colonnettes delineating the alcove and punctuating the walls.

OLD GARDEN

All too often the visit to Tsarskoe Selo is confined to the Catherine Palace, but the park and its many pavilions hold much of interest. Below the eastern façade of the Palace extends the Old Garden (STARY SAD; Старый сад); here are the Upper and Lower Baths, built by the architect Ilya Neelov in the late 1770's.

HERMITAGE

Down from the Old Garden stands the Hermitage (ERMITAZH; павильон Эрмитаж), built by Rastrelli, where receptions were held in the summer; nearby is the Hermitage Kitchen, in a remarkably composite style.

AGATE PAVILION ★

In the vicinity of the Palace the Old Garden is delineated by two of the most interesting buildings of Tsarskoe Selo: the Agate Pavilion (AGATOVY PAVILION; Агатовый павильон) and the Cameron Gallery, both built after 1780.
COLD BATHS. The first floor of the Agate Pavilion was occupied by the Tsarina's cold baths. On the second floor the AGATE BEDROOMS open on to a hanging garden, which in turn gives access to the elegant CAMERON GALLERY. There are also a large salon and two studies with walls richly covered in semi-precious agate from the Urals, after which the pavilion is named. (These rooms are currently closed to visitors.)

CATHERINE PARK

The lower reaches of the Catherine Park (EKATERININSKY PARK; Екатерининский парк) are taken up by a lake; nearby is a series of follies.

GROTTO, OR MORNING SALON. Originally decorated with thousands of seashells, the grotto was built in the reign of Elizabeth I by Rastrelli. Catherine II liked to come here from time to time, early in the morning, after her marathon work sessions.

AROUND THE LAKE. The Turkish-inspired "Admiralty" and the Chesme Column (TCHESMENSKAYA KOLLONA; Чесменская коллонна) in the middle of the lake are succeeded by the Turkish baths built by Monighetti toward 1850. The Pyramid, where Catherine II's dogs are buried, is close to the Palladian bridge. There are more monumental features: the Orlov Gate and the impressive ruined tower designed by Yury Felten
● *86*.

UPPER GARDEN. North of the Catherine Park are the Evening Hall, the Concert Hall and the Creaking Pavilion. The Great Caprice, which is an elaborate arch standing at the end of the avenue that separates Catherine Park from Alexander Park, has a pagoda-like roof supported on Ruskeala marble columns.

ALEXANDER PARK

ALEXANDER PARK (ALEKANDROVSKY PARK; Александровский парк) is named for the Grand Duke Alexander Pavlovich, the future Alexander I and favorite grandson of Catherine II.

CHINESE VILLAGE. This echoes the pavilions described, with its painted roofs (now under restoration), its theater and its various quaint bridges, such as the cross-shaped one with four ramps.

ALEXANDER PALACE (ALEKSANDROVSKY DVORETS; Александровский дворец). This classical building, built by Quarenghi in 1792 for the future Emperor, was also the favorite residence of the last members of the imperial family (closed to the public, occupied by the Army).

KAGUL OBELISK
This monument stands opposite the side wing of Catherine Palace.

THE ARCH
On the way to the Catherine Palace you pass beneath an arch; this communicates with the Lyceum, a building converted into a school in the 19th century. The poet Pushkin was educated here.

▲ PALACES ON THE OUTSKIRTS PAVLOVSK

P avlovsk is the most elegant of the summer palaces around St Petersburg, in its decoration and the quality and quantity of the objects it contains. Although PAVLOVSK (Павловск) is barely more than a couple of miles from Tsarskoe Selo it is sometimes ignored by visitors from abroad. None the less, there is a striking contrast between the majestic aspect of the latter and the more home-like character of the former. The histories of the two palaces would have been very similar had it not been for an adventure unique in the annals of the 18th century. In

order to get away from the court, and above all to visit the capitals of Western Europe and acquire works of art for their residence, Paul Petrovich and the Grand Duchess Maria Fyodorovna set out on a tour lasting over a year. They left St Petersburg on September 19, 1781 and embarked on a 428-day journey that would take them the length and breadth of Europe, with the objective of embellishing the palace of Pavlovsk.

Paul Petrovich and Maria Fyodorovna.

PAVLOVSK
The original wooden houses on the site, known as Krik and Krak, were succeeded by two small palaces, also in wood, called Marienthal ("Maria's Valley") and Paulslust ("Paul's Joy"). These also proved inadequate, and the decision was made to build yet again. The result was what we know as Pavlovsk Palace (Pavlovsky Dvorets; Павловский дворец), much larger and in brick; it was designed by Charles Cameron ● 86, one of Catherine II's favorite architects.

GREAT PALACE

STATE APARTMENTS. The central block of the building is classical in structure. On the second floor are the apartments of Paul and Maria Fyodorovna, set around a central salon known as the Greek Hall. On the Grand Duke's side this gives on to a room called the Hall of War and on the Grand Duchess's side the Hall of Peace. The décor, which was begun by Charles Cameron ● 86, was mostly completed by Vincenzo Brenna (1740–1819), an Italian artist whom Paul and Maria Fyodorovna met in Poland on their travels.

GALLERIES. After Paul I's accession in 1796 Brenna was commissioned to enlarge the palace, now an imperial residence. He heightened the two single-story side galleries

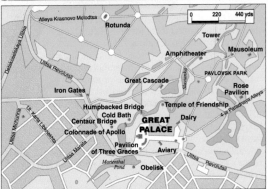

⏱ Half a day

VESTIBULE
The Vestibule (where the tour begins) was decorated by Voronikhin with twelve allegorical sculptures in the Egyptian style, very fashionable at the time. On the upper landing can still be seen the elaborate stucco décor designed by Brenna.

built by Cameron. He then added two ample pavilions to house the new Throne Room and chapel; and finally he included two other service wings, on the same quarter-circle plan.

HALL OF WAR. The carved and gilded wooden *torchères* of the Hall of War (above left) are additional tangible proof of the special talent of Russian artisans for woodwork, such as the chairs in the Greek Hall and the marquetry floors of the Grand Duchess's apartment.

BOUDOIR. The Boudoir is decorated with porphyry columns and painted pilasters brought from Italy by the royal couple (left page, center).

269

Vase from the toilet service of Maria Fyodorovna.

GRAND DUCHESS'S STATE APARTMENTS. In the apartments of Maria Fyodorovna (center) is a magnificent series of Gobelins and Savonnerie tapestries, along with a sixty-four piece toilet service in Sèvres porcelain kept in a glass cabinet opposite the bed, which was given to Paul I and the Grand Duchess by Louis XVI and Marie-Antoinette during their visit to France.

PICTURE GALLERY. In the picture gallery Russian furniture and vases relate harmoniously with European paintings and French objects in gilded bronze purchased on the orders of Paul I, who originally wanted them for his St Petersburg residence, the Mikhail Castle ▲ 229.

THE ROSE
Maria Fyodorovna dedicated a pavilion to her favorite flower, the rose, a motif which covers the chairs and everyday objects.

THRONE ROOM ★. In the Throne Room, or State Dining Room (above left), are magnificent displays of porcelain ● 64 from the various palace collections, both French (Sèvres) and Russian (St Petersburg). The dominant feature of this room is its enormous ceiling fresco by the set designer Pietro di Gottardo Gozango.

FAMILY ROOM. The Family Room on the first floor is especially touching, with personal mementos of the palace's founders, drawings of Maria Fyodorovna and a charming family portrait.

CORNER SALON. With its 1815 décor by the architect Carlo Rossi ● 86, the Corner Salon shows the evolution of taste during the reign of Alexander I.

BALLROOM. In the gay pink and blue ballroom are four major canvases by the French artist Hubert Robert, of which Paul I was particularly fond.

MUSEUM OF INTERIORS. On the third floor the Museum of Interiors exhibits a collection of Russian furniture and objects from the late 18th and 19th centuries.

" ... 1,500,000 roubles are invested in perpetuity for the upkeep of Pavlovsk .. I give to my son the Grand Duke Mikhail the castle of Pavlovsk ... the Grand Duke Mikhail will gain possession of Pavlovsk on condition that the castle, the gardens, parks, orangeries, hospital and invalids' home ... that, in a word, all the dependencies of that beautiful place, are maintained ... "
Maria Fyodorovna

> **"A HOME, A COLONNADE, A TEMPLE AT PAVLOVSK GIVE ME GREATER JOY THAN ALL THE BEAUTIES OF ITALY."**
> MARIA FYODOROVNA

PARK AT PAVLOVSK

AVIARY. Near the palace stands an aviary, designed by Cameron, in which the Grand Duchess bred her songbirds.
TEMPLE OF FRIENDSHIP. Further on is the Temple of Friendship, also built by Cameron, which symbolized the reconciliation between Paul Petrovich and Catherine II. The walls bear depictions of platonic and romantic love.

THE SLAVYANKA
On the banks of the Slavyanka, and overlooking it, are the foundation obelisk and the Marienthal staircase, formerly a landing stage.

PIL TOWER. Beyond the cast-iron bridge designed by Rossi and the amphitheater is the thatched Pil Tower.
NEW WOODS. In the New Woods overlooking the Slavyanka are the monument to Maria Fyodorovna's parents, the Duke and Duchess of Wurttemburg (their profiles appear on a marble pyramid inside) and the mausoleum of Paul I.
VANISHED PAVILIONS. Other favorite retreats of the owners of Pavlovsk (the Old Chalet, the Elizabeth Pavilion by the Slavyanka Valley, the New Chalet and the farm in the Great Star area) have disappeared since World War Two. The Great Star is formed by twelve paths which converge on a statue of Apollo at the center. A statue of a mythological figure stands at the entrance to each path.
ROSE PAVILION. This place, much loved by Maria Fyodorovna (especially after she became a widow), stands on an expanse of parkland known as the White Birch. It was here that the Dowager Empress met her son Alexander I ● *36* after his victory over Napoleon. In seventeen days the decorator Pietro Gonzaga managed to add a ballroom, dedicated to the liberator of Europe. The current restoration of this building, so dear to the creator of Pavlovsk, at a time when Russia is going through times of special difficulty, is a striking symbol of the nation's deep attachment to its history and culture.

PAVLOVSK PARK
(Pavlovsky Park; Павловский парк). The grounds of Pavlovsk, covering nearly 2,000 acres, were a major interest of Paul Petrovich and Maria Fyodorovna from the start. They beautified the estate with artificial lakes and follies. The meandering river Slavyanka served as the basis for Cameron's first landscape project.

APARTMENTS
The State Staircase leads directly to the Great Antechamber, which is followed by the Marble Dining Room and Paul I's Throne Room (the tapestries here were a gift from Louis XVI). In the White Room (below) the walls are covered in stucco by Rinaldi.

In 1766 Catherine II gave Gatchina (Гатчина) to Count Orlov. On this estate, 28 miles from St Petersburg, the architect Antonio Rinaldi ● 86 built a country residence. After 1783 Gatchina belonged to Paul Petrovich, who had it altered to some extent by Vincenzo Brenna ▲ 268. Paul I, who was always afraid of assassination, had a secret underground tunnel built, which served as an escape route leading beyond the lake to a smaller pond (where, in the 20th century, the first submarine was used). Following Paul I's assassination the palace was left empty until Nicholas I ordered its restoration in 1844.

GATCHINA PALACE

State bedroom of Maria Fyodorovna (right).

ENGLISH GARDEN
An English garden was fashioned from the original hunting estate, described by Orlov in a letter to Rousseau: "Sixty versts from St Petersburg I have a property where the knolls surrounding the lakes are an inspiration . . . to reverie." The park is filled with picturesque monuments, notably the Chesme Obelisk.

FAÇADE. Gatchina Palace (GATCHINSKY DVORETS; Гатчинский дворец), faced in limestone, is made up of a central block with galleries on either side leading to service wings. The plan is quadrilateral, with an inner courtyard.

"SQUARE" WINGS OF THE ARSENAL AND KITCHENS. Under Nicholas I the main central bulding was converted into a memorial of filial devotion, and comfortable apartments set up in the lateral wings.

INTERIOR DÉCOR. The décor of the central building nearly all dates from Rinaldi's time (elaborate marquetry floors and fine stuccos).

GATCHINA PARK

After the death of Orlov the park at Gatchina (GATCHINSKY PARK; Гатчинский парк) was embellished with several new buildings. By the White and Silver lakes are two pavilions: the Venus Pavilion, a copy of the Prince de Condé's original at Chantilly, and the Birch Pavilion, whose rustic exterior belies an interior of great refinement.

PRACTICAL INFORMATION

◆ USEFUL INFORMATION

With over five million inhabitants, St Petersburg is the most northerly of the world's largest metropolises. Its geographical location – at the mouth of the the Gulf Stream, close to the Arctic Circle – is the reason for the extreme changes and capricious variations of climate. Its location also gives rise to St Petersburg's characteristic "white nights", that period beginning around the summer solstice when days seem never-ending. Winters at this latitude are extremely hard, but even under a thick blanket of snow this ancient imperial capital is always full of charm.

ESSENTIAL DOCUMENTS

You will need a valid passport and a visa. Tourist visas are valid for a maximum of 30 days and can be obtained from the appropriate embassy, consulate, tour operators or agency. You will be required to fill out a customs declaration form on arrival and another on departure.

◆ To obtain a visa you will need a hotel reservation or written invitation, passport, three passport-size photos and a completed application form. Visas can take up to two weeks and cost £20/$20; make sure you apply in plenty of time. Courier services can also be arranged through agencies such as Intourist who offer a normal and express service.

USEFUL ADDRESSES:
◆ **UK:** CONSULAR DEPARTMENT OF THE RUSSIAN EMBASSY 5 Kensington Palace Gardens, London W8 Tel. 0171 229 8027
◆ **US:** CONSULATE GENERAL OF THE RUSSIAN FEDERATIONS 9 East 91st Street New York, NY 10128 Tel. (212) 348 0926

HEALTH

There are no required vaccinations or inoculations for St Petersburg. If you are undergoing a course of treatment it is best to take any medication you may need with you. Remember to take out travel insurance before you leave ◆ 275.

THINGS TO TAKE
◆ An umbrella
◆ Comfortable walking shoes
◆ In summer, mosquito repellent

TIME DIFFERENCE
St Petersburg is 3 hours ahead of GMT and 8 hours ahead of Eastern Standard (New York) Time.

LANGUAGE

The official language is Russian. English is spoken only in tourist areas. To enable you to find your way around the city you are recommended to acquaint yourself with the names of street and Metro stations. It would also be useful for you to familiarize yourself with the cyrillic alphabet.

MONEY ◆ 284
◆ The official currency is the rouble (an inconvertible currency). Years ago the kopeck was still in circulation (1 rouble was worth 100 kopecks), but galloping inflation has since eliminated this.
◆ Note: Only roubles minted since 1993 are valid. Those minted before this time are completely different and easy to recognize, so there is little risk of fraud. Take US dollars and make sure they are in good condition (used ones are likely to be refused) and preferably in small denominations. There are plenty of bureaux de change, so do not take the risk of changing money on the black market.
◆ You are required to depart with less money than you brought into the country.
◆ Taking roubles out of the country is prohibited.

CYRILLIC ALPHABET

Upper case	Lower case	Phon.
А	а	a
Б	б	b
В	в	v
Г	г	g
Д	д	d
Е	е	e/ye
Ё	ё	o/yo
Ж	ж	j
З	з	z
И	и	ee
-	й	i/y
К	к	k
Л	л	l
М	м	m
Н	н	n
О	о	o
П	п	p
Р	р	r
С	с	s
Т	т	t
У	у	ou
Ф	ф	f
Х	х	kh
Ц	ц	ts
Ч	ч	ch
Ш	ш	sh
Щ	щ	shch
-	ъ	-
-	ы	y
-	ь	-
Э	э	e
Ю	ю	yu
Я	я	ya

AEROFLOT
Russian International airlines

The magnificent light of the summer nights.

The Neva covered in ice.

THE "WHITE NIGHTS"

The "white nights" are one of the major tourist attractions in St Petersburg. From June 11 to July 2, dawn and dusk merge into one as the city gleams under a supernatural light. This is the perfect time for night walks along the Neva. It is also the festival season, with the participation of some of Russia's most important musicians. Tour operators and agencies offer special packages during the white nights and over the Christmas period:
♦ ST PETERSBURG TRAVEL COMPANY (INTOURIST)
Isaakievskaya Ploshchad 11
Tel. 2 10 09 05
UK:
♦ INTOURIST
219, Marsh Wall
London, E14 9PD
Tel. 0171 538 8600
US:
♦ INTOURIST
620 5th Ave, Suite 868
New York, NY 10111
Tel.(212) 757 3884

CHRISTMAS AND NEW YEAR

December has the shortest days in the year: barely five hours of sunlight each day. But it is also the time of the true Russian winter. With luck, you may see the Neva frozen over and may actually be able to walk on the icy solid Gulf of Finland. New Year's Eve celebrations are organized in most of the large hotels (the most prestigious of which is, of course, the Grand Hotel Europe), in the good restaurants, or, numbers and budget permitting, in a palace with a private caterer:
♦ Potel et Chabot
Tel. 315 63 05
♦ Ivan and K°
Tel. 294 02 52
Traditionally, the Mariinsky Theater and the Little Theater of Opera and Ballet (Maly Theater) stage Tchaikovsky's *The Nutcracker Suite.*

INDIVIDUAL OR GROUP TRAVEL?

St Petersburg does not yet really cater for the individual traveler. Tourist offices are not common, and the signs in public places are only in Russian. Attempting to organize trips out of the city can be fairly complicated.
ORGANIZED TRIPS FOR GROUPS AND INDIVIDUALS
Some tour operators offer package holidays which may include hotel reservations, visas and car rental.
TOUR OPERATORS
UK:
♦ NOBLE CALEDONIA
Tel. 0171 491 4752
♦ ART STUDY TOURS
Tel. 0171 735 8300
♦ REGENT HOLIDAYS UK
Tel. 0117 9211 711

♦ KONTAKT POINT
Tel. 0171 603 1535
♦ PROGRESSIVE TOURS
Tel. 0171 262 1676
♦ SWAN HELLENIC
Tel. 0171 831 1616
♦ THOMPSONS
Tel. 0171 433 3444
♦ SAGA
Tel. 0171 444 7202
♦ KOSMOS
Tel. 0171 464 3444
♦ BARRY MARTIN
Tel. 0171 439 1271
♦ EXPRESS VOID LTD
Tel. 0171 250 1006
♦ COX & KINGS TRAVEL
Tel. 0171 873 5001

US:
♦ AMERICAN EXPRESS VACATIONS
Tel. (800) 241 1700
♦ CARAVAN TOURS
Tel. (800) 227 2826
or (312) 321 9800
♦ OLSON-TRAVELWORLD
Tel. (800) 421 5785

or (310) 546 8400
♦ TRAFALGAR TOURS
Tel. (800) 854 0103
or (212) 689 8977
♦ MAUPINTOUR
Tel. (800) 255 4266
or (913) 843 1211
Discount packages for students can be obtained from:
♦ COUNCIL TRAVEL
Tel. (212) 661 1450
♦ EDUCATIONAL TRAVEL CENTER
Tel. (608) 256 5551
♦ TRAVEL MANAGEMENT INTERNATIONAL
Tel. (617) 661 8187
♦ TRAVEL CUTS
Tel. (416) 979 2406

CITY BREAKS

Many tour operators and travel companies offer short breaks to St Petersburg. These packages, often the most economic way of seeing the city, frequently include flight, hotel accommodation and food, and may include entrance to museums and other sights.

TRAVEL INSURANCE

Many tour operators and insurance agents sell travel insurance. In the US insurance cover is also available from:
♦ ACCESS AMERICA, INC
Tel. (800) 284 8300
♦ CAREFREE INSURANCE TRAVEL
Tel. (800) 323 3149
♦ TELE-TRIP
Tel. (800) 228 9792
♦ TRAVEL GUARD INTERNATIONAL
Tel. (800) 782 5151

AVERAGE ANNUAL TEMPERATURES (°F)												
Month	Jan	Feb	Mar	Apr	May	Jun	Jul	Aug	Sep	Oct	Nov	Dec
Max.	19	23	32	46	59	68	70	68	59	48	36	27
Min.	9	10	18	32	43	52	55	55	48	39	28	18

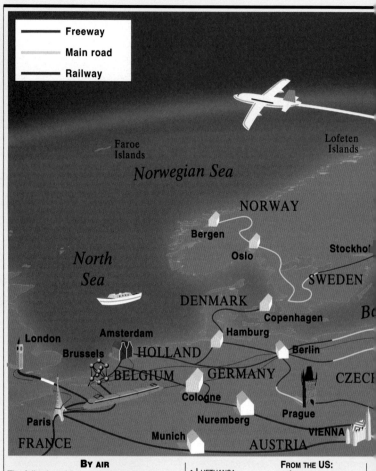

Legend:
- ——— Freeway
- ——— Main road
- ——— Railway

Faroe Islands

Lofeten Islands

Norwegian Sea

NORWAY

Bergen

Oslo

Stockhol

SWEDEN

North Sea

DENMARK

Copenhagen

Ba

London

Amsterdam

Hamburg

Berlin

Brussels

HOLLAND

BELGIUM

GERMANY

CZECH

Cologne

Paris

Nuremberg

Prague

VIENNA

FRANCE

Munich

AUSTRIA

BY AIR

The following airlines offer flights from the UK to St Petersburg:

FROM THE UK:

◆ BRITISH AIRWAYS
Tel. (01345) 222111
Regular flights from both Heathrow and Stansted. Prices start from £404 (Apex fare) up to £1,008 (club class). Outside the main tourist season there are sometimes special deals available with return flights starting as low as £299.

◆ AEROFLOT
Tel. (0171) 355 2233
Flights from Heathrow Fri., Sat., Sun. only. Prices range from £300 to £400 for a return flight, £250 for a single ticket.

◆ AUSTRIAN AIRLINES
Tel. (0171) 434 7350
There are three flights each week from Heathrow, traveling either via Vienna or Zurich. Prices from around £465 to £490 for an Apex flight (reserve at least two weeks in advance).

◆ FINNAIR
Tel. (0171) 408 1222
Flights via Helsinki. Prices range from £366 (for an Apex return ticket) to £665 for an excursion fare (valid for three months) to £914 for a business class ticket.

◆ LUFTHANSA
Tel. (01345) 737747
Flights via Frankfurt. Prices for a return ticket from £425 for an Apex fare, to £928 for an economy class fare, and £1064 for a business class ticket.

◆ SWISSAIR
Tel. (0171) 434 7300
Flights to St Petersburg via Stockholm.

FROM THE US:

◆ AEROFLOT
Tel. (800) 995 5555
Non-stop flights from New York.Prices range from $702 (coach class) to $1539 (business).

◆ BRITISH AIRWAYS
Tel. (800) 247 9297
Flights from New York with connection in London. Prices range from $768 (coach) to $3,152 (business) and $5,498 (first).

FROM THE AIRPORT

Pulkova Airport is situated approximately ten miles from St Petersburg. To get to the city center take **bus** no. 13 (Moskovskaya metro station). The bus stop is on the left on leaving the airport building. If you are intending to travel by **taxi**, it is best to reserve in advance.

Barents Sea
North Cape

Gulf of Bothnia
FINLAND

White Sea
Arkhangelsk

Lake Ladoga
Lake Onega

Helsinki
Gulf of Finland
Tallinn
ST PETERSBURG
RUSSIA

Sea
Gulf of Riga
ESTONIA
Riga
LETTONIA
Smolensk
Moscow

LITHUANIA
Vilnius

Gdansk
Warsaw
Minsk

POLAND
BELORUSSIA

Kracow
Lvov
Kiev

SLOVAKIA
Bratislava
UKRAINE

♦ DELTA AIRLINE
Tel. (800) 221 1212
Flights from New
York with connection
in Frankfurt. Prices
range from $800
(coach), through
$3,200 (business) to
$5,500 (first).

USEFUL ADDRESSES
♦ PULKOVO AIRPORT II
Tel. 104 34 44
♦ AEROFLOT
7/9, Nevsky Prospekt
Tel. 314 69 59
♦ BRITISH AIRWAYS
Nevsky Palace
Hotel
57, Nevsky Prospekt
Tel. 119 61 00
or 119 62 22
♦ FINNAIR
Pulkovo II
Tel. 104 34 39

♦ LUFTHANSA
Pulkovo II
Tel. 104 34 32
♦ SWISSAIR/SAS /
AUSTRIAN AIRLINES
– Nevsky Palace
Hotel
57, Nevsky Prospekt
Tel. 14 50 86
– Pulkovo II
Tel. 10 34 43

BY RAIL
Total journey time by
rail and ferry is
around 29 hours.
♦ Train from
Liverpool Street,
London, with ferry
crossing from

Harwich to Hook of
Holland, stopping in
Berlin.
COST: Return fare
£287 (under 26 years
of age £217)
Single ticket £163
(under 26's £124)
♦ Train from
Liverpool Street, with
ferry crossing from
Ramsgate to Ostend,
to Berlin and then on
to St Petersburg.
COST: Return £357
(under 26 years of
age £274)
Single £181 (under
26 years of age
£137)

For information and
reservations contact:
♦ BRITISH RAIL
INTERNATIONAL
Tel. (0171) 834 2345

BY ROAD
Traveling to
St Petersburg by
road is not
recommended.
Russian authorities
are unable to
guarantee any
back-up services in
case of breakdown
or other eventualities
and only certain
through routes are
advised.

BY COACH
There are no coach
services running
direct to
St Petersburg.

277

Nothing could be simpler than finding your way around the center of St Petersburg, where the main tourist attractions (the Admiralty, Peter and Paul Fortress, St Isaac's Cathedral) and the canals provide you with clear landmarks. Out of the center, it a little more difficult to find your bearings and, following in the footsteps of novelist Alexandre Dumas, say "I know . . . St Petersburg like the back of my hand. I know how to say *na prava* (right), *na leva* (left), *pachol* (go), *stoy* (stop), and *amoy* (home). Thanks to this repertoire . . . , I am well able to get by."

STREET NUMBERING

In theory all streets are numbered starting from the Neva. In practise, in the majority of cases, street numbering is as follows:

◆ from north to south and from west to east, for the mainland area of the city, situated to the south of the Neva;

◆ from south to north and from east to west for Vasilyevsky Island;

◆ from south to north and from west to east for Petrograd Island, also known as Petrogradskaya.

TOPOGRAPHY

In the heart of St Petersburg, the oldest part of the city, the streets are laid out in a radial system, the main arteries fanning out from a central point while the canals curve around them. Later areas were constructed mainly to an orthogonal design, dividing the whole area into a network of streets running at right angles to each other and forming "microdistricts" bound by the main arteries radiating out from the center.

PUBLIC TOILETS

The pictograms indicating the public conveniences feature a stylized form of the letters "М" and "Ж" of the cyrillic alphabet, the first letters of the words Мужчина (mooshtshina, man) and Женщина (zhenshtshina, woman).

GLOSSARY / Словарь		
Yes / no	da / nyet	да / нет
Hello	zdrastvuity	здравствуйте
Goodbye	dasvidanya	до свидания
Please	pazhalusta	пожалуйста
Thank you	spasiba	спасибо
Excuse me	izvinitye	извините
Do you speak . . .	vui gavarity . . .	вы говорите...
English?	pa anglisky?	по-английски ?
French?	pa frantsuzsky?	по-французски ?
I don't understand	ya ne ponimayu	я не понимаю
I don't know	ya ne znayu	я не знаю
Can you help me?	pamaguity pazhalusta	помогите пожалуйста
Is it possible to . . .?	mojna . . .?	можно . . . ?
Where?	gde?	где?
When?	kagda?	когда?
Who?	kto?	кто?
How?	shto?	что?
Leave me alone	otstan ot menia	отстань от меня
IN THE STREET		
Please can you tell me	skazhity, pazhalusta	скажите пожалуйста
How to get to. . .?	kak mne papast v . . .?	как мне попасть в...?
Do you know where . . . is?	vuy ne znayety, gde . . .?	вы не знаете, где...?
Can you show me	mozhna pakazat	можно показать
on the map?	na karty?	на карте ?
Is it far?	dalieko?	далеко ?
Can I walk there?	mozhna pishkom ?	можно пешком ?
Left/right	na leva / na prava	налево/направо
Straight ahead	priama	прямо
On the corner	v uglu	в углу
River	rieka	река
Canal	kanal	канал
Bridge	most	мост
Avenue	prospekt	проспект
Road	ulitsa	улица
Quay	naberezhnaya	набережная
Back street	pereulok	переулок
Square	ploshchad	площадь
Highway	shossé	шоссе
Boulevard	bulvar	бульвар

NOTE
Crossing the street outside of the designated areas is forbidden. Contravening this regulation may incur a fine.

БИРЖЕВОЙ мост

As the city is currently in a state of upheaval and in the process of readopting many of the pre-revolutionary street names, different signs coexist alongside each other to give the names of streets, buildings and to indicate the various public transport stops. Recently a new type of advertising has appeared in St Petersburg – newly installed street signs are now often sponsored by commercial companies; don't be surprised to find the trademark of distinctly western companies displayed under the name of the street.

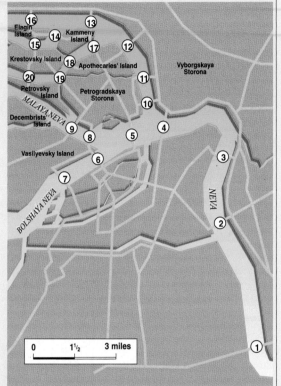

Elagin Island ⑯
Kammeny Island ⑬
⑭
⑮
⑰ ⑫
Krestovsky Island ⑱
Apothecaries' Island
Vyborgskaya Storona
⑳ ⑲
Petrovsky Island
⑪
Petrogradskaya Storona
Decembrists Island ⑩
⑨
⑧
⑤
④
NEVA
Vasilyevsky Island ⑥
③
⑦
②
BOLSHAYA NEVA
MALAYA NEVA

| 0 | 1½ | 3 miles |

①

BRIDGES

The 300 or so bridges form an integral part of St Petersburg's architectural heritage. Between them they link the 42 islands which make up the city, crossing 68 rivers or branches of the sea and 20 canals. The first (Anichkov), a wooden bridge, was constructed in 1715. At 110 yards, the Blue Bridge is the widest of them all and the Alexander Nevsky the longest (991 yards). Between April and November – that is when the rivers are not frozen – the swing bridges (20 in total) stay raised for part of the night in order to let commerce vessels through. You are advised to be aware of the bridge opening and closing times in order to avoid being stranded on the wrong island.

TIMETABLE OF SWING BRIDGE LIFTING TIMES	
1. Volodarsky:	2.10–5.40am
2. Alex. Nevskovo:	2.40–4.45am
3. Bolsheokhtinsky :	2.50–4.50am
4. Liteiny:	2.15–4.35am
5. Troitsky:	2.05–4.35am
6. Dvortsovy:	2–3am and 3.20–4.20am
7. Leitenanta Shmidta:	2.00–4.45am
8. Birzhevoy:	2.30–3.15am and 3.45–4.45am
9. Tuchkov:	2.35–3.05am and 3.45–4.45am
10. Sampsonievsky:	2.10–2.25am and 3.20–4.25am
11. Grenadersky:	2.45–3.45am and 4.20–4.50am
12. Kantemirovsky:	2.45–3.45 and 4.20–4.50am
13. Ushakovsky:	2.15–2.55 and 3.55–4.30am
14. Elagin I :	by
15. Elagin II:	special
16. Elagin III:	arrangement
17. Kamennoostrovsky:	2.15–3am and 4.05–4.55am
18. Bolshoy Krestovsky:	2.05–3.55 and 4.40–5.20am
19. Lazarevsky:	1.55–2.35am and 4.45–5.20am
20. Bolshoy Petrovsky:	1.25–2am and 5am–5.45am

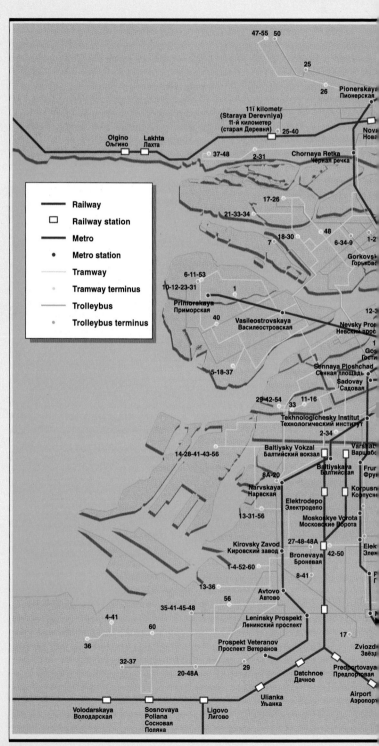

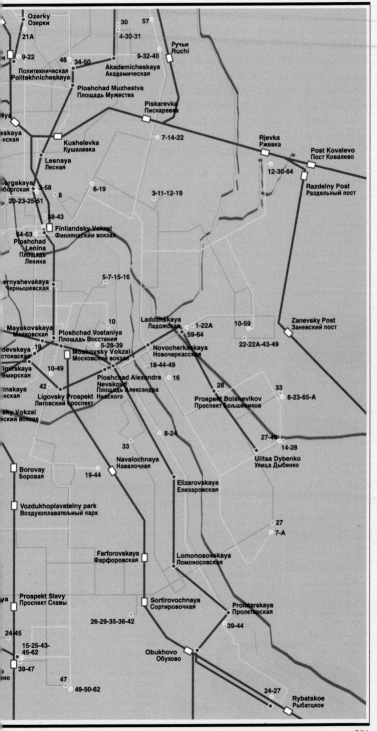

Ozerky
Озерки

21A

9-22

30   57

4-30-31

Ручьи
Ruchi

9-32-40

46   34-50

Политехническая
Politekhnicheskaya

Akademicheskaya
Академическая

Ploshchad Muzhestva
Площадь Мужества

Piskarevka
Пискаревка

skaya
нская

Kushelevka
Кушелевка

7-14-22

Rjevka
Ржевка

Post Kovalevo
Пост Ковалево

Lesnaya
Лесная

12-30-64

Razdelny Post
Раздельный пост

ergskaya
боргская   3-58

20-23-25-51   8

6-19

3-11-12-19

38-43

54-63
Ploshchad
Lenina
Площадь
Ленина

Finliandsky Vokzal
Финляндскии вокзал

ernyshevskaya
Чернышевская

5-7-15-16

Mayakovskaya
Маяковская   10

Ploshchad Vostaniya
Площадь Восстания

Ladozhskaya
Ладожская   1-22A
59-64

10-59

Zanevsky Post
Заневский пост

evskaya
стоевская   19

5-28-39

Moskovsky Vokzal
Московский вокзал

Novocherkasskaya
Новочеркасская

22-22A-43-49

imirskaya
имирская

10-49

Ploshchad Alexandra
Nevskovo
Площадь Александра
Невского

18-44-49

16

28

33

8-23-65-A

inskaya
нская   42

Ligovsky Prospekt
Лиговский проспект

Prospekt Bolshevikov
Проспект Большевиков

sky Vokzal
ский вокзал

8-24

33

27-46

14-28

Borovay
Боровая

19-44

Navalochnaya
Навалочная

Ulitsa Dybenko
Улица Дыбенко

Vozdukhoplavatelny park
Воздухоплавательный парк

Elizarovskaya
Елизаровская

27

7-A

Farforovskaya
Фарфоровская

Lomonosovskaya
Ломоносовская

Prospekt Slavy
Проспект Славы

Sortirovochnaya
Сортировочная

Proletarskaya
Пролетарская

24-45

26-29-35-36-42

39-44

15-25-43-
45-62

39-47

47

49-50-62

Obukhovo
Обухово

24-27

Rybatskoe
Рыбатцкое

The public transport network in St Petersburg, although considerable (4 metro lines, 179 bus routes, 65 tram lines, 50 trolleybus lines), is barely adequate for this city of five million inhabitants which extends over an area of 230 square miles (around 12 x 19 miles). In spite of the rundown state of the trams, buses and trolleybuses, and fairly long waits, this mode of transport can be an excellent way of getting around the historic center as the various monuments are spread over a fairly large area. For longer journeys, or if you are in a hurry, it is best to take the Metro, but avoid rush hour, when the trains are crowded (7am to 9am and 4pm to 6pm).

BUS, TROLLEYBUS AND TRAMS

Tickets are required for trips by tram (*talony*); these can be purchased from kiosks and sometimes from the driver. Tickets must be validated by punching them in the machines on board the vehicle.

◆ Tram stops are indicated by boards showing a "T" above the electric lines. Trams run from 5.30am to 12.30am.

◆ Bus stops are indicated by square yellow signs marked with the letter "A" above the sidewalk. Buses run from 5am to 12.30am.

TAXIS

In general, taxis are yellow with a "T" sign on the side or a "Taxi" sign on the roof of the car. Taxis are becoming a service purely for tourists as they are usually too expensive for local people. An approximate cost would be 2,000 roubles plus 600 roubles per half mile. It is best to agree on the price of your journey beforehand. There is a central taxi reservation number: Tel. 312 00 22, although taxis can be

ТАКСИ

hailed in the street. The average price for a taxi ride from St Petersburg to the airport is 150,000 roubles ($30). Taxis frequently congregate in front of the larger hotels (many of them foreign vehicles). These will tend to be more expensive than ones hailed in the street.

GASOLINE

Around the city center several service stations have recently appeared, all owned by the Finnish

BY CAR

Parking prohibited (on the left, odd days, on the right, even days).

Driving a private vehicle requires certain formalities and therefore some inconvenience. It is probably simpler to rent a car with driver (at western prices) through a car rental agency:

◆ Transvelltroika St Petersburg 37 Lermontovsky Prospekt, Tel. 113 72 53 or 113 72 28. Credit cards accepted.
◆ AVIS (cars, minibus): 13 Ulitsa Remeslennaya, Tel. 235 64 44 or 235 16 82. Credit cards accepted.
◆ Avtodom (cars, limousines, Mercedes minibus) 56 Nab. Moika, Tel. 315 90 43.
◆ Interavto Volvo (Mercedes, minibus) 12 Ulitsa Alexandra Nevskovo, Tel. 277 40 32 or 274 20 60. See also the car rental bureaux in the following hotels: Astoria, Moskva, Pribaltiskaya or Pulkovskaya ◆ 298.

company Neste. Regular gas and diesel are on sale. 100 Moskovsky Prospekt; 68 Maly Prospekt; 36 Ulitsa Avangardnaya; 34 Ulitsa Pulkovskoye ; 36 Nab. Obvodnovo Kanala Tel. 166 57 77.

DRIVING

◆ The highway code is much the same as that in force in Western Europe. However, at traffic lights if, along with the go signal, there is also an orange and red light showing, vehicles coming from the opposite direction have right of way.
◆ The roads are frequently in poor condition.
◆ In case of accident contact GAÏ (ГАЙ, traffic accidents): Tel. 234 2646.
◆ Wearing of seatbelts is compulsory and drinking and driving is prohibited.

METRO

The Metro (метро) is the quickest and most reliable form of public transport. There are 54 stations operating over 4 different lines. Metro stations are indicated by an enormous blue letter "M", lit up at night. The metro runs from around 5.30am to 1am. To travel you will need a token; these are available from ticket booths at the station entrances (the price is shown at the cash desk). Trains run every 1 to 2 minutes during peak hours and approximately every 5 minutes in the evening. Beware: all signs are in cyrillic script. Station entrances are marked 'вход'; city center exits 'выход'; and line transfers 'переход'. A Metro plan is displayed at each station. After each stop the name of the station is announced in the train along with that of the next destination.

	line 1 Kirovsko–Vyborgskaya		line 3 Nevsko–Vasileostrovskaya
	line 2 Moskovsko–Petrogradskaya		line 4 Pravoberejnaya
	extension project for line 2		extension project for line 4

GLOSSARY / Словарь

Entrance	vkhod	вход
Exit	vuikhod	выход
Underground passage	perekhod	переход
Breakdown	ne rabotayet	не работает
Information	spravky	справки
Public toilets	tualet	туалет
Station	vakzal	вокзал
Metro	metro	метро
Trolleybus	traleybus	троллейбус
Tram	tramvay	трамвай
Airport	airaport	аэропорт
Taxi	taxi	такси
Car	mashina	машина
Danger	apasna	опасно

MONTHLY TRAVEL PASSES

Valid for all public transport, monthly travel passes for the following month are available from Metro stations and ticket booths during the last four or five days of the previous month. If your visit is long enough, monthly passes are a very convenient method of traveling around the city. They carry the inscription 'единый'.

ЕДИНЫЙ М 188965
СЕНТЯБРЬ 09.94
МЕТРО · ТРОЛЛЕЙБУС
ТРАМВАЙ · АВТОБУС
16000 руб.

BOAT TRIPS

◆ Throughout the summer months (May to October), boat trips run along the Neva between Peter the Great monument (Decembrists' Square) and Smolny Institute, with a stop at Palace Bridge and another in front of the Summer Garden.
◆ Speed boats (which carry between 4 and 12 people) allow you to explore the city via the canals. Embark at Anichkov Bridge (on the Fontanka), at the People's Bridge (on the Moika) or on the Griboedov Canal. Approximate cost of a small boat taxi for 2 to 4 people with an individual tour and stops on request: $50.
◆ The boat company Речьфлот offers hour-long trips along the Neva. The landing stage is opposite the Hermitage Museum.

283

The recent upheavals within the former Soviet Union have affected all areas of daily life. The rate of inflation has left the rouble, the official currency, extremely unstable. Recent modernization of the telecommunications systems has brought about great improvements in the press and television. Although many aspects of life in the city are less restricted than they once were, the visitor is advised to take the same precautions as in any major city.

MONEY

Nowadays, there are a number of official bureaux de change: at the airport, at hotel

ОБМЕН ВАЛЮТЫ

receptions, in banks and in the larger stores (and sometimes in the smaller ones too). There are also some in the high streets, particularly in the city center. Opening times vary and some may be closed on a particular day of the week. Do not change money on the black market: this practise is not only illegal but also extremely risky. Bureaux de change register each transaction and this document must be presented when you pass through customs on leaving the country. Rates of exchange vary slightly between banks and bureaux. In general, the rate of exchange in hotels is less favorable than elsewhere. The dollar is the preferred currency and you are recommended to take new bills with you, as far as possible: banks are very selective when it comes to the quality of the notes they will accept.

In theory, currencies other than the rouble are not accepted as regular payment over the counter. In practise, this legislation may not always be adhered to, particularly in the stores and boutiques which are geared more to tourists. Nevertheless, roubles are the usual form of currency, and, within the country, compete against the dollar reasonably successfully. Credit cards are taken in more and more places, but are still not readily accepted everywhere. If you intend to use a credit card, enquire first. Traveler's checks are welcomed by most banks, although Eurocheques are still not widely accepted.

CRIME AND SAFETY

The media in the west is quick to report any outbreaks of crime or violence in St Petersburg. The mafia may be more in evidence, but there is no real threat as long as you are sensible: don't allow strangers to accompany you at night, always stick to the main streets and don't make a show of any expensive equipment you have.

EMERGENCY NUMBERS
Fire service: 01
Police (Militsia): 02
Ambulance: 03
GAÏ (road accidents): 234 26 46

GLOSSARY / Словарь		
Money	diengui	деньги
Rouble	rouble	рубль
Dollar	dollar	долар
Credit card	creditnaya kartochka	сpедитная карточка
Change	abmion	обмён
I would like to change	mne nuzhna abminiat	мне нужно обменять
dollars	dolary	доллары
Post	pochta	почта
Mailbox	pachtovy iashchik	почтовый ящик
Postcard	atkrytka	открытка
Envelope	kanvert	конверт
Letter	pismo	письмо
Stamp	marka	марка

PRICES

1 CUP OF TEA: 10 CENTS–$1	1 TAXI RIDE IN THE CITY: $5–15	1 TICKET TO THE THEATER: $40 OR MORE	1 MEAL IN AN AVERAGE RESTAURANT: $10–60
1 DOUBLE ROOM IN A HOTEL: $80	1 ICE CREAM IN THE STREET: 10 CENTS–$1	1 ENTRANCE TO A MUSEUM: 10 CENTS–$8	1 BOAT TRIP: $5–10

All prices are given in dollars due to the rate of inflation of the rouble.

TELEPHONE

TO CALL ST PETERSBURG FROM THE UK:
Dial 00 7 812 + local number.
FROM THE US:
Dial 011 7 812 + local number.
TO CALL THE UK:
Dial 8 10 44 + local number.
TO CALL THE US:
Get local access code from operator + 1 + US area code + local number.
TRADITIONAL PUBLIC TELEPHONES
These are for local calls only and take metro tokens (available from the station entrances). Lift receiver, wait for tone, dial number, when the call is answered insert token and speak.
MODERN PHONE BOOTHS
These phone booths (see above) can be used for all calls, including international ones and take telephone cards (sold in Marlboro kiosks, SPT, 13 Ulitsa Gorokhovaya). English instructions and prices are on display in each booth.
DIRECTORY ENQUIRIES
Dial: 09.

MAKING CALLS FROM YOUR HOTEL
The use of the

telephone varies from one hotel to another. Local calls are free. International tariffs, by contrast, tend to be extremely high (an average of $5 a minute for calls to Europe, for example). In some hotels, you need to be careful when calling abroad: after a specified time span (50 seconds at the Grand Hotel Europe, for example) you will incur charges for your call even if the person you are dialing does not answer.

MAIL

CENTRAL POST OFFICE
This is situated at 9 Ulitsa Pochtamtskaya and is open Monday to Saturday from 9am to 8pm, and Sunday from 10am to 6pm. There are facilities for sending faxes, making photocopies and changing money. (NB: hotel receptions also sell stamps.) Mail delivery varies greatly (from several days to several weeks) so if something is urgent it is best to use an express service, send a telegram or send a

package via DHL (Nevsky Palace Hotel, 57 Nevsky Prospekt, Tel. 119 61 00, Mon. to Fri., 9am to 6pm.) Mail boxes are red (local mail) and blue (air mail and destinations outside of St Petersburg). Mail boxes bear the inscription 'почта'.

HEALTH

Avoid drinking tap water or buying food from street stalls or kiosks. In the case of serious health problems contact the consulate, who will give you the name of a doctor or even recommend a hospital.

TELEVISION AND NEWSPAPERS

Most hotels subscribe to a satellite television network and many hotels carry foreign newspapers. There are also several English-language publications edited in St Petersburg which are distributed free to selected hotels, restaurants and larger department stores. Look out for *St Petersburg Press*, an extremely useful publication.

Since its growth in popularity as a holiday destination, St Petersburg is now having to cater for ever-increasing numbers of tourists. In contrast to the luxury hotel business that has recently appeared, traditional hotel accommodation is still somewhat basic. Eating out can also be unpredictable with great variations in quality and price. As for shopping, the days of extreme poverty and long lines in front of shops are now a thing of the past: you can buy anything you require, although prices may be higher than you expect.

ACCOMMODATION

HOTELS

Still somewhat inadequate, the hotel trade has improved greatly, particularly in the "luxury" category (with the renovation of the Grand Hotel Europe and the Astoria and the construction of the Nevsky Palace).

◆ Aside from these three grand hotels, which tend to be very expensive, there are a number of hotels independent of the Intourist group, fairly conveniently located, or maybe slightly out of the center, which are comfortable and reasonably priced (Pulkovskaya, Pribaltiiskaya, Gavan, Moskva, Sovetskaya, St Petersburg).

◆ Between the two categories, there are several basic hotels which are newly built (or newly renovated): Neptune, Okhtinskaya, Deson-Ladoga, Mercury, and even a floating hotel – the Peterhof.

◆ Throughout the "white nights" and over the Christmas period ◆ 274, you are recommended to

reserve well in advance.

GUESTHOUSES

A relatively recent option for the visitor to St Petersburg is the possibility of staying with a Russian family, although this type of accommodation is not very common. Most apartments in St Petersburg are only equipped with one bathroom and so a holiday of this nature would involve the visitor being more part of the family than in a traditional west-European style guesthouse.

◆ Tour operators can provide you in advance with information about the family you would be staying with, when they give you their address ◆ 275. CGTT Lepertours, Transtours, Inexco/KMP Group.

CAMPING

Olguino, 11 miles from St Petersburg, from June to Sept. Ulitsa Primorskoye Tel. 238 35 50 or 238 30 09.

YOUTH HOSTELS

28 Sovetskaya III Ulitsa Tel. 277 05 69 Fax 277 51 02

HOSTELLING
R U S S I A

Well-kept and inexpensive ($15). *Holiday* 1, Ulitsa Mikhailova Tel./Fax 542 73 64.

SHOPPING

Stores are generally open from 9am to 8pm and most are located along the Nevsky Prospekt. Many of the former shop signs still remain, so don't be surprised to find stereos for sale in what was once a bakery. Supermarkets are beginning to appear everywhere, but many stores and boutiques are of a more traditional nature. To make a purchase you must first go to the cash desk and pay for the goods you require, then collect your merchandise by showing your receipt. Language may be a problem: you will need to tell the cashier (in Russian) the name, price and quantity of the product you require. If your mastery of Russian is insufficient for you to do this, write the information on a piece of paper and show it to the cashier.

ICE CREAM

St Petersburg is famous for its ice cream (мороженое) and it is eaten in summer and winter alike. Nowadays, it is frequently imported, usually from Finland, although it is still possible to find delicious local Russian ice cream. Vanilla is the usual flavor, although fruit flavors and western-style ice creams are increasingly available.

GLOSSARY / Словарь		
Bill/check	shchiot	счёт
Menu	menyu	меню
Do you have a table?	yest svabodny stol ?	есть свободный стол ?
Can I order?	mozhna zakazat ?	можно заказать ?
Water	vada	вода
Vodka	vodka	водка
Coffee	kofe	кофе
Tea	chay	чай
Bread	khleb	хлеб
Fish	ryba	рыба
Meat	miassa	мясо
Ice cream	marozhenoy	мороженое
Hot	gariachy	горячее
Cold	khalodny	холоднее

RESTAURANTS

Fine cuisine, an excellent wine list and the best service are reserved for those who can afford to dine at the Grand Hotel Europe restaurant (ресторан). Equally good is the Dvorianskoye gnezdo restaurant, which has recently opened next to the Mariinsky Theater.

◆ There are an increasing number of middle-range restaurants which are frequently run as joint ventures with foreign companies and usually offer a choice of international or Russian menus: try the hot or cold zakusky (hors d'oeuvres, such as salads, a selection of meat or fish, caviar crepes, salmon roe and blinis); soup (bortsch: beet soup,

and shchi: cabbage soup); beef Stroganoff, pelmeni (Siberian ravioli) or chicken Kiev as main dishes, and for dessert,

pastries, honey crepes or ice cream.

◆ Dinner generally costs between $20 and $40. Your hotel reception will provide you with information (menu, price, ethnic entertainments and opening times). In peak season reserve in advance.

DRINKS

Georgian wine can be rather mediocre, and local beer may leave much to be desired. Mineral water is usually sparkling. Vodka, by contrast, is usually of an excellent quality.

◆ Avoid large "Russian" restaurants (particularly along the Nevsky) and the stolovaya (столовая) or zakussochnaya (закусочная), which are cheap canteens.

◆ There are many fast food outlets appearing in the form of small cafes (кафе) or catering vans selling hamburgers and hotdogs. Don't be confused by the traditional cafeterias which serve tea, coffee and snacks such as pirozhki (pâté) and toast. During the summer months, it is wise to avoid the pirozhki (particularly the meat variety) and also meat balls on sale on street stalls.

◆ Tap water in St Petersburg is not drinkable unless boiled first.

SOUVENIRS

There is a rich variety of crafts in St Petersburg: lacquered boxes (Palekh, Mstiora, Fedoskino, Kholuy), wooden dishes (Khokhloma), trays and boxes, glazed pottery (Gjel), matryoshka dolls (right), boxes and jewelry, enamelwork, amber jewelry, rag

dolls (which traditionally were made into tea cozies), balalaikas, wooden toys, painted lead soldiers, woolen and silk scarves . . . You will no doubt wish to bring back caviar and vodka; avoid buying from street vendors as the quality and freshness cannot be guaranteed.

MARKETS

The best time to go to the markets (рынок) is early morning (they open at 8am) when it is much quieter and altogether more pleasant. The best market is in the city center close to the Vladimirskaya Metro station (3 Kuznechny Pereulok): good choice of fruit and vegetables, good quality meat, flowers, excellent local or Siberian honey and other typical produce

– salted gherkins – and dairy products such as farmhouse cheeses and thick sour cream. Near the circus, between Engineerskaya Ulitsa and Italianskaya Ploshschad is Maple Leaf Market, Klennovaya Shossé. It is a walk-in market catering especially for tourists and sells souvenirs, icons, t-shirts and a variety of other goods. Watch out for pickpockets.

CAVIAR

In season caviar is usually sold for around $15 for 90 grams at fish shops along Nevsky Prospekt. It is best to buy the blue 90 gram tins, or glass jars with yellow lids. Check the eggs are not too congealed. If the caviar proves too salty, there is a Russian saying that the girl adding the salt was in love.

No more than two 90 gram jars per person are allowed through customs.
Hotel waiters can usually provide the best caviar, if asked cautiously.

ANTIQUES

There are a number of stores selling antiques and crafts; the largest concentration is on Ulitsa Bolshaya Konyushennaya. The DLT Store also has an antiques department.
NOTE: taking antiques and works of art out of the country incurs a 40% tax and requires special authorization (разрешение на вывоз, razrisheniey na vyvodz) which may take time to obtain.

St Petersburg is famous for its natural and architectural beauty, and also for its excellent museums and rich artistic culture. The arts have always flourished here and there is a strong tradition and appreciation of the arts in general. The widest range of events occurs in the summer, during the period of the "white nights".

MUSEUMS

A former imperial palace, the Hermitage is famous throughout the world. Sumptuous collections of paintings, objets d'art, furniture and Egyptology are housed within this

magnificent building. Its Russian art collection is particularly impressive and gives a history of Russian art from the icons of the 12th century through to the avant-garde works of the 20th century. Also worth visiting are: Ethnography Museum, Naval Museum, the Zoological Museum (one of the most important in the world), Artillery Museum, Kunstkammer Museum (Peter the Great Museum of Anthropology and Ethnography, Museum of Musical Instruments). Many palaces are now museums: Summer Palace of Peter I; Menshikov Palace; Marble Palace (Romonov Portrait Gallery); Yusupov Palace. Also worth seeing are: Pavlosk Palace; Tsarskoe Selo, Petrodvorets, Oranienbaum and Gatchina Palace . . . and don't forget the unmissable Peter and Paul Fortress and St Isaac's Cathedral. Most museums are open from 10am or 11am and close around 6pm.

NOTE

◆ In museums (and frequently at the theater), expect to see different ticket prices for Russians to those for tourists. Locals would be unable to pay the "international" prices. On the other hand, if tourists were charged the lower rates, museums would soon go out of business.
◆ Leaving your belongings in the cloakroom is compulsory in museums and theaters. There is no charge.

NIGHTLIFE

Discotheques, clubs, casinos and nightclubs are now on the increase in St Petersburg. However, there is still no real tradition of nightlife. One fashionable nightclub:
◆ STIER'S CLUB
4, Stachek Square
Tel. 186 95 22

ORGANIZED EVENINGS OUT

The company Potel et Chabot will organize on request shows and spectacles in palaces (Yusupov, Shuvalov . . .).
10 Nab. Dvortsovaya Tel. 314 60 00.

THEATER

St Petersburg has a reputation for producing excellent quality theater. Choose from the internationally famed Mariinsky Theater (formerly the Kirov), Little Theater of Opera and Ballet (Maly Theater), the Philharmonia or the Capella. More recently, the Yusupov Hotel, the Hermitage Theater, the Beloselsky-Belozersky and the Church of Smolny Convent (sacred music). For listings and reservations ask at your hotel, main theater box offices or at the venue itself. Ticket prices vary, depending on where you buy your ticket (they are cheaper at the theater than at hotel desks).
◆ Tickets are available from the central ticket office (Театральная касса) 42 Nevsky Prospekt, theater box offices or from your hotel.

MOVIE THEATERS

There are several movie theaters in St Petersburg (around twelve on the Nevsky Prospekt itself), but movies receive much less publicity than in the west. Most movies tend to be American, but there are also some Russian and a few European films on occasion.

RELIGIOUS SERVICES

The most impressive services take place in the upper nave of St Nicholas' Cathedral, Sundays, from 10am to 1pm and evenings from 6pm.

SPORT AND LEISURE

In summer go horse riding in the park on Krestovsky Island Tel. 230 78 73, hire a speed boat or sailing boat from one of two sailing clubs (Tel. 230 75 85), or play tennis at the tennis club (*Lawn Tennis:* Tel. 540 16 79). In winter, go fishing through a hole in the ice on the frozen Gulf of Finland (Tel. 238 35 50).

THEMATIC ITINERARIES

▲ 1. The Hermitage   ▼ 5. Menshikov Palace

2. Palace Square

▼ 7. Peter and Paul Fortress

▼ 9. St Nicholas' Cathedral

10. Mariinsky Theater

3. Arts Square

4. Nevsky Prospekt

▼ 8. Tsarskoe Selo   ▲ 6. Petrodvorets

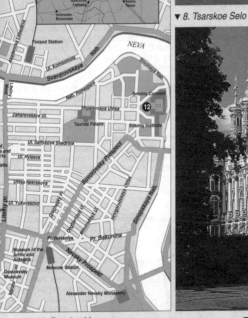

11. Russian Museum

▼ 12. Smolny

◆ ST PETERSBURG:
FOUR DIFFERENT APPROACHES

Mini cruise along the banks of the Neva.

A bird's-eye view of the city.

The cultural and historical background to St Petersburg is extremely rich and a constant source of fascination to the visitor. Whether viewed from the embankment, the air, or by underground, the various aspects of this former imperial capital never fail to captivate. These itineraries offer four ways of exploring this magnificent city.

BY BOAT

Approaching the city by boat can be an experience you will never forget (boat trips run from May to October).
PRICE: $50. DURATION: 1 hour. Depart from Anichkov Bridge, in front of Beloselsky-Belozersky Palace **(1)**. At no. 36, Fontanka stands the former Catherine Institute **(2)** and opposite, at no. 21, is the private residence of Count Shuvalov **(3)**. No. 34 is the Sheremetev Palace **(4)** which houses the Akhmatova Museum. From Bielinsky Bridge, the Church of St Simeon and St Anna **(5)** is visible. Just after Panteleimon Bridge the spectacular view over the Moika Canal encompasses the Engineers' Castle **(6)**, the Summer Garden **(7)** and the Field of Mars **(8)**. The Church of the Resurrection **(9)** is one of the most breathtaking buildings along the Griboedov Canal. On the left is the Russian Museum **(10)**. Further along, at no. 13 is the old Mutuel Credit building **(11)**, a branch of the Central Bank of Russia. At the intersection with the Nevsky Prospekt stands the Dom Knigi bookstore **(12)**. On the far side of the bridge stands Kazan Cathedral **(13)**. Opposite Bank Bridge is the Institute of Financial and Economic Science **(14)**. The Haymarket was the setting Dostoevsky chose for his novel *Crime and Punishment*. Next is St Nicholas' Cathedral **(15)**, overlooking Kryukov Canal, and set further back is the Mariinsky Theater **(16)**. Also on the Moika is New Holland **(17)** then, returning toward the center, you pass in front of Yusupov Palace **(18)** where Rasputin was assassinated. Across the Blue Bridge, with its Neptune's Scale (at flood level) **(19)**, there is a stunning view of St Isaac's Cathedral **(20)** and the statue of Nicholas I. At the intersection of Moika Canal and Winter Canal, near the Old Hermitage **(22)** and the Catherine Theater **(23)**, is the mayor Anatoly Sobshak's house **(21)**. From the mouth of the Neva there is a stunning view. From the embankment admire the Marble Palace **(24)** and Trinity Bridge. Once past Peter I's Summer Palace **(25)**, you return to the starting point, Anichkov Bridge **(1)**.

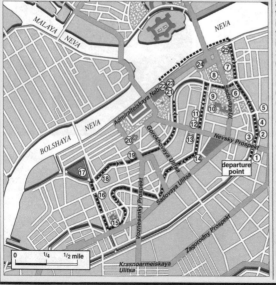

The sumptuous décor in Avtovo Station.

Narva Triumphal Arch, from tram no. 31.

BY SUBWAY

Push open the doors to the Metro, enter into vast, brightly lit lobbies and take the elevator to these underground palaces. There are 54 stations serving 4 lines, and the style of each reflects the era during which it was built. This itinerary takes you through a chronological history of the Metro.

LINE NO. 1 (RED)
Take the Metro to Ploshchad Vostanya. Line no. 1, opened in 1955, is typical of the Stalin era: these luxurious stations all have extraordinarily majestic décor. Pushkinskaya station, dedicated to Pushkin, is an excellent example with its white marble walls and red granite floor. Continue to Avtovo (stopping off briefly to see Narvskaya and Kirovsky Zavod): a richly decorated station with sixteen columns faced in patterned pressed glass. Take the train back in the opposite direction and change at Tekhnologichesky Institut (NB: the train is just opposite on the same platform).

LINE NO. 2 (BLUE)
Take line no. 2 to Nevsky Prospekt station. This line, constructed between 1960 and 1970, is more sober in style than line no. 1. Utilitarian in aspect, these stations are all very similar in appearance. At Nevsky Prospekt change onto line 3 toward Gostiny Dvor.

LINE NO. 3 (GREEN)
Built between 1960 and 1970, this line has an innovative feature: the so-called "closed" platforms are separated off from the tunnels by metal partitions which open up at the same time as those of the trains. This system is spectacular at Mayakovskaya Station, with its red-decorated walls. Change at Alexandra Nevskovo station (the chain-mail style décor is reminiscent of the Battle of Neva) onto line no. 4.

LINE NO. 4 (YELLOW)
Functional in style, each of these stations has its own unique features. Stop off to take a look at Dostoevskaya Station before continuing on to complete the tour at Sadovaya. (See ♦ 283 for Metro map.)

BY TRAM

Line no. 31 takes in a good portion of the old city (journey lasts approximately 1 hour). Take the tram from Narva Triumphal Arch (Narvskaya Metro). On the Staro-Petergovsky Prospekt is the inn of the monastery of Valaam. After the Obvodny Canal the line runs along Griboedov Canal. At Theater Square look out for the Mariinsky Theater, the Conservatoire and the statue of Rimsky-Korsakov. Before turning into Ulitsa Glinka note, on the right, the dome of St Nicholas Cathedral. The tram crosses the Moika by way of the Kisses Bridge (on the right see the dome of St Isaac's and on the left, New Holland). At Labor Square stands Nicholas Palace. Next the tram runs along Per. Konnogvardeysky (Imperial Stables).

To the right is St Isaac's Cathedral and to the left the Admiralty. From Palace Square there is a delightful view of the Hermitage, Alexander Column and the Stock Exchange. Palace Bridge brings you back to Vasilyevsky Island where you can see the Rostral Columns and the nearby Zoological Museum. Past the Malaya Neva, the tram continues to Petrogradsky Island (Fortress) and finally onto Apothecaries' Island where the Convent of St John of Kronstadt comes into view. Before taking the Metro to Chornaya Rechka, take in Kammeny Island, where the dachas of the nobility were constructed in the early 20th century.

BY HELICOPTER

On a lawn just behind Peter and Paul Fortress, a helicopter awaits, ready to take off at any time. Circling slowly over the city, it provides passengers with superb views of the city (Hermitage, Fortress, Neva, Summer Garden, Smolny, *Aurora*, Admiralty, St Isaac's).
PRICE: $20.
DURATION: 10 to 12 minutes.
Individual bookings:
♦ AVIA COMPANY BALISKY AVIALINEA 9, Ul. Razyezjaya
Tel. 104 1676
or 315 3458

PANORAMIC VIEWS
♦ Dome of St Isaac's (130 feet) gives you an excellent view over the city center.
Be warned, there are 562 steps and no elevator.
♦ Telecommunications tower (656 feet).
The view from here stretches over the city and surrounding forests as far as the Gulf of Finland.
Television center, 6 Ulitsa Chapygin, Petrogradskaya Metro.

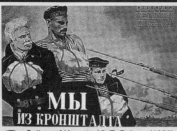

"The Sailors of Kronstadt", E. Dzigan (1936).   *The Valaam Monastery surrounded by woods.*

Those with a taste for Russian culture as it was during the reign of Peter the Great and a desire to rediscover the roots of Russia will appreciate a visit to the old city of Novgorod. Or take a boat trip to Valaam Island and savor the Nordic charm of the lakes and islands. A slightly longer journey along the rivers and lakes of Carelia will take you to Lake Onega and Kizhi Island with its extraordinary wooden architecture. For something a little more remote, visit Kronstadt, the fortified town on Kitline Island, in the Gulf of Finland.

KRONSTADT

This port, 18 miles from St Petersburg, was inaccessible to outsiders for many years. In 1703, Peter the Great built a fortress here to defend the capital. Since 1720 Kronstadt has been a major Baltic Navy base. The name is reminiscent of the sailors' revolt against Soviet control in 1921. To reach Kronstadt, sail along the dyke protecting St Petersburg from floods (excellent view of the sea).

TOWN VISIT
Begin in the heart of the town at the old shopping arcade **(1)** and St Vladimir's Church **(2)**. Continue along Obvodny Canal to the Italian Palace, now the officers' mansion, **(3)**. See Peter the Great's Lock **(4)**, the park and the Bronze Horseman **(5)**, overlooking the port **(6)**. In the Summer Garden **(7)** are monuments to the ships *Oprichnik* **(8)** and *Domashenko* **(9)**. The naval cathedral **(10)** dominates the mound. In Yakornaya Square, is a statue of Vice-Admiral Makarov **(11)** and the rock of "eternal fire" **(12)**. Opposite the cathedral notice the road around the square: each cobble-stone has a metal surround.

NOTE: guided tours are obligatory and a day pass required. This involves a phone call from your guide and presentation of a visitor's passport.

COACH TRIPS
The simplest way to see Kronstadt and Novgorod is by coach.
◆ **RESERVATIONS** can be made in St Petersburg:
– two ticket booths by Gostiny Dvor (corner of Ul. Dumskaya and Nevsky Pr. (coach departure point)
– Davran Agency Tel. 271 09 58/ or 271 36 59.
– Society for the Protection of Culture & Hist. Monuments Tel. 273 30 50.
◆ **KRONSTADT** Trip lasts 5 hours. Price: $6.
◆ **NOVGOROD** Trip lasts 12 hours. Price: $9.

KRONSTADT

Kronstadskoe Shosse

GULF OF FINLAND

Prospekt Lenina

Sovestkaya Ulitsa

Makarovskaya Ul.

Petrovskaya Ul.

Ul. Ammermana

0   ¼   ½ mile

Domes of St George of Novgorod.

The fantastic wooden architecture of Kizhi.

NOVGOROD

Founded in the 19th century, this ancient Russian city is situated 120 miles from St Petersburg and was at its commercial and cultural peak from the 12th to the 15th century. Novgorod lost its independence when it became part of Moscow in 1478 and was devastated in 1570 at the hands of Ivan the Terrible. Today it is the site of one of the richest medieval architectural heritages in the world.

A TOUR OF THE CITY
Start in the St Sophia district which is situated on the left bank of the Volkhov. This is the home of the Kremlin with its nine watch towers. The Kremlin includes St Sophia Cathedral (1045–50) **(1)**, Facettes Palace (15th century) **(2)** with its superb collection of ancient icons and its clock tower **(3)**, and the monument to the Russian Millennium (1862) **(4)**. On the right bank stretches the Commercial district with the Yaroslav courtyard, St Nicholas' Church (12th century), and several other smaller churches which date from the 13th to the 17th century. On the banks of the Volkhov stands the Merchant Court arcade; these buildings all date from the Middle

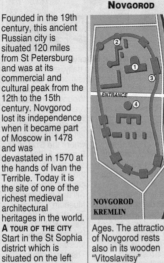

NOVGOROD KREMLIN

Ages. The attraction of Novgorod rests also in its wooden "Vitoslavitsy" architecture (Shossé Yurievskoe), a mile from the city center. Further south stands St George's Monastery with its cathedral (1119), princes' tombs and clergies' boyars.

VALAAM

To the northwest of Lake Ladoga, Carelia Island (with a surface area of 11½ sq. miles) forms part of an archipelago linking around fifty little islands. The monastery, founded here in the Middle Ages, was seized by the Swedes in 1611 and restored by order of Peter the Great in 1715. Today the monastery, which numbers around sixty monks, is also responsible for the running of a farm and an orchard. The large 19th-century monastery cathedral is currently being restored. Explore the area on foot and discover ancient chapels and *skites* (remote Anchorite monasteries) at the edge of the forest on the rocky banks of Valaam Island.
DURATION:
1 day and 2 nights.
PRICE: $70–95 (including 3 meals per day). The price varies depending on the type of room.

GETTING TO NOVGOROD:
◆ BY CAR from St Petersburg, 120 miles along the Shossé Moskovskoe.
◆ BY COACH from the intercity station, at 36, Nab. Obvodnovo Kanala.
◆ BY HELICOPTER: Tel. 104 16 76.
The following hotels are recommended to those wishing to spend more than a day in Novgorod:
◆ BERESTA PALACE HOTEL
Raion 3
Tel. (816) 347 47.
◆ INTOURIST
16, Ul. Dimitroskaya
Tel. (816) 74 642 or (816) 74 282.

KIZHI

Situated to the north of Lake Onega, Kizhi has chapels, farms, barns and a mill, all typical features of this area. The St Lazarus Chapel (14th century) is its oldest building and the Church of the Transfiguration (1714), constructed entirely from wood and surmounted by twenty-two wood-tiled domes, is the island's main attraction. Kizhi, 42 miles from Petrozavodsk, the capital of Carelia, was founded by Peter the Great on the banks of Lake Onega. After Petrozavodsk and Kizhi the boat crosses lakes Onega, Swir and Ladoga, stops at Valaam then returns to St Petersburg.
DURATION: 3 days and 4 nights. **PRICE:** $170–280 (meals inc.).

VISITS TO VALAAM, KIZHI AND CARELIA
Boat trips are available from mid May to mid October.
◆ Reservations can be made in St Petersburg at the CENTRAL TOURIST OFFICE
27, Ul. Bolshaya Koniushennaya, 1st Floor, Room 17. Tel. 311 24 45.
or the CENTRAL EXCURSION BUREAU
56, Nab. Angliiskaya Tel. 311 40 19.
◆ Boat departures: 195, Obukhovskoy Oborony Prospekt.

St Petersburg, the inspiration of Russia's most illustrious writers and poets, has become something of a myth in literature. Traveling around the city is an excellent way to rediscover the world of Pushkin's novels.

A LITERARY TOUR OF ST PETERSBURG

Start at THE PALACE OF COUNT LAVAL ▲ 195 (4 Nab. Angliiskaya, tram no. 31, trolleybus nos. 5, 22, 44 to St Isaac's Square). Here, in this aristocratic building, in May, 1828, Pushkin gave the first reading of his drama *The Brothers Godunov*. Continue along the embankment to THE BRONZE HORSEMAN ▲ 194. This statue, dedicated to Peter the Great, takes its name from Pushkin's poem. Behind the park, to the left of St Isaac's Cathedral, is the LOBANOV-ROSTOVSKY MANSION, built by Montferrand. Perch on the back of one of the two lions of the colonnade, of Carrara marble. Eugène, the ill-fated protagonist of *The Bronze Horseman*, watches Peter the Great's sinister silhouette with horror. On St Isaac's Square stands the STATUE OF NICHOLAS I ▲ 196, sworn enemy of Pushkin. On the right of Blue Bridge, on the Moika, is the NEPTUNE SCALE ▲ 197, installed in 1971, to commemorate the worst floods: 1967, 1935, 1924, 1903, 1824 (the year of *The Bronze Horseman*, a particularly disastrous flood because ground level was much lower at that time). Skirt around St Isaac's Square, past the Astoria Hotel and follow BOLSHAYA MORSKAYA ▲ 214 up to no. 26. This is where Pushkin lived from 1831 to 1832 and it was here that he planned *The Queen of Spades*. Turning left you will see, in the parallel street, PRINCESS GALITZINE'S HOUSE ▲ 213 (10 Ul. Malaya Morskaya) which served as a model for *The Queen of Spades*. Opposite, at no. 13, on the Nevsky Pr., is the apartment of a professional card player – a gambling house which Pushkin himself would probably have frequented and where, undoubtedly, Herman (in *The Queen of Spades*) would have played.

PUSHKIN MUSEUM ▲ 182
(12 Nab. Moika, open daily, except Tues. and the last Friday in the month). This is the last residence of Pushkin and his wife, Natalia Goncharova. Wounded in a duel, Pushkin died here on January 29, 1837.

◆ Stop for a break at the LITERARY CAFÉ ▲ 214 (18 Nevsky Prospekt), formerly *Wolf and Berenger*. It was here, on January 28, 1837, that Pushkin arranged to meet his second, Danzas, before the duel that was to cost him his life.
◆ For those on a more restricted budget, visit the snack bar at 57 Nab. Moika. Next continue along the Moika as far as the PUSHKIN MUSEUM ▲ 182. Pushkin's funeral was held in the IMPERIAL STABLES CHURCH ▲ 182 (1, Konyshennya Ploshchad, open daily from 9am until 7pm). Cross the square and carry on along Griboedov Canal (go past St Savior's Church), then cross the square. Take Ulitsa Ingenernaya, on the left, to Arts Square where the STATUE OF PUSHKIN ▲ 224 stands. This is one of the city's main artistic centers, where you will find the Russian Museum, Little Theater of Opera and Ballet (Maly Theater), Philharmonic, and Musical Comedy Theater. Enthusiasts can go to a performance of *Boris Godunov*, *Eugene Onegin* or *Queen of Spades*.

A FAMOUS DUEL

The scene of the duel between Pushkin and Baron Dantes is commemorated by an obelisk. Take the metro to Nevsky Prospekt station and then continue on to Chornaya Rechka (there is a statue of Pushkin in the station); next continue on foot to the scene of the duel (on Kolomyazhsky Prospekt).

USEFUL ADDRESSES

◆ CHOOSING A RESTAURANT

◆ Modest
◆◆ Good quality
◆◆◆ Top quality
◆◆◆◆ Luxury

	PAGE	ADDRESS	CUISINE	PRICE	SETTING
RESTAURANTS					
F O R T R E S S					
AUSTERIA Tel. 238 4262	306	Peter and Paul Fortress	Russian	◆◆	
IMPERIAL Tel. 234 1742	306	53, Kamennoostrovsky Prospekt	Russian	◆◆	
PIROSMANI Tel. 235 6456	306	14, Bolshoy Prospekt	Georgian	◆◆	●
TBILISI Tel. 232 9391	306	10, Sytninskaya Ulitsa	Georgian and Vegetarian	◆◆	
TÊTE À TÊTE Tel. 232 7548	306	65, Bolshoy Prospekt	Russian	◆	
VICTORY RESTAURANT Tel. 232 4143	306	24, Kamennoostrovsky Prospekt	Russian and German	◆◆	
V A S I L Y E V S K Y I S L A N D					
KALINKA Tel. 218 2866 _One of the best Russian restaurants in St Petersburg_	307	Syezdovskaya Linia	Russian	◆◆◆	
RESTAURANT SWIR Tel. 213 6321 _Floating restaurant_	307	Nab. Makarova Tuchkov Bridge	International	◆◆◆	
H E R M I T A G E					
KROUNK Tel. 273 3830	303	14, Solianoy Per.	Armenian	◆	
THE 1001 NIGHTS Tel. 312 22 65 _Immaculate oriental decoration_	303	21, Millionnaya Ulitsa	Uzbek	◆◆	●
RUSSKIE BLINI Tel. 297 0559 _Welcoming, typically Russian atmosphere_	303	13, Ulitsa Furmanova	Russian	◆	
A D M I R A L T Y					
ADAMANT Tel. 311 5575	304	72, Nab. Reki Moiki	Russian	◆◆◆	
BISTRO FRANÇAIS Tel. 315 2465	304	20, Ulitsa Galernaya	French	◆◆◆◆	●
ASTORIA CAFÉ Tel. 210 5906 _Specialty: Swedish food_	305	Astoria Hotel, Bldg. A Isaakievsky Pl.	International	◆◆◆	
DVORIANSKOE GNEZDO Tel. 312 3205 _One of the most elegant restaurants_	305	21, Ulitsa Dekabristov	French	◆◆◆◆	●
RESTAURANT ANGLETERRE Tel. 210 5906	305	Astoria Hotel, Bldg. B Isaakievsky Pl.		◆◆◆◆	
WINTER GARDEN RESTAURANT Tel. 210 5906	305	Astoria Hotel, Bldg. A Isaakievsky Pl.	International	◆◆◆◆	●
THE POLONESE Tel. 315 0339	305	45, Bolshaya Morskaya Ulitsa	Russian	◆◆◆◆	
NIKOLAI Tel. 311 1402 _In a 19th-century palace_	305	52, Bolshaya Morskaya Ulitsa	European	◆◆◆	●
1913 RESTAURANT Tel. 315 5148	305	13, Voznesensky Pr.	Russian	◆◆	
RESTAURANT SAIGON Tel. 315 8772	305	33, Ulitsa Kazanskaya 2, Voznesensky Pr.	Russian, oriental and European	◆◆	
TANDOOR Tel. 312 5310	305		Indian	◆◆	
N E V S K Y					
LITERATURE CAFÉ Tel. 312 6057	308	18, Nevsky Prospekt		◆◆	●
CAT Tel. 311 3377	308	24, Karavannaya Ulitsa	Russian	◆◆	
RESTAURANT DRUZHBA	309	Nevsky Prospekt	International	◆	
RESTAURANT EUROPE Tel. 119 6000 _Jazz brunch_	309	Hotel Europe 1, Ulitsa Mikhailovskaya	Russian International	◆◆◆◆	●
SADKO Tel. 119 6000 _Pleasant lunchtime restaurant_		Hotel Europe 1, Ulitsa Mikhailovskaya		◆◆	●

		PAGE	ADDRESS	CUISINE	PRICE	SETTING
ASSEMBLY RESTAURANT	Tel. 314 1537	309	11, Ulitsa Bolshaya Konyushennaya	Russian	♦♦	
METROPOL REST.	Tel. 311 0233	309	20–22, Ulitsa Sadovaya	Russian		
ST PETERSBURG	Tel. 314 4947	309	7, Griboedov Canal	Russian	♦♦♦	
F O N T A N K A				International		
APHRODITE	Tel. 275 7620	310	86, Nevsky Prospekt	International	♦♦♦	
BELLA LEONE	Tel. 113 1670	310	6, Vladimirsky Prospekt	International	♦♦♦	
DOMENICO'S	Tel. 272 5717	310	70, Nevsky Prospekt	Russian and European	♦♦♦	
ADMIRALTY RESTAURANT		310	Nevsky Palace Hotel 57, Nevsky Prospekt	International	♦♦♦	
IMPERIAL RESTAURANT	Tel. 275 2001	310	Nevsky Palace Hotel 57, Nevsky Prospekt	International	♦♦♦	
LANDSKRONA RESTAURANT	Tel. 275 2001	310	Nevsky Palace Hotel 57, Nevsky Prospekt	International	♦♦♦♦	●
NEVSKY RESTAURANT	Tel. 311 8993	310	71, Nevsky Prospekt	Russian	♦♦	
RESTORANTCHIK	Tel. 311 8589	310	79, Nevsky Prospekt.		♦♦	
TCHINARA	Tel. 279 1478	310	15, Ulitsa Vostaniya	Georgian	♦	
S M O L N Y						
WARSTEINER FORUM	Tel. 277 5406	310	120, Nevsky Prospekt	German	♦♦	
A R O U N D S M O L N Y						
PODVORIE	Tel. 465 1399		16, Filtrovskoe Tyarlevo		♦♦♦	●
Typical Russian cuisine and décor		312				
CAFÉS – BRASSERIES						
F O R T R E S S						
CAFÉ GROT			3, Alexandrovsky Park	Russian	♦	●
Unusual setting		306				
GRAND CAFÉ ANTWEP.	Tel. 233 9746	306	13–15, Kronversky Pr.	Russian	♦♦	
TROITSKY MOST	Tel. 232 66 93	306	2, Ulitsa Malaya Posadskaya	Vegetarian	♦♦	
N E V S K Y						
CAFÉ BALKAN	Tel. 315 4748	308	27, Nevsky Prospekt	Russian	♦	
TCHAÏKA	Tel. 311 1957	308	14, Griboedov Canal		♦♦♦	
BRASSERIE	Tel. 119 6000	309	Hotel Europe 1, Ulitsa Mikhailovskaya	International	♦♦♦	
THE MEZZANINE	Tel. 119 6000	309	Hotel Europe 1, Ulitsa Mikhailovskaya		♦♦♦	●
S M O L N Y						
CAFÉ BALSEN	Tel. 271 2811	311	142, Staro Nevsky Pr.	European	♦♦	●
SURPRISE	Tel. 277 2431	311	113, Staro Nevsky Pr.	International	♦	
FAST FOOD						
N E V S K Y						
GRILL MASTER	Tel. 110 5540	308	46, Nevsky Prospekt	Fast food	♦	
F O N T A N K A						
TCHARODEIKA	Tel. 279 0940	311	88, Nevsky Prospekt	Cafeteria	♦	
S M O L N Y						
HOT DOG		310	Staro Nevsky Prospekt	International	♦	
A R O U N D S M O L N Y						
SELF-SERVICE REST.	Tel. 470 6966	310	Pavlovsk		♦	
PETERHOF	Tel. 427 9884	312	Peterhof		♦	

◆ MUSEUMS AND PLACES OF INTEREST

	PAGE	ADDRESS	OPENING TIMES
PANORAMA			
TELEVISION TOWER TEL. 234 78 87		3, Ul. Akademika Pavlova	Open Wed.–Sun. 11am–5pm
HISTORY			
MUSEUM OF POLITICAL HISTORY TEL. 233 7113	306	214, Ul. Kubysheva	Open Fri.–Wed. 10am–6pm
PETER THE GREAT'S CABIN TEL. 232 4576	306	Petrovskaya Nab.	Open Wed.–Mon. 10am–6pm
PETER AND PAUL FORTRESS TEL. 238 4540	306	Pl. Revolutsy	Open Mon. and Thur.–Sun. 11am–6pm and Tue. 11am–5pm
LENIN MEMORIAL MUSEUM TEL. 278 1321	311	Pl. Proletarskoy Diktatury	Open Mon.–Fri. 10am–6pm and Sat. 11am–3pm
SIEGE OF LENINGRAD MUSEUM TEL. 275 7208	303	9, Solianoy Per.	Open Thur.–Tue. 10am–5pm
ST PETERSBURG HISTORY MUSEUM TEL. 311 7544	304	44, Angliiskaya Nab.	Open Thur.–Tue. 11am–5pm
PAINTING AND SCULPTURE			
MUSEUM OF THE ACADEMY OF ARTS TEL. 213 6496	307	17, Universitetskaya Nab.	Open Wed.–Sun. 11am–7pm
WINTER PALACE HERMITAGE MUSEUM TEL. 311 3725	303	36, Dvortsovaya Nab.	Open Tue.–Sat. 10.30am–6pm and Sun. 10.30am–5pm
MUSEUM OF DECORATIVE ARTS TEL. 273 3258	303	15, Solianoy Per.	Open Tue.–Sat. 11am–5pm
RUSSIAN MUSEUM TEL. 314 3448	308	2, Ingenernaya Ul.	Open Mon. 10am–5pm, Wed.–Sun. 10am– 6pm
LITERATURE			
PUSHKIN MUSEUM	303	12, Nab. Reki Moiky	
BLOK MUSEUM TEL. 113 8616	304	57, Ul. Dekabristov	Open Thur.–Mon. 11am–5pm and Tue. 11am–4pm
ANNA AKHMATOVA MUSEUM TEL. 272 2211 OR 272 1811	310	53, Liteiny Pr.	Open Tue.–Sun. 10.30am–6.30pm
DOSTOEVSKY MUSEUM TEL. 164 6950	310	5, Kuznechny Per.	Open Tue.–Sun. 10.30am–6.30pm
MUSIC AND THEATER			
MUSEUM OF MUSICAL INSTRUMENTS TEL. 314 5345 OR 314 5394	304	5, Isaakievsky Pl.	Open Wed.–Sun. noon–6pm
THEATER MUSEUM TEL. 311 2195	308	6, Pl. Ostrovsky	Open Th.–Mon. 11am–6pm and Wed. 1–7pm
SCIENCE AND NATURAL SCIENCE			
BOTANICAL MUSEUM TEL. 234 8470	306	2, Ul. Professora Popova	Open Sat.–Thur. 11am–4pm
ZOOLOGICAL MUSEUM TEL. 218 0112	307	1, Universitetskaya Nab.	Open Sat.–Thur. 11am–6pm
MUSEUM OF ANTHROPOLOGY AND ETHNOGRAPHY TEL. 218 1412	307	3, Universitetskaya Nab.	Open Sat.–Wed. 11am–6pm
LOMONOSOV MUSEUM TEL. 218 1412	307	3, Universitetskaya Nab.	Open Sat.–Wed. 11am–4.30pm
MENDELEEV MUSEUM TEL. 218 2982 OR 218 9744	307	7-9, Universitetskaya Nab.	Open Mon.–Fri. 10am–5pm
ETHNOGRAPHIC MUSEUM TEL. 219 1676 OR 219 1719	308	4, Ingenernaya Ul. 10, Pl. Iskustv	Open Tue.–Sun. 10am–6pm
MUSEUM OF THE ARCTIC AND ANTARCTIC TEL. 311 2549	310	24 A, Ul. Marata	Open Wed.–Sun. 10am–6pm

	PAGE	ADDRESS	OPENING TIMES
MILITARY ART			
CRUISER AURORA TEL. 230 5202	306	4, Petrogradskaya Nab.	Open Tue.–Thur. and Sat.–Sun. 10.30am–4pm
ARTILLERY MUSEUM TEL. 232 0296	306	Kronverkskaya Nab.	Open Tue.–Sun. 11am–6pm
NAVAL MUSEUM TEL. 218 25 01 OR 218 2502	307	4, Pl. Pushkina	Open Wed.–Sun. 10.30am–5.30pm
SUVOROV MUSEUM	311	Ul. Saltykova Shchredrina	
PALACES			
MENSHIKOV PALACE TEL. 213 1112	307	15, Universitetskaya Nab.	Open Tue.–Sun. 10.30am–4.30pm
MARBLE PALACE TEL. 312 9196	303	5, Ul. Millionaya	
SUMMER PALACE	303	Nab. Kutuzova	Open 10.30am–6pm
YUSUPOV PALACE TEL. 311 53 53 OR 314 9883	304	94, Nab. Reki Moiki	
ENGINEERS' CASTLE FORMER MIKHAILOVSKY PALACE TEL. 210 44 67 OR 210 4173	308	2, Ul. Sadovaya	Open Mon. 10am–5pm and Wed.–Sun. 10am–6pm
BELOSELSKY–BELOZERSKY PALACE TEL. 319 9990 OR 319 9792	310	41, Nevsky Pr.	Open noon–6.30pm
PETERHOF	312	Peterhof	
GRAND PALACE TEL. 427 9527			Open Tue.–Sun., 11am–6pm May–Sep. and 11am–5pm Oct.–Apr.
MONPLAISIR TEL. 427 9129			Open Thur.–Tue. 11am–6pm, May–Sep.
HERMITAGE			Open Wed.–Mon. 11am–6pm
MARLY			Open Wed.–Mon. 11am–6pm
COTTAGE TEL. 427 9953			Open Sat.–Thur. 11am–6pm, May–Sep.; Sat.–Sun. 10.30am–5pm, Oct.–Apr.
CATHERINE PAVILION			Open Fri.–Wed. 11am–6pm
BENOIS FAMILY MUSEUM			Open Tue.–Sun. 11am–6pm
ORANIENBAUM	312	Oranienbaum	
CHINESE PALACE			Open Wed.–Mon. 11am–5pm, in summer
"SLIDING HILL" PAVILION			Open Wed.–Mon. 11am–5pm
CHINESE KITCHEN			Open Wed.–Mon. 11am–5pm
PETER III'S PALACE			Open Wed.–Mon. 11am–5pm
CAVALRY HOUSE			Open Wed.–Mon. 11am–5pm
PAVLOVSK PAL. TEL. 470 6214	312	Pavlovsk	Open Sat.–Thur. 10am–6pm
TSARSKOE SELO	312	Tsarskoe Selo	
CATHERINE PALACE			Open Wed.–Mon. 11am–5pm
PUSHKIN MUSEUM			Open Wed.–Mon. 10am–4pm
GATCHINA PALACE	312	Gatchina	Open Tue.–Sun. 10am–6pm
RELIGION AND CHURCH SERVICES			
MOSQUE	306	7, Pl. Maxima Gorkovo	Open Sat.–Thur. noon–7pm
CHURCH OF ANDREEVSKY		Ul. Kamskaya	Open 9am–8pm
SMOLENSK CEMETERY	307	Ul. Kamskaya	
ST ISAAC'S CATHEDRAL	304	Isaakievsky Pl.	Open Thur.–Tue. 11am–6pm
MUSEUM OF RELIGIOUS HISTORY KAZAN CATHEDRAL TEL. 314 5856	308	10, Ul. Plekhanova	Open Mon.–Tue. and Thur.–Fri. 11am–6pm, Sat.–Sun. 12.30–6pm
ST NICHOLAS' CATHEDRAL	304	1/3 Nikolskaya Pl.	
VLADIMIRSKAYA CHURCH	310	Pl. Vladimirskaya	Open 8am–9pm
ALEXANDER NEVSKY MONASTERY	311		
CHURCH OF THE ANNUNCIATION			Open Fri.–Wed. 10.30am–7pm
TRINITY CATHEDRAL			Open 8am–2pm and 5–6pm
CEMETERIES		Pl. Alexandra Nevskovo	Open Fri.–Wed. 11am–6pm
SMOLNY MONASTERY	311	Pl. Rastrelli	Open Thur.–Tue. 11am–6pm and Wed.

USEFUL INFORMATION

TOUR OPERATORS

IN THE UK:

◆ NOBLE CALEDONIA
11 Charles Street
London W1
Tel. 0171 491 4752
One of the forerunners for tourism in Russia.

◆ VOYAGES JULES VERNES
20, Dorset Square
London W1
Tel. 0171 723 5066
Offers luxury cruises and train journeys and high-class guided tours.

◆ REGENT HOLIDAYS UK
15, John Street
Bristol BS1 2HR
Tel. 0117 9211711

◆ PROGRESSIVE TOURS
12, Porchester Place
London W2 2BS
Tel. 0171 262 1676
Organizes hotels, excursions, tickets and visas.

◆ ABERCROMBIE & KENT
Sloane Square House
Holbein Place
London SW1
Tel. 0717 262 1676

◆ COX & KINGS TRAVEL
4th Floor, Gordon House
10 Greencoat Place
London SW1
Tel. 0171 873 5001

IN THE US:

◆ AMERICAN EXPRESS VACATIONS
Tel. (800) 241 1700

◆ CARAVAN TOURS
Tel. (800) 227 2826
or (312) 321 9800

◆ OLSON-TRAVELWORLD
Tel. (800) 421 5785
or (310) 546 8400

◆ TRAFALGAR TOURS
Tel. (800) 854 0103
or (212) 689 8977

◆ MAUPINTOUR
Tel. (800) 255 4266
or (913) 843 1211

◆ COUNCIL TRAVEL
Tel. (212) 661 1450
There are also branches at college campuses throughout the US.

◆ TRAVEL MANAGEMENT INTERNATIONAL
Tel. (617) 661 5551

◆ TRAVEL CUTS
Tel. (416) 979 2406

IN ST PETERSBURG:

◆ PETER'S GUIDES
Tel. 812 713 4459
Intourist trained individual guides. Contact Anna.

◆ VALERA
Tel. 812 278 0195
Experienced individual guide.

◆ KOSMOS LTD
Local tourism firm.
Tel. 812 213 1121
or 812 218 7743
Contact: Vladimir Kazhebnikov.

GENERAL

EMERGENCIES

FIRE BRIGADE
Tel. 01

POLICE
Tel. 02

EMERGENCY MEDICAL ASSISTANCE
Tel. 03

INGOSSTRAKH
17, Ul. Zakharievskaya
Tel. 273 0625
In case of road accidents.

AMERICAN MEDICAL CENTER
77, Nab. Fontanky
Tel. 119 6101

BANK, BUREAUX DE CHANGE

AMERICAN EXPRESS
Grand Hotel Europe
1/7, Ul. Mikhailovskaya
Open Mon.–Fri.
9am–5pm,
Sat. 9am–11pm

AEROFLOT BANK
26, Griboedov Canal
Open 9am–9pm
One of the best rates of exchange in St Petersburg. Very popular.

INKOM BANK
57, Nevsky Prospekt
Tel. 113 19 70

SVERBANK
80, Nevsky Prospekt
Open 10am–2pm
and 3–8pm
Closed Sun.
Bureau de change open until 6pm. Not the best rates of exchange, but takes Visa, Mastercard, American Express, Thomas Cook travelers' checks.

VNESHTORGOVYBANK
29, Ul. Bolshaya Morskaya
Open 10am–1pm
and 2–5.30pm,
Fri. 10am–4.30pm
One of the best exchange rates in the city. A branch of Aeroflot.

MONEY

Should you need to wire money from the US contact

◆ AMERICAN EXPRESS MONEYGRAM
Tel. (800) 543 4080

◆ WESTERN UNION
Tel. (800) 325 6000

TRANSPORT

CENTRAL RESERVATION AND TICKET OFFICE
24, Griboedov Canal
Tel. 201
Open Mon.–Sat. 8am–8pm, Sun. 8am–4pm
For international connections: ticket booths nos. 90 to 105 on the second floor.

BALTIC STATION
120, Nab. Obvodnovo Canal
Tel. 168 2972

FINLAND STATION
6, Pl. Lenina
Tel. 168 7685

MOSCOW STATION
9, Ul. Poltavskaya
Tel. 168 0111

WARSAW STATION
118, Nab. Obvodnovo Canal
Tel. 168 2972

VITEBSK STATION
52, Zagorodny Prospekt
Tel. 168 5390

PORT
Pl. Morskoy Slavy
Tel. 355 19 02

CAR RENTAL

AVIS
13, Ul. Remeslennaya
Tel. 235 64 44

AUTODOM
56, Nab. Reki Moiki
Tel. 315 90 43

INTERAVTO
12, Ul. Alex. Nevskovo
Tel. 113 72 53

TRANSVELTROIKA
37, Lermontovsky Prospekt
Tel. 113 72 53

TOURIST OFFICES

CENTRAL TRAVEL BUREAU
27, Ul. Bolshaya Konyushennaya
Tel. 315 30 74
Open 10am–6pm during the winter and
10am–7pm throughout the summer months
Closed Sun.
Organized tours of Russia.

TOURIST OFFICE
SERVICE BUREAU
Astoria Hotel
Isaakievsky Ploshchad,
Bldg. B, 1st floor,
at the end, on the right.
Trolleybus nos. 5 and 22
Tel. 210 50 40
Open 9am–5pm

PRACTICAL INFORMATION

UK CONSULATE
Pl. Proletarskoy Diktatury
Smolninsky Raeya
194215
Tel. (812) 119 6036

US CONSULATE
15, Furshtadtskaya Ulitsa
Tel. 275 1701

CENTRAL POST OFFICE
9, Ul. Pochtamskaya
Open Mon.–Sat.
9am–8pm
Sun. 10am–6pm

POST, PACKAGES, TELEGRAMS
14, Ul. Furmanova
Open 9am–1pm
and 1.30–8pm
Closed Sat.–Sun.
and public holidays.

POST AND TELEPHONE
5, Bolshaya Morskaya
Open 8am–10.30pm

POST OFFICE
EMS EXPRESS
MAIL SERVICE
4, Konnogvardeisky Bl.
Entrance no. 2
Tel. 311 96 71
or 311 92 88
Open Mon.–Fri.
9am–8pm, Sat.–Sun.
10am–6pm

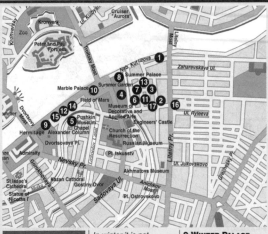

HERMITAGE

PRACTICAL INFORMATION

1 PHARMACY
6, Nab. Kutuzova
Open 9am–7pm
Closed Sat. and Sun.

2 PHARMACY
12, Ul. Pestelia
and Ul. Mokhovaya
Open Mon.–Fri.
9am–8pm, Sat.–Sun.
11am–5pm
*Contact lenses and
accessories.*

**3 POST, PACKAGES,
TELEGRAMS**
14, Ul. Furmanova
Open 9am–1pm
and 1.30–8pm
Closed Sat., Sun. and
public holidays.

CULTURE

4 SUMMER GARDEN
Open 8am–10pm in
summer, 8am–7pm in
winter. Closed Tue. and
the last Mon. of the
month.

*In winter it is not
possible to see the
statues. The tea shop
and café are open from
10.30am to 6pm.*

5 PUSHKIN MUSEUM
12, Nab. Reki Moiki
*Closed for maintenance
work from October
1994.*

**6 MUSEUM OF
DECORATIVE ARTS**
15, Solianoy Per.
Open 11am–5pm
Closed Sun. and Mon.

**7 SIEGE OF
LENINGRAD MUSEUM**
9, Solianoy Prospekt
Tel. 275 72 08
Open 10am–5pm
Closed Wed.

8 SUMMER PALACE
Nab. Kutuzova
Open 10.30am–6pm
Closed Tue. and the last
Mon. of the month, and
from November until the
end of March.

**9 WINTER PALACE
AND THE HERMITAGE
MUSEUM**
36, Nab. Dvortsovaya
Nevsky Prospekt metro
station, trolleybus
nos. 1, 9 and 10
Tel. 311 37 25
Open Tue.–Sat.
10.30am–6pm,
Sun. 10.30am–5pm
Closed Mon.
*Ticket office closes one
hour before museum
closing time.*

10 MARBLE PALACE
5, Ul. Millionnaya
Tel. 312 91 96
*Entrance to the palace
is through the
Field of Mars.*

RESTAURANTS

11 KROUNK
14, Solianoy Per.
Tel. 273 3830
Open noon–10pm
*Cool, rather formal
atmosphere.
Armenian cuisine.
Price: around $7.*
⌂

**12 ★ THE 1001
NIGHTS**
21, Ul. Millionnaya
Tel. 312 22 65
or 314 52 66
Open noon–midnight
*Located in a basement.
Immaculate oriental
décor. Hushed
atmosphere.
Specialty of the house is
a dish called "plov"
(a type of rice-based
couscous, with meat,
vegetables and raisins).
Uzbek cuisine.*
⌂ **C**

13 ★ RUSSKIE BLINI
13, Ul. Furmanova
Open 11am–6pm
Closed Sat.–Sun.
Tel. 279 0559
*This small restaurant
has a friendly, typically
Russian atmosphere
where you share tables
with the other patrons.
Service is fast. This
popular restaurant tends
to get extremely busy
around 1.30pm.
Specialty: Russian
pancakes.
Price: $3.*

SHOPPING

14 BOSKO
8, Ul. Millionnaya
Open 11am–7pm
Closed Sun.
Jewelry.

**15 PETROPOL
GALLERY**
27, Ul. Millionnaya
Five minutes from
Dvortsovaya Pl.
*Sale and display of
various items including
Russian ivory
miniatures.
Visa and Mastercard
credit cards are
accepted.*

16 YAN TEA HOUSE
24, Liteiny Prospekt
and Ul. Pestelia
Open 11am–7pm
Closed Sat. and Sun.
*Specializes in loose
tea imported from
Denmark. Good range
of products.*

17 OU FONTANKY
8, Ul. Pestelia
Open 11am–2pm
and 3–7pm
Closed Sun.
*Stationery, pictures
and also an antiques
department.*

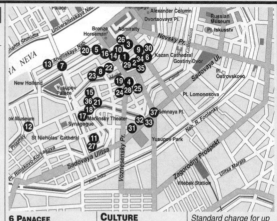

ADMIRALTY

PRACTICAL INFORMATION

TOUR OPERATORS

1 AREA
Astoria Hotel
Isaakievsky Pl.
Entrance at no. 39,
Ul. Bolshaya Morskaya
Tel. 210 50 81 / 210 50 82
Fax 210 50 84
Open 9am–5pm
*Specializes in tours to
Helsinki and
surrounding areas.*

2 DELTA AIRLINE-CSA-
BALKAN AIRLINES
36, Bolshaya Morskaya
Open Mon.–Fri.
9am–1pm and 2–5pm
Closed Sat. and Sun.

3 FINNAIR
19, Ul. Malaya Morskaya
Open Mon.–Fri.
9am–5pm Closed Sat.
and Sun.
*Airport office.
Tel. 104 36 29.*

4 LUFTHANSA
7, Voznesensky Pr.
Tel. 104 34 32
Open Mon.–Fri.
9am–5.30pm
Closed Sat. and Sun.

4 MALEV HUNGARIAN
AIRLINES
7, Voznesensky Pr.
Open Mon.–Fri.
9am–5pm. Closed Sat.
and Sun.
*Accepts Visa and
American Express.*

5 EMS EXPRESS
MAIL SERVICE
4, Konnogvardeisky Bl.
Entrance no. 2
Tel. 311 96 71 / 311 92 88
Open Mon.–Fri.
9am–8pm, Sat.–Sun.
10am–6pm
*Express mail service
(3 to 5 days to Europe).*

1 TOURIST OFFICE
SERVICE BUREAU
Astoria Hotel, Bldg. B
Isaakievsky Pl.
Bldg. B, 1st floor
at the end on the right
Trolleybus nos. 5 and 22
Tel. 210 50 40
Open 9am–5pm

6 PANACEE
PHARMACY
17, Ul. Gorokhovaya
Tel. 314 05 85
Open Mon.–Fri. 9am–
7pm, Sat. 11am– 6pm
and Sun. 11am–4pm

7 PHARMACY
Pl. Truda
Buses no. 1, 5, 11
and 33
Open Mon.–Sat.
8am–8pm. Closed Sun.

8 CENTRAL POST
OFFICE
9, Ul. Pochtamskaya
Open Mon.–Fri.
9am–8pm
Sat.–Sun. 10am–6pm

1 FOREIGN
NEWSPAPERS
Astoria Hotel,
Isaakievsky Pl.
Open 8am–7pm
*There is a newspaper
kiosk in each of the
hotel's buildings.*

9 VNESHTORGOVY-
BANK
29, Ul. Bolshaya
Morskaya
Open 10am–1pm
and 2–5.30pm,
Fri. 10am–4.30pm
*The best exchange
rates in St Petersburg.*

CULTURE

10 ST ISAAC'S
CATHEDRAL
Isaakievsky Pl.
Trolleybus nos. 5 and 22
Tel. 315 97 32
Museum open
11am–6pm,
Panoramas: 11am–5pm
Closed Wed.

11 ST NICHOLAS'
CATHEDRAL
1/3, Nikolskaya Pl.
Tel. 114 08 62

12 BLOK MUSEUM
57, Ul. Dekabristov
Tel. 113 86 16
Open Thur.–Mon. 11am–
5pm, Tue. 11am–4pm

13 ST PETERSBURG'S
HISTORY MUSEUM
44, Nab. Angliiskaya
Tel. 311 75 44
Open 11am–5pm
Closed Wed. and the last
Tue. in the month.

14 MUSEUM OF
MUSICAL INSTRUMENTS
5, Isaakievsky Pl.
Tel. 314 53 45 / 314 53 94
Open noon–6pm
Closed Mon. and Tue.

15 YUSUPOV PALACE
94, Nab. Reki Moiki
Tel. 311 53 53 / 314 98 83
*Guided tours only:
available in Russian
and other languages.*

*Standard charge for up
to three people.*

16 CENTRAL
EXHIBITION HALL
(MANÈGE)
1, Isaakievsky Pl.
Tel. 314 82 53
Open 11am–7pm
Closed Thur.
Box office open until 6pm.

THEATER

17 MARIINSKY
THEATER
Teatralnaya Pl.
Tel. 114 12 11
Ballet and opera.

18 MUSICAL COMEDY
THEATER
Ul. Glinky
*Box office opening hours:
noon–3pm and 4–8pm.*

RESTAURANTS

19 ADAMANT
72, Nab. Reki Moiki
Tel. 311 55 75
Open noon–midnight
*On the Moika. Open
until 11pm. Russian
cuisine. Dishes: $2–20.*
⌂ 🄲

20 BISTRO FRANÇAIS
20, Ul. Galernaya
Tel. 315 24 65
*Beautiful red house,
with French-
style décor.
Expensive.
French
cuisine.*
⌂ 🄲
🅐

1 ASTORIA CAFÉ
Astoria Hotel, Bldg. A
Isaakievsky Pl.
Trolleybus nos. 5 and 22
Tel. 210 59 06
Open 12.30–3.30pm
*Specialty: Swedish
buffet (smorgasbord).
International cuisine.
Price: $30*
⌂ 🇨 ⛶

21 ★ DVORIANSKOE GNEZDO
21, Ul. Dekabristov
Tel. 312 32 05
Fax 311 88 69
Open 1–11pm
*One of St Petersburg's
most elegant
restaurants. Sumptuous
setting, imaginative
menu, much in demand.
Credit cards: Visa and
Mastercard only.
French cuisine.
Price: $50–75 (inc. wine).*
🅿 ⌂ ⛶ ⛪ 🏠

1 RESTAURANT ANGLETERRE
Astoria Hotel, Bldg. B
Isaakievsky Pl.
Tel. 210 59 06
Open noon–midnight

1 WINTER GARDEN RESTAURANT
Astoria Hotel, Bldg. A
Isaakievsky Pl.,
Trolleybus nos. 5
and 22
Tel. 210 59 06
Open noon–midnight
*Last orders 11pm.
Visa and Mastercard
only. International
cuisine.
Price: $11–40.*
⌂ 🇨 ⛶ ⛪

22 ★ THE POLONESE
45, Ul. Bolshaya
Morskaya
Tel. 315 03 39 / 315 03 19
Open noon–midnight
*Situated on the
premises of the
Composers' Union.
Three rooms.
Magnificent setting all in
wood, quiet
atmosphere. Making a
reservation the day
before guarantees you
the pleasure of enjoying
your meal with a duo or
quartet playing in the
background.
Russian cuisine.*
⌂ 🇨 ⛶

23 NIKOLAI
52, Ul. Bolshaya
Morskaya
Tel. 311 14 02
Open noon–11pm
Closed Sun.
*In the Dom Arkhitektov,
19th-century palace.
Beautiful setting.
European cuisine.
Price: $15–40.*
⌂ 🇨

24 1913 RESTAURANT
13 Voznesensky Pr.
Tel. 315 51 48
Open noon–11pm
*Not particularly warm
atmosphere. Bar open
to non-diners.
Imaginative drinks and
cocktails menu.
Russian cuisine.
Dishes: $1–9.*
⌂ 🇨

25 ★ RESTAURANT SAIGON
33 Ul. Plekhanova
Sennaya Pl. or
Sadovaya metros
Open noon–11pm
*This is not an Asian
restaurant. Pleasant
setting in bamboo.
Last orders 10pm.
Russian, oriental and
European cuisine.
Dishes: $1–6.*
⌂ 🇨

26 TANDOOR
2, Voznesensky Pr.
Trolleybus nos. 5 and 22
Tel. 312 53 10
Fax 312 38 86
*Pleasant, though rather
dark, setting. Good
quality service (the
waiters speak English).
Specialties: "murg chaat"
and mutton "shahi" curry.
Indian cuisine.
Price: around $25.*
⌂ 🇨 ⛶

HOTELS

1 ASTORIA
39, Ul. Bolshaya
Morskaya
Tel. 298 38 14
Fax 315 96 68
*Exceptional location at
the foot of St Isaac's
Cathedral. Rooms and
suites. Swimming pool,
car rental, international
newspapers.*
☐

NEPTUNE
93 A, Nab. Obvodnovo
Kanala
Tel. 210 18 11
*Small, quiet, modern
hotel.*

PULKOVSKAYA
1, Ploshchad Pobedy
*Halfway between the
city center and the
airport.*
Tel. 264 51 22
Fax 264 63 96

SHOPPING

27 AUTO-STOP
24, Nab. Kanala
Kriukova
Tel. 310 06 08
Open 9am–8pm
Car parts and repairs.

28 CONCOR
Voznesensky Prospekt
and Pirogova Prospekt
Tel. 117 20 57
Open Mon.–Fri.
11am–3pm and 4–7pm,
Sat. 11am–5.40pm
Closed Sun.
Contact lenses.

29 ARTISTS' UNION GALLERY
38, Ul. Bolshaya
Morskaya
Tel. 315 74 14
Open Tue.–Sat.
1–8pm, Sun. 1–7pm
Closed Mon.

30 YAKHONT
24, Ul. Bolshaya
Morskaya
Open Mon.–Fri.
10am–2pm and
3pm–7pm,
Sat. 10am–4pm
Closed Sun.
Jewelry.

31 KOZHI & MEKHA
51, Ul. Sadovaya
Sennaya Pl. metro
Open Mon.–Sat.
10am–2pm and
3–7pm
Closed Sun.
*Furs, leather clothing
and children's wear,
all locally made in
St Petersburg. Limited
range of goods but
all very reasonably
priced.*

32 KODAK
45, Ul. Sadovaya
Sennaya Pl. metro
*Various brands of film.
Express photo
developing service.*

33 SKYF
42, Ul. Sadovaya
Sennaya Pl. metro
*Wide choice of
perfumes, leather goods,
scarves . . . from Italy.
Everything is priced in
dollars.*

34 PHOTO SERVICE
30, Ul. Bolshaya
Morskaya
Open 9am–8pm
*Photo developing
service, passport
photos and visiting
cards.*

35 ROT FRONT
34, Ul. Bolshaya
Morskaya
Open Mon.–Fri.
10am–2pm and 3–7pm.
Closed Sat.–Sun.
*Wide range of
St Petersburg furs
at reasonable prices.
Stock tends to vary.*

36 SERVICE STATION
Teatralnaya Pl.
*Situated behind the
statue of Rimsky-
Korsakov*
Open 7am–11pm

37 YVES ROCHER
Sennaya Pl.
Open Mon.–Sat.
10am–8pm, Sun.
11am–4pm
*Express mail service
(3 to 5 days to
Europe).*

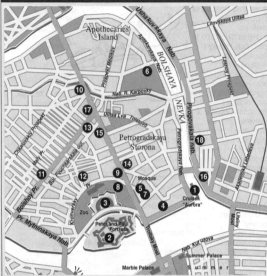

12 TBILISI
10, Ul. Sytninskaya
Tel. 232 93 91
Open noon–10pm
Good food. Wines are rather pricy. Georgian and vegetarian cuisine.
Price: $10–25.
⌂ **C** ▭

13 TÊTE-À-TÊTE
65, Bolshoy Prospekt
Tel. 232 75 48
Open 1pm–5pm and 7pm–midnight
Pleasant, intimate atmosphere.
Russian cuisine.
Price: around $10.
⌂ **C**

14 TROITSKY MOST
2, Ul. Malaya Posadskaya
Gorkovskaya metro
Tel. 232 66 93
Open 11.15am 15–4.20pm
Snack, pizzeria.
Vegetarian cuisine.
Price: up to $10.

15 VICTORY RESTAURANT
24, Kamennoostrovsky
Pr. Gorkovskaya metro
Tel. 232 41 43
Tel. 232 51 30
Open noon–midnight
Floor shows. Russian and German cuisine.
Price: $12–15.
C ▭··

HOTELS

16 ST PETERSBURG
5/2, Vyborgskaya Nab.
Tel. 542 9101
Fax 248 8002
Restaurant, sauna, boutiques. View of the city.

SHOPPING

17 BOOKSTORE
40, Kamennoostrovsky Prospekt.
Petrogradskaya metro
Open Mon.–Fri. 10am–2pm and 3–7pm,
Sat. 10am–2pm and 3–6pm
Closed Sun.

18 STOCKMAN
1, Finliandsky Prospekt
Pl. Lenina metro, behind St Petersburg Hotel
Open 10am–8pm
Well-stocked western supermarket. Bureau de change at the entrance.

FORTRESS

CULTURAL LIFE

1 CRUISER "AURORA"
4, Nab. Petrogradskaya
Bus no. 49 or Gorkovskaya metro
Tel. 230 52 02
Open Tue.–Thur. and Sat.–Sun. 10.30am–4pm
Closed Mon. and Fri.

2 PETER AND PAUL FORTRESS
Pl. Revolutsy
Gorkovskaya metro
Tel. 238 4540
Open Thur.–Mon. 11am–6pm, Tue. 11am–5pm
Closed Wed. and last Tue. of the month.

3 ARTILLERY MUSEUM
Nab. Kronverkskaya
Gorkovskaya metro
Tel. 232 02 96
Open 11am–6pm
Closed Mon. and last Tue. of the month.

4 HOUSE OF PETER THE GREAT
Nab. Petrovskaya
Gorkovskaya metro
Tel. 232 4576
Open 10am–6pm
Closed Tue. and the last Mon. of the month.
Ticket office closes at at 5pm.

5 MOSQUE
7, Pl. Maxima Gorkovo
Gorkovskaya metro
Open noon–7pm
Closed Fri.
Women are expected to wear headscarves.

6 BOTANICAL MUSEUM
2, Ul. Prof. Popova
Petrogradskaya metro
Tel. 234 84 70
Open 11am–4pm
Closed Fri.

7 MUSEUM OF POLITICAL HISTORY
214, Ul. Kuibysheva
Gorkovskaya metro
Tel. 233 7113
Open 10am–6pm
Closed Thur.
Guided tours by arrangement.

RESTAURANTS

2 AUSTERIA
Peter and Paul Fortress
Gorkovskaya metro
Tel. 238 4262
Open noon–midnight
Jazz band from 7pm each evening, except Wed. Good value and friendly atmosphere. Russian cuisine. Specialties: blini with caviar, "zakusky", "shchi".
⌂ **C**

8 CAFÉ GROT
3, Alexandrovsky Park
Gorkovskaya metro
Open 10.30am–8pm
Café, snack bar in an artificial cave. Unusual setting for a drink and a snack.
Russian cuisine.
Moderate prices.
⌂ **C**

9 GRAND CAFÉ ANTWERPEN
13–15, Kronversky Pr.
Gorkovskaya metro
Tel. 233 97 46
Open noon–midnight
Jazz pianist every evening. Friendly. Russian and European cuisine.
Price: $50
P ⌂ **C**

10 IMPERIAL
53, Kamennoostrovsky
Pr. Petrogradskaya metro Tel. 234 17 42
Open noon–midnight
Classical music. Russian cuisine.
⌂ ▭··

11 ★ PIROSMANI
14, Bolshoy Prospekt
Petrogradskaya metro
Tel. 235 64 56
Open noon–11pm
Original quiet setting, good food. Specialties: kebabs, cheesecake. Reserve in advance.
Georgian cuisine.
Price: $20–30 (including drinks).
⌂

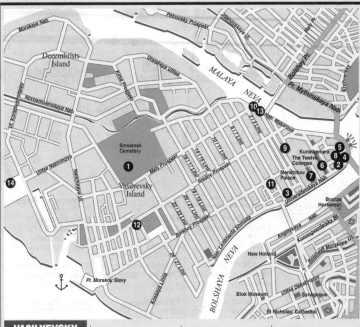

VASILYEVSKY ISLAND

CULTURAL LIFE

1 SMOLENSK CEMETERY
Ul. Kamskaya
Primorskaya metro,
bus no. 41.
*Women are advised to
wear skirt and headscarf.*

2 MUSEUM OF ANTHROPOLOGY AND ETHNOLOGY
3, Nab. Universitetskaya
Trolleybus no. 10
and bus nos 7 and 10
Tel. 218 1412
Open 11am–6pm
Closed Thur. and Fri.
*Ticket office closes at
4.45pm. Guided tours in
English by appointment.*

3 MUSEUM OF THE ACADEMY OF ARTS
17, Nab. Universitetskaya
Trolleybus no. 10
Tel. 213 6496
Open 11am–7pm
Closed Mon. and Tue.
*Guided tours in
Russian.*

4 LOMONOSOV MUSEUM
3, Nab. Universitetskaya
Tel. 218 1412
Open 11am–4.30pm
Closed Thur. and Fri.

5 NAVAL MUSEUM
4, Pushkina Pl.
Tramway nos 21, 26 and
31, bus nos. 10 and 45
Tel. 218 2501
or 218 2502
Open 10.30am–5.30pm
Closed Mon., Tue. and
last Thur. of the month.
*Parking. Guided tours
in Russian. Ticket
office open until
4.45pm.*

6 MENDELEEV MUSEUM
7–9, Nab. Universitetskaya
Trolleybus no. 10
Tel. 218 29 82
or 218 97 44
Open 10am–5pm
Closed Sat. and Sun.
*Central building of the
university, to the left of
the lobby. Reserve in
advance. Tours in
English are available by
arrangement.*

7 MENSHIKOV PALACE
15, Nab. Universitetskaya
Trolleybus no.10
Tel. 213 1112
Open 10.30am–4.30pm
Closed Mon.
*Guided tours in
Russian every
15 minutes. Tours in
English are available by
previous
arrangement.*

8 ZOOLOGICAL MUSEUM
1, Nab.Universitetskaya
Tel. 218 0112
Open 11am–6pm
Closed Fri. and pub. hols.
*Ticket office open until
5pm. Guided tours in
Russian.*

RESTAURANTS

9 KALINKA
Syezdovskaya Linia
Vasileostrovskaya metro
Tel. 218 2866 / 213 3718
Open noon–midnight
*One of the best
Russian restaurants in
St Petersburg. Folk
events every evening.
Price: around $40.*
⌂ ▭

10 RESTAURANT SWIR
On hotel boat Peterhof
Nab. Makarova
Vasileostrovskaya metro
Tel. 213 6321
Open noon–11pm
*International cuisine.
Menu: $33.*
⌂ ↦

SHOPPING

11 ANDREEVSKY MARKET
21, Bolshoy Prospekt,
opposite Andreevsky
Church, Trolleybus nos.
10 and 23 and bus 7,
128, 151 and 152
Open 9am–8pm
Large covered market.

HOTELS

12 GAVAN
88, Sredny Prospekt
Tel. 356 8504

13 PETERHOF
Nab. Makarova
Tel. 213 63 21
Fax 213 31 58
Floating hotel.

14 PRIBALTISKAYA
14, Ul. Korablestroiteley
Tel. 356 3001
Fax 356 0094
*The largest hotel in
St Petersburg.
Beautiful view over the
Gulf of Finland.*

307

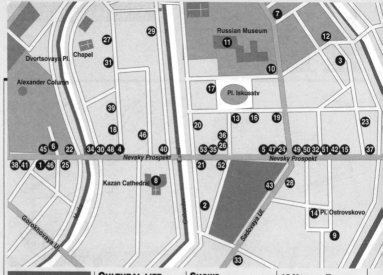

Russian Museum

Dvortsovaya Pl.   Chapel

Alexander Column

Pl. Iskusstv

Nevsky Prospekt   Nevsky Prospekt

Kazan Cathedral

Pl. Ostrovskovo

Gorokhovaya Ul.

Sadovaya Ul.

Griboedov Canal

NEVSKY PROSPEKT

PRACTICAL INFORMATION

1 AEROFLOT
7–9, Nevsky Pr.
Open Mon.–Fri.
8am–1pm and 2–8pm,
Sat.–Sun. and public
holidays 8am–1pm and
2–6pm
*Airport agency is open
24 hours a day. Accepts
bank cards.*

2 AEROFLOT BANK
26, Griboedov Canal
Open 9am–9pm
*Some of the best rates
in St Petersburg.*

3 ENERGOMASHBANK
1, Ul. Karavannaya
Open 10am–8pm

4 PETROPHARM PHARMACY
22, Nevsky Pr.
Tel. 311 20 77
Open Mon.–Fri. 8am–
9pm, Sat. 10am–8pm
Closed Sun. and 3rd
Thur. of the month.
*Open all night (9pm–
8am) 14, Ul. Bolshaya
Konyuchennaya*

5 POST OFFICE
42A, Nevsky Prospekt
Open 9am–12.30pm
and 1–8pm
Closed Sat. and Sun.

6 POST OFFICE, TELEPHONE
5, Bolshaya Morskaya
Open 8am–10.30pm

5 TELEPHONE, TELEGRAMS
42A, Nevsky Prospekt
Open Mon.–Sat. 8am–
12.30pm and 1–9pm

CULTURAL LIFE

7 ENGINEERS' CASTLE (MIKHAIL GARDENS)
2, Sadovaya Ul.
Tel. 210 44 67
or 210 41 73
Open Mon. 10am–5pm,
Wed.–Sun. 10am–6pm
Temporary exhibitions.

8 MUSEUM OF RELIGIOUS HISTORY
Kazan Cathedral
10, Ul. Plekhanova
Tel. 314 58 56
Open Mon.–Tue.
and Thur.–Fri.
11am–6pm, Sat.–Sun.
12.30–6pm
Closed Wed.
*Ticket office closes at
5pm.*

9 THEATER MUSEUM
6, Pl. Ostrovsky
Tel. 311 21 95
Open Thur.–Mon.
11am–6pm,
Wed. 1–7pm
Closed Tue. and
the last Fri. of the
month

10 ETHNOGRAPHIC MUSEUM
4, Ingenernaya Ul. and
10, Ploschad Iskustv
Tel. 219 16 76
or 219 17 19
Open 10am–6pm
Closed Mon. and
the last Fri. of the
month.
*Ticket office closes at
5pm.*

11 RUSSIAN MUSEUM
2, Ingenernaya Ul.
Tel. 314 34 48
Open Mon.
10am–5pm,
Wed.–Sun.
10am–6pm
Closed Tue.

SHOWS

12 CIRCUS
3, Nab. Reki Fontanky
Tel. 210 43 90
*Box office open
11am–2pm and 3–7pm.
Performances Mon.–Sat.
7pm, Sun. 11.30am, 3pm
and 7pm.*

13 PHILARMONIA
30, Nevsky Pr. and
2, Mikhailovskaya Ul.
Tel. 110 42 57
*Classical music. Box
office open
Mon.–Sat. 11am–3pm
and 4–7.30pm
Sun. 11am–4pm
and 5–7.30pm
on day of concert.*

14 PUSHKIN THEATER
Pl. Ostrovsky
Tel. 110 41 03
or 312 15 45
*Box office open
Mon.–Fri. 11am–3pm
and 4–7.15pm,
Sat.–Sun. 11am–6pm
15. Performances
Mon.–Fri. 11am, 7pm,
Sat.–Sun. 11am, 6pm.*

15 COMEDY THEATER
56, Nevsky Pr.
Tel. 312 45 55
*Box office open
11am–1.30pm and
2.30pm–8pm.*

16 MUSICAL COMEDY THEATER
11, Italyanskaya Ul.

17 LITTLE THEATER OF OPERA AND BALLET
1, pl. Iskusstv
Gostiny Dvor metro
Tel. 219 19 78
*Box office open
11am–3pm and
4–8pm.*

18 VARIETY THEATER
27, Bolshaya
Konyushennaya Ul.
Tel. 314 66 61
*Box office open
11am–3pm and 4–7pm.*

19 KOMISSARIEVSKAYA DRAMATIC THEATER
Italianskaya Ul.

RESTAURANTS

21 CAFÉ BALKAN
27, Nevsky Pr.
Open 11am–10pm
Tel. 315 4748
*Russian cuisine.
Dishes: $1–6..*
C

20 TCHAIKA
14, Kanal Griboedova
Tel. 311 1957
*English-style pub.
Cosmopolitan clientele.*

22 LITERATURE CAFÉ (LITERATURNOE KAFE)
18, Nevsky Prospekt
Tel. 312 6057
Open noon –5pm
and 7–11pm
*Famous as the last
place Pushkin visited on
his way to the duel that
killed him. An excellent
place for tea. Entrance:
$1. Dishes: $2–7.*
⌂ C ♫

23 CAT
22 Stremmannaya Ulitsa
Tel. 311 3377
Open noon –11pm
*Pleasant setting.
International cuisine.
Prices: around $15.*
⌂ C

24 GRILL MASTER
46, Nevsky Prospekt
Tel. 110 55 40
Open 8am 30–10pm
*Hamburger: around
$11.50 pizza: $1.*

308

25 RESTAURANT DRUZHBA
15, Nevsky Prospekt
Tel. 315 0927
Swift service.
A little noisy.
Russian cuisine.
Dishes: $2–3.
🅒

26 RESTAURANT EUROPE
Hotel Europe
1, Mikhailovskaya Ul.
Tel. 119 6000
Fax 119 6001
Open 7am–10am
and 6pm–midnight
Closed at lunchtime and
Sun. evening
Sunday lunchtime jazz,
very popular (lunch $35)
noon –3pm.
Hotel Europe also has a
brasserie (international
cuisine, dishes: $7–25),
open 11am–midnight;
Sadko restaurant
(dishes: $4–16) open
noon–1am, pleasant
lunches. The
Mezzanine tea room is
highly recommended,
open 10am–9pm;
and the Lobby Bar
open 11am–1am.
International cuisine.
Dishes: $9–32.
🅒 ▭

27 ASSEMBLY RESTAURANT
11, Bolshaya
Konyuchennaya Ul.
metro Nevsky Pr.
Tel. 314 1537
Open 24 hours
Gypsy music and
classical guitar. Russian
cuisine.
Dishes: $3–9.

28 METROPOL RESTAURANT
20–22 Sadovaya Ul.
Tel. 311 0233
Open noon –midnight
Russian cuisine.
🅒

29 RESTAURANT ST PETERSBURG
5, Griboedov Canal
Nevsky Pr. metro
Tel. 314 4947
Open noon–2am
Floor show at 9pm.
Russian cuisine.
Dishes: $8–23.
🅒 ▭

HOTEL

26 GRAND HOTEL EUROPE
7, Mikhailovskaya Ul.
Tel. 119 60 0
One of the most
prestigious hotels in the
city. Reception and
bureau de change open
24 hours. Brasserie,
nightclub, sauna,
swimming pool.
☎ ▭

SHOPPING

30 AGFA
20, Nevsky Prospekt
Open 10am–8pm
Closed Sun.
One-hour photo
developing service.

31 ANTIQUARY
13, Bolshaya
Konyoshennaya Ul.
Open 11am–2pm
and 3–7pm
Very good antiquarian
boutique. Sells icons,
musical instruments,
silverware. There are
still bargains to
be found here.
Bureau de
change.
Credobank
11am–6pm
nearby.

32 ANTIQUITIES
52A, Nevsky Pr.
Open 11am–2pm
and 3–7pm
Pictures and antiques.
Expensive. Remember
the 40% tax if taking
objets d'art out of the
country.

33 APRAKSIN DVOR
32, Sadovaya Ulitsa
Shopping mall made up
of little boutiques.

34 ART GALLERY
20, Nevsky Prospekt
Tel. 311 0106
Open noon –7pm
Pictures and antiques.

35 KRISTAL JEWELERS
34, Nevsky Prospekt
Open Mon.–Fri.
10am–2pm and 3–7pm,
Sat. 11am–4pm

36 SAMOTSVETY JEWELERS
4, Mikhailovskaya Ul.
Open Mon.–Sat.
10am–2pm and 3–7pm
Range of amber.

37 KNIZHNAYA LAVKA
Nevsky Prospekt
Open 10am–2pm
and 3–7pm
Closed Mon. and Sun.
Bookstore which also
sells compact discs.

38 DEMION
3, Nevsky Prospekt
Open Mon.–Sat.
10am–2pm and 3–7pm
Closed Sun.
Jewelry and showroom
for precious stones and
articles in wood.

39 DLT
Bolshaya
Konyuchennaya Ul.
Open Mon.–Sat.
10am–8pm, Sun.
11am–6pm
Department store.

40 DOM KNIGI BOOKSTORE
28, Nevsky Prospekt
Open 9am–8pm
Closed Sun.
One of the best
bookstores in
St Petersburg.

41 FLOWERS
5, Nevsky Prospekt
Open 8am–2pm
and 3–8pm
Fresh and artificial
flowers. To order
flowers:
Tel. 312 16 26.

42 ELISEEV
56, Nevsky Prospekt
Open 9am–1pm
and 2–9pm
Closed Sun.
Excellent food store,
very attractive and
extremely popular.

43 GOSTINY DVOR A–Z SUPERMARKET
2nd floor of Gostiny
Dvor
West European style
supermarket. One of the
best general stores in
the city.

44 KODAK EXPRESS
7A, Malaya
Konyuchennaya Ul.
Open 9am–9pm
One-hour express
photo developing
service.

45 ISKUSTVO
16, Nevsky Prospekt
Open 10am–2pm
and 3–7pm
Art books and books
on Russian culture,
watercolors,
paintings.

46 MIR
13, Nevsky Prospekt
Open Mon.–Sat.
10am–2pm and 3–7pm
Books and souvenirs.

47 PÂTISSERIE SEVER
44, Nevsky Prospekt
Open 10am–1pm
and 2–8pm
Excellent patisserie.

48 HOUSE OF MILITARY BOOKS
20, Nevsky Prospekt
Open Mon.–Fri.
10am–2pm and 3–7pm,
Sat. 10am–2pm
and 3–6pm
Wide range of books.
Art gallery. Stationery
and photocopying on
the 2nd floor. Models of
military buildings.

49 PASSAGE SUPERMARKET
48, Nevsky Prospekt
Open Mon.–Sat.
11am–9pm
West European style
supermarket. Tends to
be rather expensive.

50 CHINA, CRYSTAL, GLASS
62, Nevsky Prospekt
Open Mon.–Sat.
11am–2pm and 3–8pm

51 WELLA SALON
54, Nevsky Prospekt
Tel. 312 30 26
Open Mon.–Sat.
9am–9pm
Unisex hair salon.

52 ART GALLERY
29, Nevsky Prospekt
Open Wed.–Sat.
10am–2pm and 3–7pm
Closed Sun. and Mon.
Portraitists in front of
the store.

53 ELISEEV SUPERMARKET
32, Nevsky Pr.
Open Mon.–Fri.
8am–9pm, Sat.
9am–9pm
and Sun. 10am–6pm
Popular store.

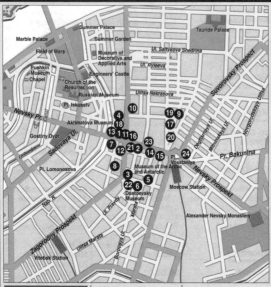

FONTANKA

PRACTICAL INFORMATION

1 SVERBANK
80, Nevsky Prospekt
Open 10am–2pm
and 3–8pm
Closed Sun.
*Bureau de change open
until 6pm, not
particularly good rates,
but does take Visa,
Mastercard, American
Express, Thomas Cook
travelers' checks.*

2 DHL
Nevsky Palace Hotel
57, Nevsky Prospekt
Tel. 119 6100
Open Mon.–Fri. 9am–
6pm. Closed Sat.–Sun.

CULTURAL LIFE

3 VLADIMIRSKAYA CHURCH
Vladimirskaya Pl.
Vladimirskaya
and Dostoevskaya metro
Open 8am–9pm
Undergoing restoration.

4 ANNA AKHMATOVA MUSEUM
53, Liteiny Prospekt
Mayakovskaya metro;
trolleybus nos. 3, 8, 15, 19
Tel. 272 2211
or 272 1811
Open Tue.–Sun.
10.30am–6.30pm
Closed Mon. and the last
Wed. of the month.

5 MUSEUM OF THE ARCTIC AND ANTARCTIC
24A, Ul. Marata
Tel. 311 2549
Open 10am–6pm
Closed Mon. and Tue.

6 DOSTOEVSKY MUSEUM
5, Kuznechny Prospekt
Dostoevskaya and
Vladimirskaya metro
Tel. 164 69 50
Open 10.30am–6.30pm
Closed Mon. and last
Wed. of the month.
*Ticket office open until
5.30pm.*

7 BELOSELSKY-BELOZERSKY PALACE
41, Nevsky Prospekt
Mayakovskaya metro
Tel. 319 9990
or 319 9792
Fax 311 1750
Open noon–6.30pm
*For information on
guided tours:
Tel. 312 36 44.*

SHOWS

8 LITTLE (MALY) DRAMATIC THEATER
18, Ul. Rubinsteina
Mayakovskaya,
Vladimirskaya and
Dostoevskaya metro
Tel. 113 20 78
or 113 20 28
*Ticket office open
noon–3pm and
4–7pm.*

9 BOLSHOY KONTSERNY ZAL
6, Ligovsky Prospekt
Vostaniya Pl. metro
Tel. 275 1273
*Ticket office open
11am–8pm.
Offers all types of
performances: concerts,
dance . . .*

7 ST PETERSBURG CULTURAL CENTER
Beloselsky-Belozersky
Palace
41, Nevsky Prospekt
Tel. 315 5236
*Dance, chamber music,
folklore, thematic
evenings. Ticket office
open noon–6pm, and
7pm on days when
there are concerts.*

10 THEATER
51, Liteiny Prospekt
Tel. 273 5335
*Box office open
11am–3pm
and 4–7pm.*

RESTAURANTS

2 ADMIRALTY RESTAURANT
Nevsky Palace Hotel
57, Nevsky Prospekt
Open noon–11pm
*Also has a branch in
the Nevsky Palace
Hotel: Bierstube
(international cuisine)
open from 5pm;
Lobby Bar and
Vienna Café,
open from 10am.
International cuisine.
Price: $25–30.*
C ▭

11 APHRODITE
86, Nevsky Prospekt
Mayakovskaya metro.
Tel. 275 7620
Open noon–midnight
*International cuisine.
Visa and Mastercard.
Price: around $25.*
C ▭

12 BELLA LEONE
9, Vladimirsky Prospekt
Tel. 113 1670
Fax 113 1673
Open 1pm–midnight
*International cuisine.
Price: $30–40.*
C

13 DOMENICO'S
70, Nevsky Prospekt
Tel. 272 5717
Open noon–6am
*Discotheque from
10pm. Russian and
European specialties.
Price: $10–20.*
C

2 IMPERIAL RESTAURANT
Nevsky Palace Hotel
57, Nevsky Prospekt
Tel. 275 2001 or 850 1500
Fax 850 15 01
Open Mon.–Sat.
7am–11am and 7–11pm,
Sun. noon–3pm
*Smorgasbord.
International cuisine.
Price: $35.*
C ▭

2 LANDSKRONA RESTAURANT
Nevsky Palace Hotel
8th Floor
57, Nevsky Prospekt
Tel. 275 2001
Fax 850 1501
Open 7pm–midnight
*Evening dress
obligatory.
International cuisine.
Price: around $100
(inc. drinks).*
C ▭ ⦿

14 NEVSKY RESTAURANT
71, Nevsky Prospekt and Ul. Marata
Mayakovskaya metro
Tel. 311 8993 / 311 3806
Open 11am–6pm and 19am–11.30pm
Orchestra. Russian cuisine. Dishes: $3–4.

15 RESTORANTCHIK
79, Nevsky Prospekt
Tel. 311 8589
Music from 8pm. Russian cuisine. Dishes: $1.50–3.

16 TCHARODEIKA
88, Nevsky Prospekt
Tel. 279 0940
Quiet, unassuming restaurant (dishes: $1.50–6), open 11am–5am; cafeteria friendly but often crowded. Open 10am–10pm; café open 11am–11pm. Russian cuisine.

17 TCHINARA
15, Ul. Vostaniya
Vostaniya Pl.
Tel. 279 1478
Open 11am–10pm
Specialties: "basturma", "chalhlaik". Georgian cuisine. Price: $4–6.

HOTEL

2 NEVSKY PALACE HOTEL
57, Nevsky Prospekt
Tel. and fax 275 2001 or 850 1500
Swimming pool, sauna, commercial gallery, bureau de change. One of the best hotels in St Petersburg with the Grand Hotel Europe. Includes the Vienna Café, Imperial and Landskrona restaurants, a brasserie and a beer bar (open until 1am). The Vasily Samoilov Museum is also here.

SHOPPING

18 BABYLON
61–3 Liteiny Prospekt
Tel. 279 0148 or 273 4212
Open 11am–7pm
Closed Sun.
Visa, Mastercard and Amex. Electrical goods, Konica film, women's and children's wear.

18 BABYLON
69, Nevsky Prospekt
Tel. 314 6237
Open 11am–7pm
Closed Sun.
Food. Mastercard, Visa and American Express.

19 NORDIA FLOWERS
36 Ul. Zhukovskovo
Vostaniya Pl. metro
Open Mon.–Sat. 9am–2pm and 3–8pm, Sun. 10am–6pm
Interflora.

20 HOLIDAY
51, Ligovsky Prospekt
Open 24 hours
Supermarket.

21 KHUDOZHESTVENYE PROMYSLY
51, Nevsky Prospekt
Tel. 113 1495
Open Mon.–Sat. 11am–7.30pm, Sun. 11am–6pm
Souvenirs.

22 KUZNETSHNY RYNOK
Kuznetdhny Per.
Vladimirskaya metro
Open 8am–7pm
Covered food market.

23 RUSSIAN SOUVENIRS
94, Nevsky Prospekt
Open. Mon.–Sat. 10am–8pm, Sun. 10am–6pm

24 M & S SUPERMARKET
Pl. Vostaniya and Goncharnaya Ul.
Vostaniya Pl. metro
Open 24 hours

SMOLNY

PRACTICAL INFORMATION

BUREAU DE CHANGE
140, Staro Nevsky Pr.
Mayakovskaya metro
Open 10am–7pm

POST OFFICE
Staro Nevsky Prospekt
Mayakovskaya metro
Open 10am–7pm
Closed Sun.

CULTURAL LIFE

ALEXANDER NEVSKY MONASTERY
Alexandra Nevskovo Pl.
Alex. Nevskovo metro, bus nos. 21, 30, 118, 118a and 160.
Tel. 274 2635
CHURCH OF THE ANNUNCIATION
Open 10.30am–7pm

Closed Thur.
TRINITY CATHEDRAL
Open 8am–2pm; 5–6pm
CEMETERIES
Open 11am–6pm
Closed Thur.

SMOLNY MONASTERY
Pl. Rastrelli
Shernyshevskaya metro, bus nos. 46, 58, 134, 136 and 137
Open Thur.–Tue. 11am–6pm, Wed. 11am–5pm
Concerts (choirs and musical ensembles). Tickets available inside the building, program posted outside.

LENIN MEMORIAL MUSEUM
Proletarskoy Diktatury Pl.
Trolleybus no. 5
Tel. 278 1321
Open Mon.–Fri. 10am–6pm, Sat. 11am–3pm
Closed Sun.

SUVOROV MUSEUM
Ul. Saltykova Shchedrina
Chernyshevskaya metro
Closed for repairs.

RESTAURANTS

CAFÉ BALSEN
142, Staro Nevsky Pr.
Vostaniya Pl. metro
Tel. 271 2811
Open noon–midnight
Friendly café. Orchestra each evening. European cuisine. Specialties: salad bar, salmon in Pernod sauce. Price: around $10.

HOT DOG
Staro Nevsky Prospekt
Open 11am–3pm and 4–9pm
Fast food. International cuisine.

SURPRISE
113, Staro Nevsky Pr.

Tel. 277 2431
Open 11am–10pm
Specialties: cakes, Italian ice cream and snacks. International cuisine.

WARSTEINER FORUM
120, Nevsky Prospekt
Tel. 277 5406
Open noon–2am
Vostaniya Pl. metro
Good lunchtime venue. German cuisine. Price: around $7.

HOTELS

MERCURY
39, Ul. Bolshaya Morskaya
Tel. 119 6444
Fax 278 1977
Small quiet hotel.

MOSKVA
2, Pl. Alexander Nevskovo
Tel. 274 3001
Fax 274 2130

OKHTINSKAYA
4, Bolsheokhtinsky Pr.
Tel. 227 4438
Fax 227 2618
Recently built hotel in an industrial area, close to the Smolny Monastery.

SHOPPING

PETERSBURG
42, Ul. Petra Lavrova
Alex. Nevsk. Pl. metro
Tel. 273 03 41
Open 10am–7pm
Antiques, art gallery.

SOFRINO
Staro Nevsky Prospekt
Alexandra Nevski Pl. metro
Open 11am–2pm and 3–6pm
Antiques.

GATCHINA

Twenty-eight miles to the south of St Petersburg. By train: (55 mins.) depart from Baltic Station (120, Nab. Obvodnovo Kanala, Baltiskaya metro station).

CULTURAL LIFE

GATCHINA PALACE
Museum open 10am–6pm. Closed Mon.

ORANIENBAUM

Twenty-five miles to the west of St Petersburg. By train (55 mins.) from Baltic Station (120, Nab. Obvodnovo Kanala, Baltiskaya metro station).

CULTURAL LIFE

CHINESE KITCHEN
Open 11am–5pm
Closed Tue.

CAVALRY HOUSE
Open 11am–5pm
Closed Tue.

"SLIDING HILL" PAVILION
Open 11am–5pm
Closed Tue.

PETER III's PALACE
Open 11am–5pm
Closed Tue.

CHINESE PALACE
Open 11am–5pm
Closed Tue. and winter

PAVLOVSK

Eighteen miles to the south of St Petersburg. By train: (40 mins.) depart from Baltic (120, Nab. Obvodnovo Kanala) or Vitebsk (52, Zagorodny Pr.) stations. At Pavlovsk, cross the park on foot and take bus nos. 370 or 383. The 370 reaches Pavlovsk at Tsarskoe Selo.

CULTURAL LIFE

PALACE
Tel. 470 6214 / 470 2156
Open 10am–6pm
Closed Fri.

RESTAURANTS

PODVORIE
16, Filtrovskoe Tyarlevo on the edge of the park
Tel. 465 1399
Fax 465 1499
Often stages folk entertainment. Russian cuisine.

SELF-SERVICE RESTAURANT
In the left wing of the palace
Tel. 470 6966

PETERHOF

To get there: take the hovercraft (30 mins.) from the Hermitage port, or the train from Baltic Station (120, Nab. Obvodnovo Kanala), then bus nos.350, 351, 351A, 352, 353, 354 or 356.

CULTURAL LIFE

COTTAGE
Tel. 427 9953
Open Sat.–Thur. 11am–6pm (May 11– Sep.); Sat.–Sun. 10.30am–5pm (Oct.–May 10)

THE HERMITAGE
Open 11am–6pm
Closed Tue.

GREAT PALACE
Tel. 427 9527
Open 11am–6pm (May 11–Sep.) and 11am–5pm (Oct.–May 10). Closed Mon. and the last Tue. of the month

MARLY
Open 11am–6pm
Closed Tue.

BENOIS FAMILY MUSEUM
Open Tue.–Sun.
11am–6pm

MONPLAISIR PALACE
Tel. 427 9129
Open 11am–6pm

Closed Wed. and Oct.–May 10

CATHERINE PAVILION
Open Fri.–Wed.
11am–6pm

RESTAURANTS

PETERHOF
To the right of the Great Palace
Tel. 427 98 84

SHOPPING

STORES
Ground floor of the Great Palace

TSARSKOE SELO

Seventeen miles to the south of St Petersburg. By train: (30 mins.) from Baltic (120, Nab. Obvodnovo Kanala) or Vitebsk (52, Zagorodny Pr.) stations. By bus: no. 371 or 382. The 370 reaches Pavlovsk at Tsarskoe Selo.

CULTURAL LIFE

PUSHKIN MUSEUM
Open 10am–4pm
Closed Tue.

CATHERINE PALACE
Open 10am–5pm
Closed Tue.

APPENDICES

◆ BIBLIOGRAPHY

ESSENTIAL
◆ READING ◆

◆ KELLY (L.) ED.: *St Petersburg – a travellers' companion*, Constable, London, 1981
◆ OMETEV (B.) and STUART (J.): *St Petersburg: portrait of an imperial city*, Cassell, London, 1990
◆ KROPTOPKIN (PRINCE PIOTR): *Memoirs of a revolutionist*, Dover Publications Inc., New York, 1971
◆ PIPES (R.): *Russia before the revolution*, Weidenfeld & Nicolson, London and Alfred A. Knopf, New York, 1934
◆ DOSTOEVSKY (F.): *Crime and Punishment*, trans. PEVEAR (R.) and VOLOKHONSKY (L.), Everyman's Library, London and Alfred A. Knopf, New York, 1993
◆ PUSHKIN (A.): *The Captain's Daughter and other stories*, trans. DEBRECZENY (P.) and VOLOKHONSKY (L.), Everyman's Library, London, 1994
◆ WILMOT (M.) and (C.): *The Russian Journals of Martha and Catherine Wilmot*, ed. MARCHIONESS OF LONDONDERRY and HYDE (H.M.), Macmillan & Co., London, 1934

GENERAL
◆ INTEREST ◆

◆ FALLOWEL (D.): *One hot summer in St Petersburg*, Jonathan Cape, London, 1994.
◆ GUNTER (J.): *Inside Russia Today*, Hamish Hamilton, London, 1958
◆ MARSDEN (C.A.): *Palmyra of the North. The first days of St Petersburg*, Faber & Faber, London, 1942
◆ MILLER (W.M.): *Russians as People*, Dutton, New York, 1961
◆ REED (J.): *Ten Days that Shook the World*, Modern Books, London, 1928
◆ SIMPSON (C.): *This is Russia*, Hodder and Stoughton, London 1965
◆ WERTH (A.): *Leningrad*, Hamish Hamilton, London, 1944
◆ WILSON (E.): *To the Finland Station*, Secker & Warburg, London
◆ WILTSHIRE (S.): *Floating cities: Venice, Amsterdam, Leningrad – and Moscow*, Michael Joseph, London, 1991

CONTEMPORARY
◆ ACCOUNTS ◆

◆ BOURKE (R.S.): *St Petersburg and Moscow, a Visit to the Court of the Czar*, Vol. II, London, 1846
◆ BREMNER (R.): *Excursions in the Interior of Russia*, Henry Colburn, London, 1839
◆ COXE (W.): *Travels into Poland, Russia, Sweden and Denmark, interspersed with historical relations and political inquiries*, S. Price et al., Dublin, 1784
◆ CUSTINE (MARQUIS A.L.L. DE): *Letters from Russia*, trans. and ed. BUSS (V.), Penguin Books, Harmondsworth, 1991
◆ DISBROWE (C.A.A.) ED.: *Original Letters from Russia, 1825–28*, privately printed, London, 1878
◆ GRANVILLE (A.B.): *St Petersburg, A Journal of Travels to and from that capital, London, 1828*
◆ HAKLUYT (R.): *The Principal Voyages of the English Nation*, Dent, London, Everyman Edition, 1926, Oxford, 1553
◆ HERZEN (A.): *My Past and Thoughts*, trans. GARNETT (C.) and HIGGENS (H.), Chatto & Windus, London, 1968
◆ MASSON (C.F.P.): *Secret Memoirs of the Court of Petersburg*, P. Wogan, Dublin, 1801
◆ PALÉOLOGUE (M.): *An Ambassador's Memoirs 1914–1917*, trans. F.A. Holt, London 1924–5
◆ PARKINSON (J.): *A Tour of Russia, Siberia and the Crimea, 1792–1794*, London, 1971
◆ RITCHIE (L.): *A Journey to St Petersburg and Moscow*, Heath's Picturesque Annual, London, 1836
◆ STEPHENS (J.L.): *Incidents of Travel in the Russian and Turkish Empires*, Vol. II, London, 1839
◆ VAN DER POST (L.): *Journey into Russia*, Penguin Books, Harmondsworth, 1965
◆ WARD, Mrs.: *Letters from a Lady who resided some years in Russia*, London, 1775
◆ DE WASSENAER (C.): *A visit to St Petersburg 1824–25*, Michael Russell, Colby (Norfolk), 1994

◆ HISTORY ◆

◆ CLARKSON (J.D.): *A History of Russia from the Ninth Century*, Longmans, London, 1961
◆ HINGLEY (R.F.): *A Concise History of Russia*, Thames & Hudson, London, 1972
◆ HOETZSCH (O.):*The Evolution of Russia*, Thames & Hudson, London, 1966
◆ PARES (B.): *A History of Russia*, Jonathan Cape, London, 1947

IMPERIAL
◆ RUSSIA ◆

◆ BADDELEY (J.F.): *Russia in the Eighties*, Longman & Co., London, 1921
◆ BARROW (SIR J.): *The Life of Peter the Great*, William Tegg, L, 1874
◆ ANTHONY (K.): *Memoirs of Catherine the Great*, Alfred A. Knopf, New York and London, 1927
◆ GREY (I.): *Peter the Great, Emperor of all Russia*, J.B. Lippincott & Co., Philadelphia and New York, 1960
◆ HINGLEY (R.F.): *The Tsars*, Corgi, London, 1973
◆ LAMB (H.A.): *The City and the Tsar, Peter the Great and the move to the West 1648–1762*, Doubleday & Co., Garden City, New York, 1951
◆ MAZOUR (A.): *The First Russian Revolution, 1825*, University of California Press, Berkeley, 1937
◆ MOSSE (W.E.): *Alexander II and the Modernisation of Russia*, Collier, New York, 1962
◆ OLDENBOURG (Z.): *Catherine de Russie*, trans. CARTER (A.), Heinemann, London, 1965
◆ SCHUYLER (E.): *Passages from the life of Peter the Great*, Sampson, Low & Co., London, 1881

THE REVOLUTION
◆ AND AFTER ◆

◆ CARR (E.H.): *The Bolshevik Revolution*, 3 vols., Macmillan, New York, 1951–3
◆ CONQUEST (R.): *The Great Terror: Stalin's Purges in the Thirties*, Macmillan, London, 1968
◆ DEUTSCHER (I.): *Stalin*, Penguin Books, Harmondsworth, 1966
◆ DEUTSCHER (I.): *The Unfinished Revolution. Russia 1917–1967*, George Macauley Trevelyan Lectures, Oxford University Press, Oxford, 1967
◆ HINGLEY (R.F.): *Russian Revolution*, Bodley Head, London, 1970
◆ KENNEDY (R.F.): *13 Days: The Cuban Missile Crisis*, Macmillan/Pan, London, 1969
◆ LUKACS (J.): *A History of the Cold War*, Doubleday, New York, 1962
◆ McCAULEY (M.): *Bread and Justice: state and society in Petrograd, 1917–1922*, Clarendon Press, Oxford, 1991
◆ McKEAN (R.B.): *St Petersburg between the revolutions: workers and revolutionaries*, Yale University Press, New Haven (Conn.), 1989
◆ MANDEL (D.): *The Petrograd Workers and the Soviet Seizure of Power*, Macmillan, London, 1984
◆ MOOREHEAD (A.): *The Russian Revolution*, Harper, New York, 1958
◆ PAGE (B.), LEITCH (D.) AND KNIGHTLEY (P.): *Philby – The Spy who Betrayed a Generation*, Andre Deutsch, London, 1968
◆ PHILBY (K.): *My Silent War*, MacGibbon & Kee, London, 1968
◆ TROTSKY (L.): *My Life*, Grosset & Dunlap, New York, 1960
◆ SALISBURY (H.E.): *The 900 Days: The Siege of Leningrad*, Harper & Row, New York, 1969
◆ WADE (R.A): *Red Guards and workers' militias in the Russian Revolution*, Stanford University Press, Stanford, 1984
◆ WOLFE (B.D.): *Three Who made a revolution*, Lenin, Trotsky, Stalin, Dial Press, New York, 1961
◆ ZAGORIA (D.): *The Sino-Soviet Conflict*, Oxford University Press, Oxford, 1962

RELIGION
◆ AND SOCIETY ◆

◆ BACH (M.): *God and the Soviets*, Thomas Y. Crowell, New York, 1958
◆ BATER (J.H.): *St Petersburg: Industrialisation and Change*, Edward Arnold, London, 1976
◆ BOURDEAUX (M.): *Religious Ferment in Russia. Protestant Opposition to Soviet Religious Policy*, Macmillan, London, 1968
◆ NEUBERGER (J.): *Hooliganism: crime, culture and power in St Petersburg*, University of California Press, Berkeley, c. 1993

ART AND
◆ ARCHITECTURE ◆

◆ ANIKST (M.) ED.: *Soviet Commercial Design of the Twenties*, Thames & Hudson, London, 1987
◆ BELYAKOVA (Z.) AND DENISOV (Y.):

St Petersburg, A Bird's Eye View, London, 1993
◆ BILLINGTON (J.H.): *The Icon and the Axe: an interpretive history of Russian culture*, Alfred A. Knopf, (New York, 1967
◆ CONWAY (SIR W.M.): *Art Treasure in Soviet Russia*, Edward Arnold & Co., London, 1925
◆ COOKE (C.): *Architectural Drawings of the Russian Avant-Garde*, Museum of Modern Art, New York, 1990
◆ DESCARGUES (P.): *The Hermitage*, trans. DELAVENAY (K), Thames & Hudson, London, 1961
◆ ELLIOTT (D.): *New Worlds: Russian Art and Society 1900–1937*, Thames & Hudson, London, 1989
◆ ELLIOTT (D.): *Photography in Russia, 1840–1940*, Thames & Hudson, London, 1992
◆ HAMILTON (G.H.): *The Art and Architecture of Russia*, Penguin Books, Harmondsworth, 1954
◆ KAGANOVITCH (A.L.): *Arts of Russia, 17th and 18th centuries*, trans. HOGARTH (J.) et al, Nagel, Geneva, Paris and Munich, 1968
◆ KAGANOVITCH (A.L.): *Splendours of Leningrad*, trans. BERTIN (G.), Barrie and Rockliff – the Cresset Press, 1969
◆ KAHN-MAGOMEDOV (S.O.): *Pioneers of Soviet Architecture, the Search for new Solutions in the 1920's and 1930's*, Thames & Hudson, London, 1987
◆ KENNETT (V.) and KENNETT (A.): *The Palaces of Leningrad*, Thames & Hudson, London, 1973
◆ LUKOMSKI (G.K.): *Charles Cameron, 1740–1812*, trans. and ed. DE GREN (N.), Nicholson & Watson, Commodore Press, London, 1943
◆ OPOLOVNIKOV (A.) AND OPOLOVNIKOV (Y.), BUXTON (D.) ED.: *The Wooden Architecture of Russia*, Thames & Hudson, London, 1989
◆ RICE (T.T.): *A Concise History of Russian art*, Thames & Hudson, London, 1963
◆ RUBLE (B.A.): *Leningrad: shaping a Soviet city*, University of California Press, Berkeley, 1990
◆ SALMINA-HASKELL (L.): *Panoramic Views of St Petersburg, 1716–1835*, Ashmolean Museum, Oxford, 1993
◆ SARABIANOV (D.V.): *Russian Art*, Thames & Hudson, London, 1990

◆ SHUDAKOV (G.): *Pioneers of Soviet Photography*, Thames & Hudson, London, 1983
◆ STRIZHENOVA (T.): *Soviet Costume and Textiles 1917–1945*, Thames & Hudson, London, 1991
◆ TOLSTOY (V.), BIBIKOVA (I.) AND COOKE (C.) EDS.: *Street Art of the Revolution*, Thames & Hudson, London, 1990
◆ YABLONSKAYA (M.N.): *Women Artists of Russia's New Age 1900–1935*, Thames & Hudson, London, 1990

◆ PAINTING ◆

◆ BARKHATOVA (E.): *Russian Constructivist Posters*, Thames & Hudson, London, 1992
◆ BUCKMAN (D.): *Leonid Pasternak: a Russian Impressionist 1862–1945*, Maltzahn Gallery, London, 1975
◆ GODIN (A.M.): *The Artist and the City – Petersburg – Petrograd – Leningrad*, Khudozhnik, Leningrad, 1978
◆ *The State Hermitage: masterpieces from the museum's collection*, Booth Clibborn edition, Abrams, New York

◆ LITERATURE ◆

◆ BIELY (A.): *St Petersburg*, trans. COURNOS (J.), Grove Press Inc., New York, 1959
◆ BRODSKY (J.): *Less than One: Selected Essays*, Farrar, Strauss & Giroux, New York, 1986
◆ CHEKHOV (A.): *The Lady with the Dog*, trans. PEVEAR (R.) and VOLKOKHONSKY (L.), Everyman's Library, London and Alfred A. Knopf, New York, 1993
◆ DOSTOEVSKY (F.): *the Best Short Stories of Dostoevsky*, trans. MAGARSHACK (D.), the Modern Library, New York, 1955
◆ GOGOL (N.): *The Overcoat and Other Stories*, trans. GARNETT (C.), Chatto & Windus, London, 1923
◆ GOGOL (N.): *Tales of Good and Evil*, trans. DUDDINGION (N.), Everyman's Library, London and Alfred A. Knopf, New York, 1992
◆ GONCHAROV (I.): *Oblomov*, trans. DUDDINGTON (N.), Everyman's Library, London and Alfred A. Knopf, New York, 1992
◆ HERZEN (A.): *My past and Thoughts*, trans. GARNETT (C.), Chatto & Windus, London, 1975

◆ IGNATIEFF (M.): *The Russian Album*, Chatto & Windus, London, 1987
◆ NABOKOV (V.) TRANS.: *Eugene Onegin: a novel in verse by Alexander Pushkin*, trans. NABOKOV (V.), Routledge & Kegan Paul, London, 1964
◆ NABOKOV (V.): *Speak Memory – an Autobiography Revisited*, Weidenfeld and Nicolson, London, 1960
◆ PUSHKIN (A.): *Selected Poems of Alexander Pushkin*, trans. THOMAS (D.M.), Secker & Warburg, London, 1982
◆ PUSHKIN (A.): *The Letters of Alexander Pushkin*, trans. SHAW (J.T.), Wisconsin, 1967
◆ TOLSTOY (L.N.): *Anna Karenina*, trans. MAUDE (L.) and (A.) Everyman's Library, London and Alfred A. Knopf, New York, 1992
◆ TOLSTOY (L.N.): *War and Peace*, trans. MAUDE (L.) and (A.) Everyman's Library, London and Alfred A. Knopf, New York, 1992

◆ JOURNAL ◆

◆ GERHARDIE (W.): *Memories of St Petersburg*, 'The Listener', 1953

ACKNOWLEDMENTS
Grateful acknowledgment is made to the following for permission to reprint previously published material:

◆ ASSOCIATED UNIVERSITY PRESSES: Excerpt from "Tristia" #88 page 77, from *Poems of Mandelstam* by Osip Mandelstam, translated by R.H. Morrison copyright © 1990 by The Associated University Presses. Reprinted by permission

◆ FARRAR, STRAUS & GIROUX, INC.: Excerpt from "Less Than One" from *Less Than One* by Joseph Brodsky, copyright © 1986 by Joseph Brodsky; excerpt from *Turgenev's Literary Reminiscences*, translated by David Magarshack, copyright © by Farrar, Straus & Cudahy, Inc., copyright renewed 1986 by Elsie D. Magarshack. Reprinted by permission of Farrar, Straus & Giroux, Inc.

◆ GROVE/ATLANTIC, INC.: Excerpt from *St. Petersburg* by Andrei Biely, translated by John Cournos, copyright © 1959 by Grove Press, Inc. Reprinted by permission of Grove/Atlantic, Inc.

◆ JOHN JOHNSON (AUTHORS' AGENT) LIMITED: Excerpt from "The Bronze Horseman" from *Selected Poems* by Alexander Pushkin, translated by D.M. Thomas, translation copyright © 1982 by D.M. Thomas (London: Secker & Warburg Ltd). Reprinted by permission of John Johnson (Authors' Agent) Limited.

◆ NEW DIRECTIONS PUBLISHING CORP.: Excerpt fom *Futility* by William Gerhardie, copyright © 1971 by The Estate of William Gerhardie. Reprinted by permission of New Directions Publishing Corp.

◆ RANDOM HOUSE, INC.: Excerpt from "White Nights" from *The Best Short Stories of Fyodor Dostoyevsky* by Fyodor Dostoyevsky, translated by David Margarshack, translation copyright © 1955 by Random House, Inc. Reprinted by permission of Random House, Inc.

◆ VIKING PENGUIN: Letter to M.P. Chekhova, Petersburg, Jan. 14, 1891, from *The Letters of Anton Chekhov* by Anton Chekhov, translated by Avrahm Yarmolinsky, translation copyright © 1947, 1968 by The Viking Press, Inc., copyright © 1973 by Avrahm Yarmolinsky. Reprinted by permission of Viking Penguin, a division of Penguin books USA Inc.

◆ VINTAGE BOOKS: Excerpt from *Speak Memory* by Vladimir Nabokov, copyright © 1989 by The Estate of Vladimir Nabokov. Reprinted by permission of Vintage Books, a division of Random House, Inc.

◆ A.P. WATT LTD and CHATTO & WINDUS: Excerpt from "The Nevsky Prospect" from *The Overcoat and Other Stories* by Nikolai Gogol, translated by Constance Garnett, copyright © 1923 by Mrs Edward Garnett. Reprinted by permission of A.P. Watt Ltd and Chatto & Windus on behalf of The Executors of The Estate of Constance Garnett.